Intelligent IT Offshoring to India

Also by Wolfgang Messner

RIGHTSHORE!
Successfully Industrialize SAP Projects Offshore (*co-editor*)

WORKING WITH INDIA
The Softer Aspects of a Successful Collaboration with the Indian
IT & BPO Industry

Intelligent IT Offshoring to India

Roadmaps for Emerging Business Landscapes

Wolfgang Messner

palgrave
macmillan

First published 2010 by
PALGRAVE MACMILLAN

Palgrave Macmillan in the UK is an imprint of Macmillan Publishers Limited, registered in England, company number 785998, of Houndmills, Basingstoke, Hampshire RG21 6XS.

Palgrave Macmillan in the US is a division of St Martin's Press LLC, 175 Fifth Avenue, New York, NY 10010.

Palgrave Macmillan is the global academic imprint of the above companies and has companies and representatives throughout the world.

Palgrave® and Macmillan® are registered trademarks in the United States, the United Kingdom, Europe and other countries.

ISBN 978–0–230–24626–3

This book is printed on paper suitable for recycling and made from fully managed and sustained forest sources. Logging, pulping and manufacturing processes are expected to conform to the environmental regulations of the country of origin.

A catalogue record for this book is available from the British Library.

A catalog record for this book is available from the Library of Congress.

10 9 8 7 6 5 4 3 2 1
19 18 17 16 15 14 13 12 11 10

Printed and bound in Great Britain by
CPI Antony Rowe, Chippenham and Eastbourne

Contents

List of Figures, Tables and Case Studies

Figures

Tables

Case Studies

List of Abbreviations

AD	Application development
AD&M	Application development and maintenance
AG	Aktiengesellschaft (incorporated company)
AM	Application maintenance
AMO	Account management office
ARC	Asset reconstruction companies
BCM	Business continuity management
BEA	Bureau of Economic Analysis
BIA	Business impact analysis
BO	Back office
BOT	Build–operate–transfer model
BPO	Business process outsourcing
CAGE	Acronym for global distances (see Chapter 1)
CAGR	Compound annual growth rate
CBT	Computer-based training
CCM	Captive critical mass
CCTV	Closed circuit television
CEO	Chief Executive Officer
CFO	Chief Financial Officer
CIO	Chief Information Officer
CMM	Capability maturity model
COLA	Cost-of-living adjustment
COR	Charge-out rate
CRM	Customer relationship management
CV	Curriculum vitae
CxO	One of the C-level executives (CEO, CFO, CIO, ...)
DDC	Distributed delivery coordinator
DIPP	Department of Industrial Policy and Promotion

DTH	Direct-to-home
EDA	Electronic design automation
EN	English-speaking
ERP	Enterprise resource planning
FDA	Food and Drug Administration
FDI	Foreign direct investment
FIO	Firm of Indian origin
FIPB	Foreign Investment Promotion Board
FO	Front office
FTE	Full-time equivalent
GBP	British currency (UK pound)
GDP	Gross domestic product
GE	German-speaking
HR	Human resources
IC	Integrated circuit
IIM	Indian Institute of Management
IIT	Indian Institute of Technology
IM	Infrastructure management
IRR	Internal rate of return
IS	Information system
ISO	International Organization for Standardization
IT	Information technology
ITES	Information technology enabled services
JIT	Just in time
KAP	Knowledge acquisition process
KPI	Key performance indicator
KT	Knowledge transfer
LeT	Lashkar-e-Tayaaba
MARC	Minimum acceptable recovery configuration
Max / Min	Maximum / minimum
MBA	Master of Business Administration

MMO	Multisourcing management office
MNC	Multi-national company
NASSCOM	National Association of Software and Services Companies
NCR	New Delhi National Capital Region
NSG	National security guard
ORC	Offshore resource centre
PGSEM	Postgraduate programme in software enterprise management
PMO	Project management office
Q	Quarter
QMS	Quality management system
RFI	Request for information
RFP	Request for proposal
RIA	Rich Internet applications
ROI	Return on investment
RPD	Relationship performance dashboard
RTO	Recovery time objective
SaaS	Software as a service
SARS	Severe acute respiratory syndrome
SDLC	Software development lifecycle
SEI	Carnegie Mellon Software Engineering Institute
SEZ	Special economic zone
SIMI	Students Islamic Movement of India
SLA	Service level agreement
S-LEAN RFP™	Acronym for a five-step RFP process (see Chapter 5)
SME	Small- and medium-sized enterprise
SOA	Service-oriented architecture
SoW	Statement of work
SPI	Software process improvement
STP	Software technology park scheme
TMS	Transactive memory system

UK	United Kingdom
UNCTAD	United Nations Conference on Trade and Development
USA	United States of America
USD	US currency (dollar)
WAN	Wide area network

Preface

This book draws upon my fourteen years of rich India experience between 1995 and 2009. In 1995, I joined the IT organization of Deutsche Bank AG in Frankfurt am Main, Germany, as a business analyst and project manager. Right from the first day I was asked to interact with Indian colleagues from our daughter company Deutsche Software India Pvt Ltd – later this model became known as captive offshoring. These colleagues were sent on a work permit basis to work alongside us, understand the business and take work back to India. Later this became known as onsite assignment or landed resources. Without any methods for distributed delivery or any intercultural training on either side, we tried working together with them as if with our own developers sitting in the room across the corridor – later this approach was nicknamed 'prolonged workbench'. When I was sent to India in 1998 on my first expatriate assignment as project manager for a team of twenty-five Indian colleagues to implement the Euro changes into the core banking system, I very soon realized that our approach was a failure and that successfully working together with a team halfway across the globe required adherence to stringent communication protocols, methods, and most important, the definition of clear expectations, deliverable packages, and milestones. In India, the IT industry was just entering a relatively mature stage with most companies having achieved formal quality certification. However, the concept of distributed delivery remained foreign to my Western colleagues; convincing and educating them was an unplanned, major, but most necessary, task.

In the years to come I was privileged to marry Pratibha, then an Indian IT engineer who moved on to become a successful manager for operational risk and service transitions with a major international bank. I was allowed to see and experience India, its industry, people and culture, not only from an outside-in, but more importantly from an inside-out perspective. My efforts to understand the softer aspects of successfully navigating in India's IT industry culminated in my book *Working with India*, published by Springer in early 2009. On the professional front, I went on to work as a consultant for a wide variety of European companies on information system landscapes and the clever use of business information systems for supporting marketing strategies. In 2005 I was invited to teach a postgraduate course at the prestigious Indian Institute of Management, Bangalore, giving me a first-hand insight into a part of the education system on the subcontinent. After joining Capgemini, I was asked to again relocate to India and as director, to coordinate the delivery of our packaged application development projects for Central European clients. In close cooperation with both Western and Indian colleagues we further refined Capgemini's mature distributed delivery framework, termed Rightshore®. Together with my valued colleagues Anja Hendel and Frank Thun I edited offshore delivery concepts and case studies for our book *Rightshore! Successfully Industrialize SAP Projects Offshore*, published by Springer in 2008.

Looking back over those years, a number of things have matured in the IT offshoring market. First and foremost, clients have become wiser and more knowledgeable about IT landscape planning and outsourcing; naïve assumptions about offshoring no longer prevail today. Second, we hardly ever refer to IT companies as 'vendors' or 'subcontractors' any more. These terms imply a commodity view of IT and were used in the days when efforts were shifting from harnessing IT as an instrument creating strategic competitive advantage to providing services at the lowest possible cost. Repetitive mass production by cheap knowledge workers in India was supposed to work magic and lower overall IT costs, thereby freeing company employees to focus on building core competencies. Sometimes this worked and such successes were overly publicized, causing many companies to jump onto the India bandwagon. Following a natural human tendency, failures rarely made it to the headlines. Today, we have a more sophisticated understanding of IT. At the bottom layer, commoditized IT services systems and applications fuel the industry across industry sectors and make your company run as well as the competition. At the middle layer, IT supports industry-specific business processes following best practice standards. And at the top of the IT programme sits the part which creates competitive advantage. All three layers together, when operated in harmony, create value for the enterprise and its customers. Outsourcing and offshoring can be used as an instrument to enable and support all three layers, albeit in different forms, as I will show you in this book.

There are no greater business changes and challenges than the economic downturn which started with a financial crisis at the end of 2008. Companies all around the world now need to initiate changes that will allow business survival; I am convinced that offshoring can be a great help in this phase and can also ensure that companies stand a chance of emerging from this downturn in better shape than they were before.

I have written this book because I have seen the ups and downs of *ad hoc* offshoring, the issues involved in intercultural communication, and the still inherent lack of understanding about India's IT industry in the Western world. I have also seen the tremendous benefits of offshoring when it is implemented in a disciplined manner.

I have examined how offshoring can help to support business priorities in an economic downturn. Looking at relevant aspects of information technology, vendor management, India's IT growth phenomenon and intercultural collaboration from a client perspective, I have mapped the findings to India offshoring endeavours at a tactical, strategic or transformational level. In this process, I have reviewed – and also quoted in this book – a great deal of academic and practitioner literature, related it to my own experience and translated it to the needs of clients who are at the beginning or in the middle of an India offshore adventure.

The goal of this book is not to hand you a generic map, but to enable you to understand the drivers and inhibitors of offshoring to India; this will allow you to build your own roadmap and confidently enter into a learned discussion about the 'India option' in your company with leadership and employees, with analysts, and most importantly, with multi-national suppliers or firms of Indian origin.

Target audience

This book is written for people who want to provide strength and guidance in offshoring IT development and maintenance work to India. This task is not for the faint-hearted, during stable economic times and especially not in a downturn. Nor is it for the C-level executives alone. While the CIO is certainly at the centre of the action, everyone in both the business functions and IT departments has an important role to play. Hence this book is designed for the CEO, CFO, CIO, senior IT managers, and business unit leaders who look to manage a relationship with Indian offshore providers in order to better weather turbulent economic times.

Content and structure

The book opens with an explanation of offshoring, industrialization, and the role India plays in this context; it suggests a lifecycle approach to offshoring and examines how offshoring can help to achieve business and information technology priorities in a downturn. The positive as well as negative levers of the offshore business case are highlighted.

Providing a framework for assessing your company's organizational and technical 'India readiness', the book moves on to provide practical advice on offshore sourcing governance, the changes which need to be implemented in the company's own processes, and how the offshore journey can best be started. It bridges the gap between understanding India's country risk, correlating it with company risk, and providing a path to normalize the effects with a stringent business continuity plan. After considering the differences between a captive scenario and contracting with external Indian pure players or multi-national providers, the book offers a practical and lean five-step provider selection process (S-LEAN RFP™), which is centred around successfully running the offshore project and managing the relationship with the provider. This requires an understanding of the stakeholder segments involved, a stringent construct of measures to analyse and improve the offshore link, and an adoption of new skills in the front office. It closes by encouraging an understanding of the different cultural pre-programming of Indians and giving concrete advice on how to bridge the communication gap.

The idea of this book is to help C-level executives and IT project managers to cross the border to India by seeing the world as it really is, rather than in idealized terms. The book embodies the three *R*s. First, it is *relevant* because I have written it around company needs in the current changing economic climate; I have kept the discussion grounded in reality by focusing on where offshoring can save costs, create value, and how the offshore relationship can be managed to better achieve this. The frameworks and analysis provided can easily be customized by companies around the world considering offshoring IT development to India. Second, the book is *real* in the sense of combining my own personal business experience with rigorous academic research. I have now spent several years, at various points over the last decade, evaluating India offshore potential for international corporations, organizing India offshore projects, interacting with other Western and Indian practitioners, and – last but not least – living and travelling in India. Third, the book is *readable* due to its many examples, tables and illustrations. I have kept the book short and to the point – I know that your time is precious!

Enjoy the book!

WOLFGANG MESSNER
Principal, Capgemini

Any opinions expressed in this book are those of the author and not necessarily a view held by Capgemini as well.

S-LEAN RFP™ is an original trademark and used for the first time in this book.

About the Author

Wolfgang Messner started his career in 1995 as a business analyst and international project manager for Deutsche Bank AG. As early as 1998, he was assigned to Deutsche Bank's Indian subsidiary Deutsche Software (India) Pvt Ltd as expatriate project manager; his teams in Bangalore were instrumental in making the core banking system compliant with the new Euro currency. Between 1999 and 2006, he worked as a consultant for major European companies on business transformation projects with a focus on customer relationship management (CRM). In 2005, he accepted an invitation from the Indian Institute of Management Bangalore (IIM-B) and conducted a postgraduate MBA/PGSEM course as visiting professor. After joining Capgemini in Germany in 2006, he again moved to India from early 2007 to mid-2009, ramping up the company's offshore delivery capabilities for Central Europe. He is now a Principal with Capgemini in Germany; besides holding responsibility for offshore delivery, he focuses his consulting work on managing the relationship with Indian providers, the offshore lifecycle, and offshore governance structures.

Wolfgang Messner holds a doctorate in marketing from the University of Kassel (Germany), an MBA from the University of Wales (UK), and an advanced degree in computing science (Dipl.-Inform.) from the Technical University Munich (Germany). He has authored more than 25 papers in international journals and magazines, together with two books on offshoring to India. *Working with India: The Softer Aspects of a Successful Collaboration with the Indian IT & BPO Industry* was published in early 2009 by Springer and *Rightshore! Successfully Industrialize SAP Projects Offshore*, co-edited with Anja Hendel and Frank Thun, in 2008. Both books remain at the top of outsourcing bestseller lists.

Wolfgang Messner is married to Pratibha, an Indian national, and lives in Munich, Germany. His personal webpage can be found at http://www.wolfgangmessner.com

1
Offshoring: India's Playground

Offshoring is a contentious topic. Policy makers, business executives, thought leaders, and even presidential candidates express strong and often conflicting opinions about deploying young college graduates in emerging countries to take over service and IT development functions that were previously performed in a company's home location.

Offshoring at its core is not new. Relocating jobs to cut costs has happened in the past as well. In the 1980s many manufacturing plants in the north-eastern states of the USA moved to the South and South-west to save money; in Europe many companies have subsidiaries in eastern Europe where salaries are lower. Even before the fall of the Iron Curtain, in Germany for example, companies moved some units into then remote areas bordering their eastern European neighbours to make use of the salary difference within the country. In the UK, for instance, substantial salary differences between London and Manchester can be found.

With the onset of the current economic crisis, which started with a financial meltdown in late 2008, of course companies all around the world initiated changes to survive the downturn. In this context, offshoring to India again entered the limelight.

So what is new and special about this offshoring phenomenon, the industrialization concept, and the India debate? Let us first look at a few definitions and concepts to establish a common platform of terminology.

Offshoring terminology

Definitions

Often the terms offshoring and outsourcing are confused. *Outsourcing* is the act of obtaining services from an external source, that is, one whose business is incorporated outside the boundaries of the firm; it is a basic redefinition of the company around core competencies and long-term external relationships with suppliers. This redefinition happens with two objectives in mind. First, the value to the end customer should be increased. Second, the corporation should work at the highest productivity levels possible. Key to the definition of outsourcing is the concept of ongoing management and service delivery at prescribed performance levels. Outsourcing thus does not include hiring contract workers or short-term, project-based work provided by third parties; this is commonly referred to as body shopping or staff augmentation.[1] While outsourcing has traditionally meant having work performed, *cosourcing*, a rather new term,[2] is about a client and a provider melding their resources to accomplish the client's work. Both cooperate so closely that the provider can replace or augment the client's IT competencies. Another newly coined expression, *smartsourcing* is a paradigm telling you to focus on what you can do best while letting an external provider take responsibility for cost control and innovating change in non-core operations.[3] We can probably expect a few more such terms to surface in the next few years.[4] However, the added value of such artificial terms is rather limited; just consider the opposite of cosourcing or smartsourcing – would this be 'anti-sourcing' or 'dumbsourcing'?

Looking at places of service delivery, outsourced services may be provided domestically, that is, *onsite* in the company's own location and buildings, or *offsite* at the service provider's location. Offsite outsourcing, which makes use of in-country salary differences, is sometimes referred to as *closeshoring*.[5] Outsourced services may also be provided internationally and this is referred to as *offshoring*, *nearshoring*, or *farshoring*.[6]

With *offshoring* one participates in worldwide markets and does the things which are most appropriate and cost-effective in the respective markets. Offshoring concerns sourcing rather than sales activities, and it supports global or domestic rather than local operations.[7] *Nearshoring* is a derivative of the term offshoring and means sourcing activities from a foreign country which is relatively close in distance and/or time-zone. Examples are American companies nearshoring to Mexico or Canada, Austrian or German firms looking into Poland, Rumania, or Slovakia, and Japanese conglomerates sourcing from China, which would be a typical offshoring country for the USA or Europe. Sometimes *farshoring* is used to contrast sourcing from faraway countries like India with nearshoring.

Insourcing refers to bringing work back from outsourcing service providers into the home company and providing it as shared services. *Homeshoring* is the use of telecommuters.[8] Concepts like *Rightshore*®, a registered trademark of Capgemini, describe the art of delivering the right parts of a process from the right mix of locations.

In addition to international outsourcing, offshoring also comprises short-term project work and replacement of home company resources with more cost-effective international 'bodies', which is called body shopping or staff augmentation.

In this book, I will simply refer to *offshoring* as sourcing work from India and I will use the term *onsite* or *onshore* as work conducted at the company's home location.

Offshoring fields

Today, many multi-national companies and increasingly also small- and medium-sized enterprises (SMEs) pursue offshoring almost compulsively. Figure 1.1 shows that in every industry sector represented, more than 50 per cent of all companies now already offshore some of their IT function; health/pharma/biotech and financial services are leading with 78 and 71 per cent respectively.

Offshoring activities typically take place in four different fields: Application Development (AD), Application Maintenance (AM),

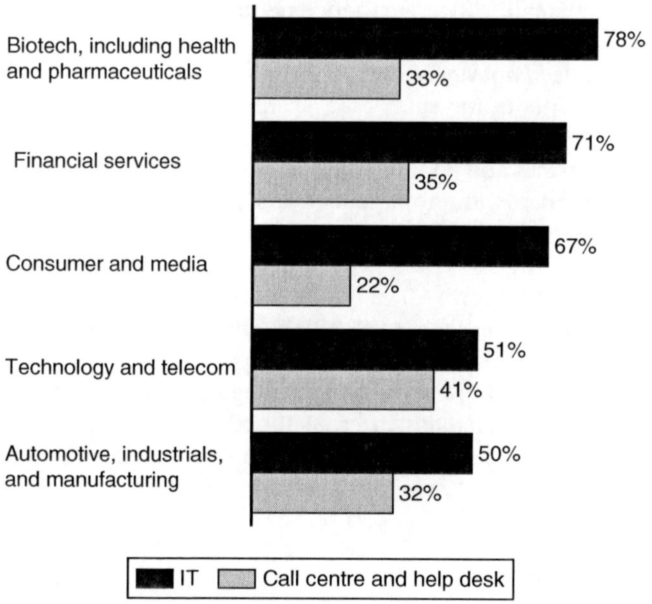

Figure 1.1 Percentage of firms offshoring
Source: Lewin and Couto (2006), p. 74. This is a study by Duke University in cooperation with Booz Allen Hamilton, US firms only.

Infrastructure Maintenance (IM), and Business Process Outsourcing (BPO).[9] Knowing about them is important for your discussions with providers as the organizational structure of many provider companies is built around these four areas; different account managers will be dealing with you for these different fields, charge-out rates of Indian resources may be substantially different, as may the kind of people working in these areas and their qualifications.

- *Application Development (AD)* is essentially computer programming with the target of developing new custom-built software, enhancing applications, consolidating and migrating applications, or configuring a standard commercial application package. Application development ends with the go-live and a short period of post-go-live support; afterwards application maintenance takes over.
- *Application Maintenance (AM)* supports the capture and resolution of maintenance requests for existing applications in order to ensure their smooth operation. Activities are around request management, incident management, processing of requests, identifying workarounds, providing resolutions, and analysing the root cause of issues. Sometimes small software enhancements are also covered under AM projects.
- *Infrastructure Maintenance (IM)* is the management of essential operation components for such core IT functions as systems, network and data storage management; it further includes security, end-user desktop services and application operations. It seeks to ensure adherence to standards, interoperability among organizational units, and effectiveness of change management procedures. Automated infrastructure maintenance services are delivered from a central point to anywhere in the world.
- *Business Process Outsourcing (BPO)* involves the contracting of the operations and responsibilities of a specific business function or process to an offshore vendor. It is categorized into back-office outsourcing, which includes internal functions like human resources, payroll, or finance, and front-office outsourcing, which is about customer-related services.

Levels of offshoring

When you look at the different ways in which offshoring is used in companies, you can identify three levels of offshoring: tactical,

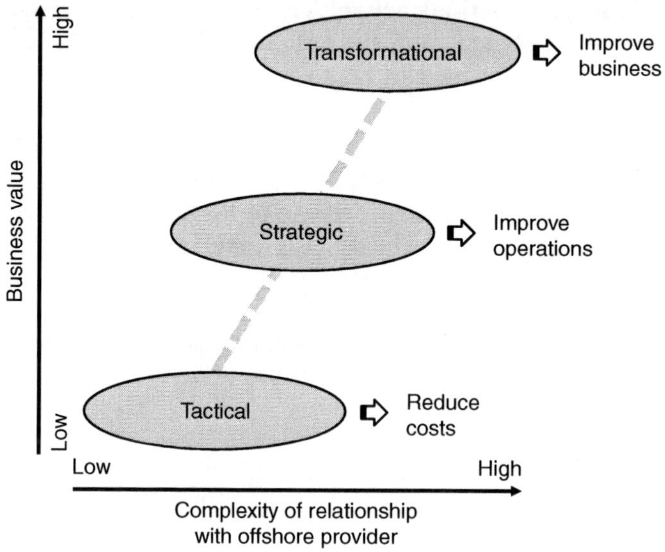

Figure 1.2 Levels of offshoring
Source: Based on the classification in Cohen and Young (2006).

strategic, and transformational.[10] The same terminology is also used for levels of outsourcing and this makes sense, because as we have seen before, offshoring is outsourcing with participation in worldwide markets.

If your company has been under intense financial pressure in recent years and has already turned to offshoring IT work and thereby driven cost out of the organization, then the obvious question is: what comes next? The levels of offshoring will show you the way ahead (see Figure 1.2).

Tactical offshoring

The drivers for tactical offshoring are usually tied to specific problems experienced by a company which have to be addressed directly and quickly. You may want to go for tactical offshoring, if your company faces the following corporate troubles:

- Need to generate immediate cost savings through labour arbitrage and an increase in efficiency
- Absence of resources or talent in your own company or the home market

Thus the focus of tactical offshoring is on constructing the right contract, getting the job delivered, and holding the vendor to the contract. All work is done under the existing rules of your IT organization.

Strategic offshoring

When companies aim to reap greater value from offshoring relationships, the strategic scope grows significantly. It is no longer about getting a specific job done, but about improving operations and integrating the scope of services. The relationship between your company and the supplier matures into a partnership between business equals with the emphasis on mutual benefit. You may decide to go for strategic offshoring if you face the following challenges in addition to the ones listed under tactical offshoring:

- Too much effort spent on managing multiple offshore vendors
- Need to free internal resources for higher value jobs

The primary focus is not on costs, but on improvement – which, of course, normally leads to reduced costs, higher quality and speed. At this stage, offshoring is used as part of the process of redefining your IT department. Your contract terms should focus on results, improvements and governance of a beneficial relationship with the provider. The level of trust required between you and the provider is elevated to a high level and thus a close alignment of interests becomes essential.

Transformational offshoring

With the third stage, the offshore provider is no longer seen as a tool, but becomes a powerful ally in the battle for introducing change into your IT department. You seek the experience in industrialization and innovation that the provider brings from the outside into your IT department. Thus there will be a shift from the operational task focus to the outcome, from simply cutting costs to creating value, from controlling the provider to asking the provider to help manage uncertainty, and from aligning with basically unchanged IT processes to aligning with offshore industrialized development and maintenance processes that help to support your strategic goals.

Such transformational offshoring projects assume that the specific services cannot be defined precisely at the very beginning of the project; instead, you need to agree with the provider on a baseline, a final goal, and satisfactory ways of measuring progress.[11]

Case Study 1: Voyage from application development to nearshore and offshore maintenance

Chemo AG is a pseudonym for one of the world's largest independent chemical companies with headquarters in Europe. It refines crude oil, produces gasoline blending components, and manufactures chemicals, polymers, and polyolefins; close to 90 per cent of its sales revenues are from the USA and Europe.

Chemo AG selected Adiuvo, a pseudonym for a multi-national IT service provider, to build a new ERP application. After successful implementation and go-live, Chemo AG intended to support this new application through an outsourced team at Adiuvo's delivery centre in Poland. Four clear imperatives drove the decision, thereby maximizing cost savings and minimizing risk through technology adaptation:

- Gain flexible access to development capacity to balance variations in demand
- Reap financial benefits by increasing productivity through a factory approach, fully utilizing factor cost differences in emerging countries, and transforming maintenance costs into variable costs
- Leverage development experience for maintenance support and enable a smooth transition
- Adhere to programming standards to provide high quality systems

During the initial phase of this nearshore application support project, most of the work was delivered onsite; Polish developers travelled to Chemo AG's headquarters on a weekly basis, interacted with their colleagues at Chemo AG and made the required changes to the programs. Only very few developers actually worked out of Adiuvo's nearshore delivery centre in Poland. For Chemo AG, this was almost as good as working together with home-country consultants: the Polish developers spoke the same language and they could interact face to face on most occasions. However, the initial cost savings were minimal and therefore Chemo AG and Adiuvo jointly decided on restricting the onsite presence of Polish developers to between 40 and 50 per cent; as an additional benefit, Chemo's employees would get accustomed to working in a distributed delivery mode. Through this setup, not only were substantial financial benefits reaped for Chemo AG over a period of four years, but release upgrades and international roll-outs in Asia were also supported. Experience showed that on average a capacity of 125 person days per month was sufficient to run and continuously improve Chemo's ERP system.

After around four years of operation, Chemo AG decided to further leverage cost arbitrage by utilizing offshore resources in India, to enhance the industrialization effect through embedding the application maintenance team in bigger delivery factories, and to increase the re-usability of code. This also meant a shift from a rather tactical offshoring approach to a more strategic one. In an evolutionary transition approach with clear knowledge transfer processes and exit criteria, the Polish developers were replaced one by one with offshore resources from Adiuvo's delivery centre in Bangalore. In the first three months, a production loss of 50 per cent was experienced, which was caused by knowledge transfer and getting accustomed to working across cultures. Subsequently, the production loss was brought down to 10 per cent. Notwithstanding these overheads, Chemo AG was able to more than double its overall cost savings as compared to the earlier nearshore approach. This was all in the initial stages before industrialization could really kick in and everybody expected further efficiency gains in the months to come.

However, the worldwide economic meltdown put even more cost pressure on Chemo AG. Despite all the projected and already proven cost savings through global delivery models, the result was not an increase in offshore utilization, but an inshoring fall-back strategy. Chemo AG had earlier merged with an American competitor who still largely followed an in-house software development approach. As a result of the recession, some of its own American IT employees had become idle and a business case showed clearly that the costs involved in laying them off would not be recuperated in the medium term through continuous offshoring. Hence, reverse knowledge transfer processes were set up and Adiuvo supported the inshoring of the application maintenance, thereby phasing out its Indian developers one by one with clear end dates.

Case Study 1 and its very surprising end illustrate that, when embarking on global delivery models, one needs to expect change and be ready for it. The choice of a trusted offshore partner makes it easier to ride these waves and reap the maximum benefits, from a financial, quality, and relationship perspective. This case study has also provided evidence that offshore projects do not necessarily have to be big in numbers in order to be a success – even smaller projects with 125 person days per month can be successfully and profitably run from India.

What is special about offshore industrialization?

I have seen many companies focusing foremost on cost cutting through offshoring. They may have actually achieved short-term cost savings by participating in worldwide labour markets, but failed to evolve their IT functions. Why?

- They have moved work offshore before fixing their internal IT development processes.
- They have lost sight of the bigger picture of enhancing IT performance.

Companies should strive not only for factor cost savings, but especially for cost-effectiveness and efficiency in their IT projects. A critical component in this journey is the industrialization of application development and maintenance. Offshoring to India is a good way to access the skills, tools, and scalability needed to industrialize.

What does industrialization of IT delivery mean? It means relying on standard systems, processes, methods, and tools for efficiency and effectiveness. With such standardization, one does not have to re-invent the wheel anew for each and every project. Or, in industrialization terms, the assembly will happen along the factory's production line. Processes of IT work can be standardized, work can be segmented and then dispersed globally, including to India, for the most efficient outcome. In his groundbreaking 2004 *Harvard Business Review* article on the services revolution, Uday Kamarkhar suggests,

> Think of technology as creating an information assembly line; information today can be standardized, built to order, assembled from components, picked, packed, stored, and shipped, all using processes resembling manufacturing. Industrialized information becomes steadily more efficient, less expensive, and more highly automated. The costs of logistics and storage are minimal; only labor and intellectual property matter. (Kamarkhar, 2004)

In practical terms, the use of specialized tools, templates, and prefabricated code pieces, together with flexible capacity management through quick staffing and de-staffing of a highly specialized workforce, makes the industrialized software factory work.

Of course, industrialization can equally well be achieved through outsourcing within the home country, through nearshoring or through offshoring to countries other than India. However, India has one unique advantage over home country outsourcing and other near- or offshoring locations, and this advantage comes from a relatively mature process-driven industry and the sheer numbers of IT developers. Some 1.47 million Indians[12] are currently working in the export-oriented and domestic software business. Offshoring and industrialization are hence levers which reinforce each other and only together manage to create maximum value. Figure 1.3 highlights the differences between offshoring and industrialization.

Services companies with India operations are currently moving towards IT industrialization.[13] It was a natural trend driven by customer

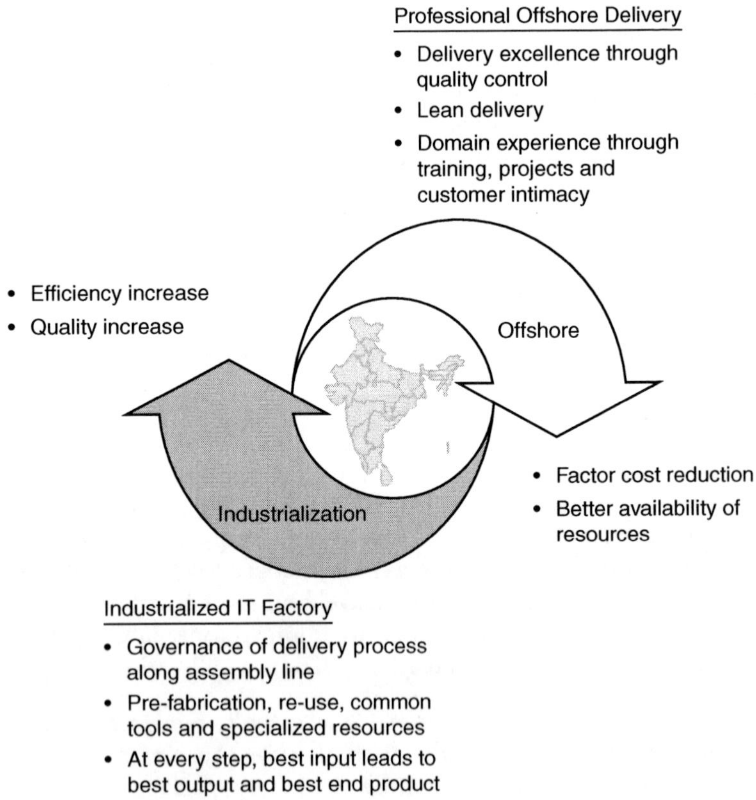

Figure 1.3 Industrialization and offshoring

expectations; offshore projects should be not only cheaper because of factor cost differences, but also on time, on budget, and more efficient. This is where the standardization of IT development processes comes in. It is a gradual shift from cost efficiency to service efficiency and delivery process management rather than project management. Project managers and team leaders now need to know how to set up, maintain, control and tune a production chain in which each deliverable is built by various people.[14] At the heart of the industrialization revolution is standardization of processes and deliverables, appropriate use of technology and specialized training of processes, tools, and standards.

Leading organizations estimate the effort savings potential through India offshore industrialization to be around 25 per cent compared with normal (onsite) project delivery with a more or less strict application of best practices. Figure 1.4 shows how these benefits can be achieved. This journey has to be made by service providers and their clients together; they depend on each other, their cooperation and thrift to drive things forward. An isolated approach does not lead anywhere – and here lies the danger for isolated captive centres; they may be left behind, as I will discuss later in Chapter 5.

Let us look in detail at Figure 1.4. The lowest quadrant shows a company engaging with an offshore provider for the first time; cost factor savings are immediate, but the project effort will go up by some 20 per cent due to knowledge transfer, communication overheads and initial misunderstandings. At this point, do not misinterpret effort increase as cost increase; due to factor cost savings, a 20 per cent effort overhead will still result in a substantial overall cost saving through factor cost differences. As the Indian service provider gains experience with your specific environment, the project effort can be slightly reduced, but an effort overhead of about 10 per cent compared with pure onsite delivery typically remains. Only when the offshore provider builds up domain expertise on top of customer knowledge and you, as customer of the service provider, can offer more than one single project to enable economies of scale, are there going to be savings in person days in addition to the cheaper factor costs. The real offshore industrialization effect kicks in when several clients across industry verticals offshore their work to the same offshore provider and economies of scale allow the provider to set up a proper process-driven delivery model.

IT service providers now need to focus their resources on the areas they want to industrialize and they need to concentrate their marketing and project acquisition activities on those key areas. Simply selling some headcount numbers here and there no longer leads anywhere.

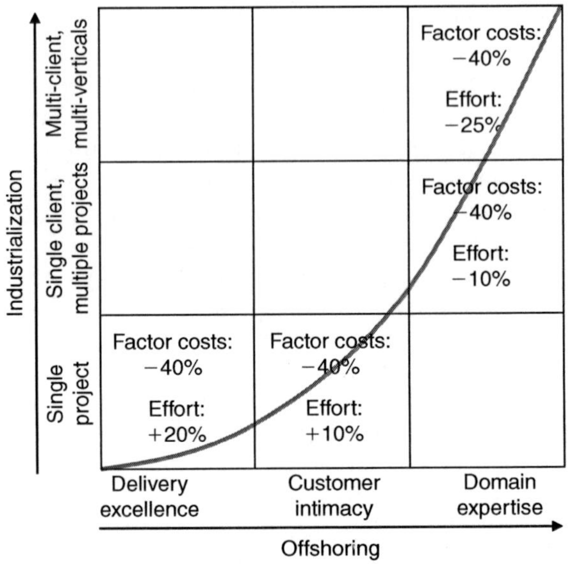

Figure 1.4 The benefits of industrialization and offshoring

Opportunistic sales behaviour has no place when it comes to reaping the benefits of industrialization.

This new industry trend has a serious effect on your selection of possible providers. Small companies do not have the necessary employee numbers to man the factory model, unless of course they operate in a very small 'niche' technology area or market; they will not be able to reap the full benefits of offshore industrialization and will be confined to standard offshore delivery models, applying standardized best practices wherever possible. I will return to this issue when we discuss provider selection in your evaluation process in Chapter 5.

For the next section, let us stay with offshoring and look at the role that India plays in this game.

The 'world is flat' syndrome

The fact that India became involved in the information technology offshoring game only after the opening of their markets in 1991, and in sizeable numbers really only after the turn of the last century, with almost one million direct employees[15] in the export-oriented software development and maintenance business at the beginning of 2009, makes its story quite unique. In addition, the Government of India supports the export-oriented IT and BPO industry by providing generous tax savings known as the Software Technology Park scheme (STP). India's IT industry also quickly adopted the software process improvement (SPI) standards ISO9000 in the early 1990s and the Capability Maturity Model (CMM) less than ten years later. Today, more than half of the total high-maturity organizations in the database of the Carnegie Mellon Software Engineering Institute (SEI) are from India.[16] Of course, India's high growth rate had to be managed by solid and controlled processes and thus SPI attracted the attention of management. It is an attempt to fight commoditization, ensure delivery quality, and move away from the notion of 'cheap is cheap'.

Still, offshoring is not a rite of passage. There are horror stories about failed offshoring endeavours, cultural clashes, quality problems, data thefts – and companies moving away from India for these very reasons. I know of CIOs who bravely state that they do not believe in offshoring. This is what makes offshoring contentious not only from a political, but also from a delivery success perspective. I have seen problems myself in more than a decade of personal involvement with offshore delivery; however, the reason for them is not always exclusively to be found on the Indian side. It generally takes two parties to create a problem. But when executives are asked about offshoring to India, they often spout slogans rather than substance. I have collected a few of these *pro* and *con* statements in Figure 1.5; they would indeed be amusing if they did not strike so frighteningly close to home.

New York Times columnist Thomas Friedman started the 'world is flat' syndrome with his 2005 book *The World is Flat*, which has been on various bestseller lists for many weeks and even today, in its second edition, can still be found in the bestselling section of many bookshops. Friedman says he was on a trip to India 'to understand why the Indians ... were taking our work, why they had become such an important pool for the outsourcing of service and information technology work' (Friedman, 2005, pp. 4–5). His personal account was written as a result of this expedition; at more than 450 pages, the book is long, but unfortunately it includes no charts, tables, footnotes or references and is thus very difficult to engage with.[17]

Today it goes without saying that technologies, communication media and standards do enable connectivity and collaboration across the world. In addition, certain services can be performed or developed at a location different from where they are delivered.

Nevertheless, it is a long way from these findings to pronouncing a flat world, where distances do not matter any more. Borders and differences

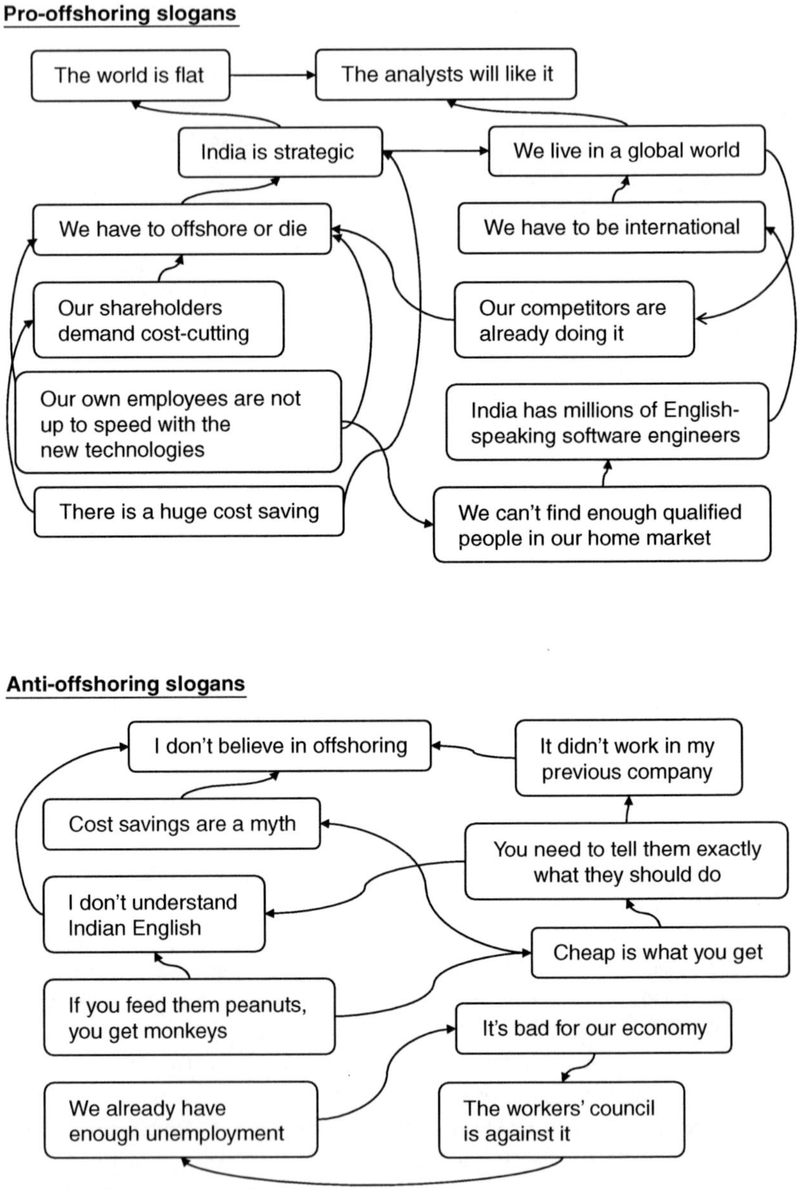

Figure 1.5 A web of offshoring slogans

do matter in the real world; distances can be found in four different dimensions, the so-called CAGE dimensions:[18]

- *Cultural distance* refers to the attributes of people that are engrained into them during their upbringing and childhood.
- *Administrative distance* attributes are found among administrative, regulatory, legal, and policy frameworks that are enforced by governments.
- *Geographical distance* is the physical distance between two countries, their time zone differences, differences in climates, and absence of common land borders.
- *Economic distance* is about the differences in economic mechanisms that affect cross-border relationships, for example, economic size, amount of trade and per capita income.

In the light of these real and existing differences between Western countries and India, the question becomes: how can we best carve out, agree on and implement a global delivery model that overcomes the obstacles of distance and at the same time makes full use of the advantages that India's IT industry has to offer?

The following chapters of this book are not about who, on either side of the CAGE difference dimensions, is right or wrong – this would be a never-ending debate adding no value to the business priorities of a changing business landscape. I will show you in which scenarios offshoring can be beneficial for meeting your targets, give you enough background information so that you can confidently talk with providers, and explain what you should do to make it work. As we shall see, almost one million people were directly employed in India's export-oriented software business in 2009 – and they must be doing something useful!

India: economic powerhouse or the third world?

Many books have been written about the awakening of the Indian tiger and many of them paint a picture of globalization apocalypse.[19] In the previous section I have argued against the 'world is flat' syndrome which has so frequently made it to the news. True, India's growth story is amazing and its wealth has become a topic of debate not only in India, but also in newspapers, pubs and even presidential campaigns of the Western world. In 2004 in the USA, Democratic candidate John Kerry built his campaign against the then President George W. Bush on the fears of Americans losing jobs to India. In May 2008, both President George W. Bush and his Secretary of State Condoleezza Rice blamed the increased spending capacity of India's growing middle class for contributing to the global rise of food prices. And at the end of 2008, presidential candidate Barack Obama won votes by promising to protect US interests through reducing offshoring jobs; he made it to the White House as President.

You should not be blinded by such high profile statements. When you are on your first business trip to India, and no later, you will notice that not everything is bright in this country. A night approach by plane to an Indian metropolis like New Delhi, Mumbai, or Bangalore does not feel like landing in New York, London, or Dubai. Where are all the lights illuminating these giants at night? There may be a power cut and parts of the city are either in darkness or running on a diesel back-up generator; many districts still do not have street lights. During the day, the picture becomes clearer. Airports like Mumbai are surrounded by mushrooming and encroaching slums in which millions of people live; an estimated 40 per cent of Mumbai's population lives in slums. At this point you need some facts.

Despite being the fourth largest economy in the world, based on purchasing power adjusted GDP, 25 per cent of India's population lives below the poverty line and the unemployment rate is estimated at 9.5 per cent.[20] Depending on the region, between 27 and 55 per cent of India's children under the age of four are malnourished.[21] 61 per cent of India's population cannot read or write at all – neither English nor any of the many local languages. This part of the population is on the edge of society and life is a daily struggle for them.

When you reach your luxury five-star airport hotel or one of the business parks the next day, you move from the real India into the virtual India, and the picture looks different again. Of course, in total the economic situation also looks different. For many years India saw a GDP annual growth rate of 8.5 per cent or even more. In 2009, and as an effect of the global economic meltdown, it has come down to seven per cent; still a very high growth percentage compared to some shrinking economies in the western hemisphere. A good 55 per cent of the GDP is attributed to the services sector – in which only 28 per cent of the labour force finds employment. Agriculture and industry are both areas for concern. With regard to agriculture, 60 per cent of the country's workforce contributes only 16.6 per cent to the GDP. Despite favourable monsoon seasons in recent years, water mismanagement and a lack of adequate storage facilities both lead to a lot of wasted produce. It is sad to see that India's children are malnourished while food supplies are rotting away or being eaten by rats in ramshackle warehouses.

In India itself, people are extremely proud of their country's achievement and feel irritated when it is still seen as a magical oriental place, full of snakes and tigers. Instead, if India wins or loses a cricket match, it becomes a national issue. And if an Indian company buys a Western competitor, it is a symbolic move. In February 2007, the Tata Group bought Corus, the British Steel company, and in early 2008, it took over the brands of Jaguar and Land Rover from Ford. The last deal was not too successful; in late 2008, Tata had to ask the British government for a bailout in the form of a GBP 500m loan guarantee to secure the jobs at their Jaguar plant in the United Kingdom.[22] Understandably, nothing much is written about this part of the story in the Indian press.

In a nutshell, India is in many ways still a developing nation – and will continue to be so for many years to come. In other ways, it is moving forward at the speed of light. When offshoring work to India, this dichotomy surfaces in one way or the other. In later chapters, I will show you concrete examples of managing business continuity risk (Chapter 4) and intercultural communication (Chapter 7). For now, we need to understand more about India's IT industry, how it has suddenly evolved from nowhere, its current status, and where it is heading in the next few years.

India's IT story

Late start in 1991

In 1991, the long running fiscal deficit precipitated an economic crisis in India, the country was *de facto* bankrupt, and the government was forced to relax controls over the movement of foreign capital. Indian IT firms, led by Infosys, Tata Consultancy Services (TCS), and Wipro, which were beginning to outgrow the limited domestic market, took the opportunity of starting to serve the IT needs of foreign customers by sending their employees as temporary workers to onsite assignments as 'landed resources'; this business model quickly became known as *bodyshopping*. Multi-national IT players started seeing a market opportunity in India as well, but they only came to India in big numbers after the year 2000.

The introduction in 1999 of the Software Technology Park (STP) scheme, with major tax savings for the export market, further encouraged this development. As a side effect, Indian IT companies quickly lost interest in serving the domestic market with its lower margin and now also less beneficial tax structures; some companies focused almost exclusively on the export market.

The STP scheme also kick-started the business process outsourcing (BPO) industry. Indians, being clever, argued that a workplace in a call centre is also equipped with a computer and coined the new umbrella term ITES, which stands for IT Enabled Services and is supposed to include application development, maintenance, infrastructure management and business process outsourcing. At the end of the discussion, the Government of India granted the BPO industry the same tax reliefs as the STP scheme.

Millennium Bug boom times from 1999 to 2001

The next two waves of demand for Indian software developers came in shortly before the turn of the last century. Around the world, panic struck IT managers, their CIOs, and CEOs about a possible 'millennium bug' in their corporate software systems. Some pieces of code developed earlier in the twentieth century only provided two digits for the year, instead of four (for example, 99 instead of 1999). On 1 January 2000, the date on the computer system would then read 01-01-00, possibly causing the operating system to interpret it as 01-01-1900 instead of 01-01-2000. All the data fields had to be extended, the program code recompiled, and the full software tested again. This job was of course very laborious, time-consuming, and at the same time not very demanding. The developed world was happy to find Indian computer scientists at comparatively cheap daily rates. Almost at the same time, many European countries introduced the common Euro currency; all core banking systems and also many corporate accounting systems had to be adapted to handle two currencies at the same time, and finally convert accounts from a legacy currency to the new Euro. The demand for Indian resources was huge, and the Indian IT industry, being rather unprepared, faced its first challenge in providing enough personnel to meet the global demand. Many graduates from related disciplines – engineering, mathematics, sciences, and commerce – signed up for programming classes and found a short cut into the software industry. Even doctors, architects and civil servants were lured away from their jobs into the better-paying world of information technology. It was in this environment that the Indian IT industry introduced walk-in interviews in an attempt to industrialize and speed up the recruitment process. The HR department together with senior specialists and project managers teamed up, rented a hotel for a weekend and invited candidates to simply show up with their curriculum vitae, but without any previous registration. First, members of the HR department matched the CV against openings, conducted an attitude interview and passed the candidate on to a specialist for a technical interview. The candidate would then be asked to solve various programming tasks in his domain expertise. On successful completion of this second interview, the project manager in the third room would decide whether to recruit the candidate onto the project. In the year 2009 and in the middle of an economic downturn, this now sounds like a fairytale of a long-forgotten past. Nonetheless, these stories are true and I had the opportunity to witness these market dynamics myself. At that time, I was an (expatriate) project manager in India and hired quite a number of good employees through this channel. Notwithstanding, there were many fakes to be filtered out and I particularly remember one candidate who claimed to be an expert on artificial intelligence. Not that I needed these skills for my Euro project, but it attracted my attention, and I asked him about neural networks. After a little bit of quizzing he had to admit that he knew a friend who knew something about it. Needless to say, I showed him the door.

During this first India IT hype, in the financial year 2000/1, the export market with a revenue of 6.2 billion USD managed for the first time to outgrow the domestic market with 5.9 billion USD. From now on India would be an important player in the IT offshore business (see Figure 1.6).

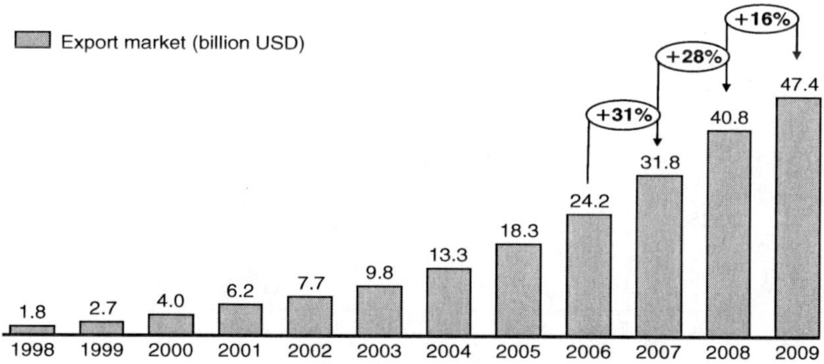

Figure 1.6 Revenue generated by the Indian IT industry

Note: I first showed this diagram in my previous book Messner (2009a), p. 67; here it is limited to the export industry and updated with the most recent data, which is collected from Nasscom (2009). Note that the Indian financial year does not follow the calendar year, so the financial year 2009 runs from April 2008 to March 2009.

Source: Nasscom (Feb 2009). Figures include IT services, engineering services, R&D, S/W products, ITES-BPO, and hardware.

Back in 1991, the Indian IT industry started as a labour-arbitrage bodyshop; through the introduction of quality models like ISO and CMM it provided process support and guidance to all its new and very young employees. While the financial year 2001/2 did not see much of an increase in the revenue generated through IT services from India, by 2002/3, Indian IT engineers had not only learnt how to solve problems, but started to gain experience in re-engineering processes and making process flows more effective. This was when the rollercoaster ride of the Indian IT boom really kicked off.

The industry overheats in 2007/08

The worldwide IT service market grew from USD 677 billion in 2006 to 748 billion in 2007 and 819 billion in 2008.[23] Within this market, the global sourcing industry was at USD 79 billion in 2008;[24] India had a 51 per cent market share of USD 40.8 billion. Offshore delivery was growing at 14.5 per cent in Europe and 18 per cent in North America, thereby soaking up more and more market share;[25] revenue from Indian IT exports reached USD 40.8 billion in the financial year 2008 and 47.4 billion in 2009. This is a compound annual growth rate (CAGR) of 16 per cent. There was strong optimism in the industry that a target of USD 60 billion would be achieved by 2010.[26]

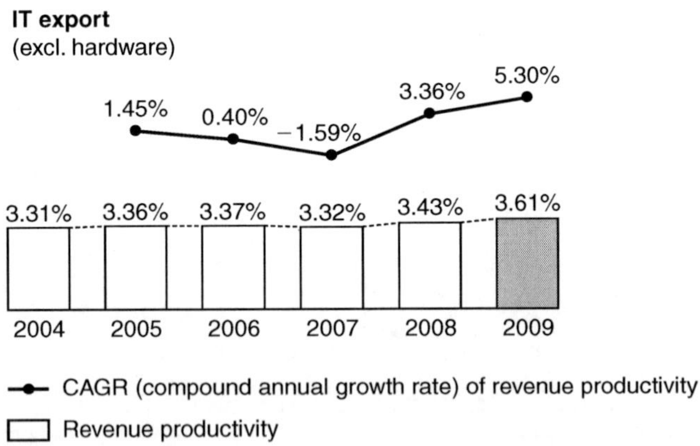

Figure 1.7 Revenue productivity of the Indian export IT industry
Note: I first showed this diagram in my previous book Messner (2009a), p. 71; here it is updated with the most recent data. Note that the Indian financial year does not follow the calendar year, so the financial year 2009 runs from April 2008 to March 2009.

In the financial year 2007/8, the entire IT industry grew at a staggering rate of 33 per cent and the export industry at 28 per cent. However, this fantastic growth was mainly due to an explosive increase of manpower. The charge-out rates to Western customers were only adjusted to the rise and fall of the rupee. Figure 1.7 shows that the industry's revenue productivity remained fairly stable between 3.31 per cent and 3.43 per cent in the years 2003/4 to 2007/8; in fact it even had a negative compound annual growth rate in 2006/7 and only picked up again in 2007/8. In comparison, the BPO industry shows less than half of IT's revenue productivity.[27] In other words, India's IT industry was thriving on adding people with similar skill levels and winning projects at the same level in the value creation chain, rather than focusing on higher value services.[28] As a business model this is not endlessly scalable and difficult to sustain. Interestingly, in the financial year 2008/9, both the export IT and BPO industries seem to have matured and revenue productivity went up by 5.3 per cent to 3.61 per cent and by 4.08 per cent to 1.62 per cent respectively. Despite the looming downturn this has been the biggest increase in the industry's value added in recent years.

Let us now look at the climbing headcount curve of India's IT industry (Figure 1.8). In 2006/7 and 2007/8, the industry added around 25 per cent new personnel each year! In absolute numbers this is between 330,000 and 390,000 additional people every year, and even more in terms of new joiners as there are also people leaving the industry to set up a business on their own or migrating to the USA, for instance. This has caused great pressure on the HR functions of Indian IT providers. Salaries shot up in a competition for talent and at the same time most providers were forced to make some compromises on formal educational requirements and took in less qualified people as well. Employees began to show little loyalty to their employers, but were more interested in their next salary increase, their kind of assignments, and their career advancement. Some companies took a decision to set up additional offices outside India's established IT corridors in so-called tier II and tier III cities. I will discuss these trends further on page 30.

The Indian IT industry was not only greedy in terms of adding thousands of new staff to their employee base every week, but in 2008 they suddenly became alarmed about the scheduled ending of the ten-year tax relief offered by the STP scheme. On the grounds that the industry was still not mature enough to compete with other international players and markets, they argued for a further prolongation of the tax reliefs. The Indian government gave in and prolonged the STP scheme for

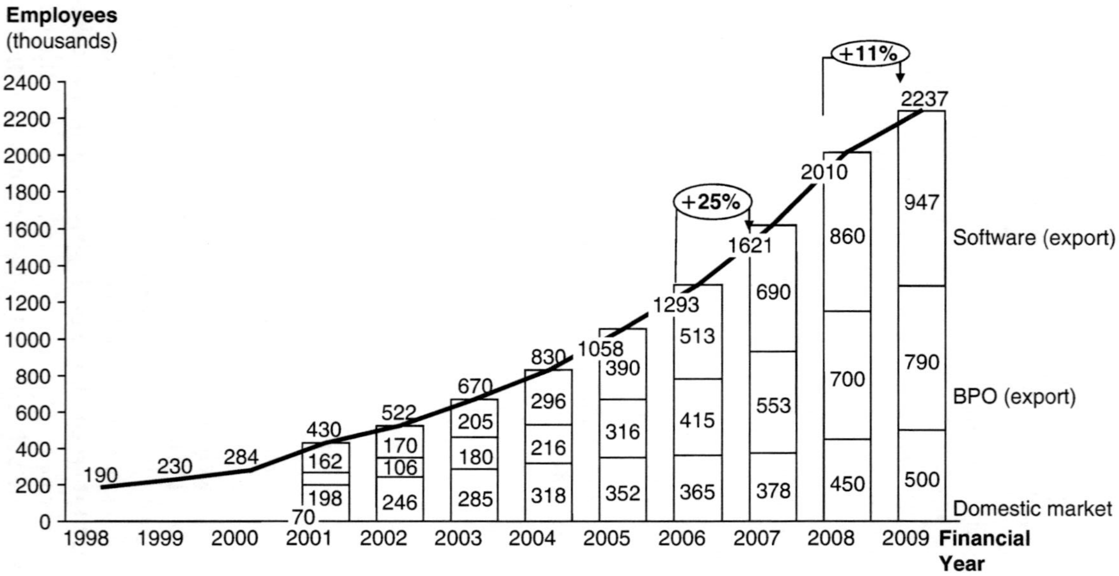

Figure 1.8 Headcount increase in the Indian IT industry

Source: Data based on Nasscom (2009).

Note: I first showed this diagram in my previous book Messner (2009a), p. 68; here it is updated with the most recent data, which is collected from Nasscom (2009). The figures do not include employees working in the IT hardware domain. Note that the Indian financial year does not follow the calendar year, so the financial year 2009 runs from April 2008 to March 2009.

another year until March 2010; later in 2009, another one-year extension to 2011 was announced.

The worldwide meltdown hits India in 2009

In this environment of job exuberance, the financial meltdown of October 2008 was initially met with disbelief. From an Indian viewpoint, this was considered to be unfair, and it was beginning to spoil many individual expectations. Suddenly the IT companies introduced recruitment freezes, bonuses were cut and salary increments reduced. A fierce charge-out rate war started, companies bidding lower and lower rates just to keep their employees busy and avoid lay-offs. There are cases where Indian IT providers have increased the weekly working hours in order to be able to bill more hours and thus make up for the lower charge-out rates. Many companies have introduced a concept of a 'virtual bench', in which they ask employees to stay at home and pay them only a fraction of their normal salary (or nothing at all). If there is a project, they would be called back and given their full salary again. Some companies have also started dismissing employees. Employees being fired in the Indian IT industry? Of course, all on the grounds of underperformance. This was quite a change and shock for the pampered IT engineers, who suddenly found their financial dreams lying shattered on the ground. Unfortunately, the Indian team managers and HR departments are not fully trained and experienced in handling this professionally, so there are cases of employees being harassed by their superiors and 'forced' to put in their papers 'voluntarily' in return for a favourable reference. Even though only an estimated five per cent of jobs are at stake,[30] fear has gripped the entire community of IT professionals. This industry problem quickly spills over to society at large. A spending freeze by software engineers has already led to empty pubs and restaurants, some of them even offering recession discounts. The real estate prices are sliding, it has become difficult for software engineers to get a loan from private banks and IT is no longer the preferred profession for grooms in arranged marriages.

In terms of overall headcount, Figure 1.8 shows a reduced growth rate of only 11 per cent for the Indian financial year 2008/9 (April 2008 to March 2009), as compared to 25 per cent in the two previous years. We can very much expect a zero growth rate for the financial year 2009/10, if figures are reported honestly. The industry is most likely not going to shrink, but remain stable as many Western companies will be reconsidering their IT value chain and will be looking even more carefully into options for managing their cost base.

Apart from the worldwide recession, two more problems hit the industry at the beginning of 2009; only this time they were home-made.

The World Bank banned three Indian IT firms from doing business with them due to improper behaviour; the ineligible firms were Wipro for four years (2007–2011) for providing improper benefits to World Bank staff, Megasoft for four years (2007–2011) for participating in a joint venture with bank staff while also conducting business with the World Bank, and Satyam for eight years (2008–2016) for giving improper benefits to bank staff and failing to maintain documentation to support fees charged for its subcontractors.[31]

For Satyam, it was the least of its problems. In the first week of 2009, its founder and chairman, B Ramalinga Raju, admitted to the country's biggest financial fraud. On 16 December 2008, Satyam shareholders had reacted negatively towards Satyam's bid to acquire Raju's family-owned company Maytas Infrastructure[32] for USD 1.6 billion. On 2 January 2009, Raju disclosed to the stock exchange that his family had pledged all its shares to institutional lenders. Three of the independent directors resigned. On 7 January, Raju confessed having faked the balance sheet, making up accrued interest, understating liability, and overstating debtors' positions.[33] He was later suspected to have faked employee numbers as well, having transferred substantial amounts of imaginary salary payments to his own private account. India was stunned at the magnitude of this corporate drama. The *Indian Economic Times* covered the news on its front page and termed Satyam a big lie,[34] subtly referring to the Sanskrit translation of Satyam – which is 'truth'. At many points in the first quarter, it was feared that the company could not pay salaries to its employees. India's government reacted quickly and introduced a government-controlled board to oversee the functioning and later sale of the company to Mahindra. All Satyam employees were taken by surprise, but given the market situation, they could do little else but fear for their salary payments and jobs. I have personally received a sizeable number of emails from Satyam employees asking if I had a job for them. Let us just imagine for a moment that the Satyam fall-out had happened only half a year earlier when the entire Indian IT industry was still recruiting on a grand scale. On hearing the bad news about their employer, the 40,000 plus employees would all have reached out to headhunters and other companies and many of them would probably have found a new job. Satyam as a company would have evaporated in no time; clients would have had to shift their projects to other vendors in a hurry. Only the economic crisis has prevented this from happening and saved the employee base of Satyam.

Critical analysis of India's IT industry

Offshore vendors, Indian associations, and the press never tire of promoting India as the El Dorado for offshoring IT and BPO services. They build their arguments around the British heritage, the industry's maturity levels and quality norms (ISO and CMM respectively), the support of India's Government, foreign investments in India, English language proficiency, and – of course – the ready availability of talent. Together these form a flywheel of success,[35] graphically depicted in Figure 1.9, and a compelling proposition to potential customers.

While all these arguments are certainly true in one form or another, a somewhat more critical view helps to build realistic expectations, align project setups accordingly, and finally deliver more successful India offshore projects. In the next section, I am going to critically analyse this flywheel of success, looking at positives as well as limitations. Without all these perspectives you will not have the complete picture to evaluate the 'India option' independently and correctly for your own company.

Figure 1.9 The Indian IT flywheel of success: a boilerplate version

Heritage

Indians are proud of their independence from the British colonial powers and celebrate Independence Day each year on 15 August, not only in government quarters in New Delhi, but on every road and in every village. In short, Indians are proud of having shaken off their colonial past and become independent. Democracy was introduced in the aftermath of independence and it is certainly true that India is the world's biggest democracy in terms of the number of its citizen. Having said this, I would estimate that at least two-thirds of the population does not know how the political system of the country functions, is bribed into voting for a certain party, and on election day is loaded onto a truck and driven to the polling station with clear instructions.

After independence, India tried a policy of non-alignment. As a member of the Commonwealth it had to balance relationships with Great Britain and a friendship move towards the Soviet Union, which was necessary due to conflicts with China and US support for Pakistan. Only the financial crisis of 1991 and India's *de facto* bankruptcy forced the country to open itself up to the Western world for trade and investment. Hence, India's much famed openness to the West is not even twenty years old – and certainly did not come voluntarily.

On a different note, the concept of zero as a number and not merely a symbol for separation is attributed to India; the Indian scholar Pingala in the 4th century BC used binary numbers in the form of short and long syllables similar to Morse code, in 628 AD Brahmagupta for the first time published rules governing zero in his book *Brahmasputha Siddhanta* (The Opening of the Universe), and by the 9th century AD practical calculations were carried out using zero, which was treated like any other number. Some people therefore attribute a certain mathematical inclination to Indians. This argument, however, could not be more ridiculous. During the days of the great Indian mathematicians, science was studied only by a tiny elite sub-group of Brahmins; if the idea that such extraordinary genes would have been passed across so many generations is already far-fetched, today's IT industry employs people from so many diverse backgrounds that only a tiny number would be related to the great mathematicians of ancient times.

CMM/ISO

Software process improvement (SPI) is a true Indian success story. In the early 1990s, the quality norm ISO9000 was introduced and in the late 1990s, when CMM was introduced, almost the entire Indian IT industry applied for re-certification. While process improvements are usually a tedious and slow process, the fast adaptation in India throws up one question: why? The Indian software industry had to convince their customers thousands of miles away that they could provide a high quality service. ISO and CMM as globally accepted quality models were a key factor in this argument. The need to reduce risk in fixed-price contracts required some formalities at the offshore interface and a stringent monitoring of all activities. And, most importantly in my opinion, albeit rarely ever mentioned, the high growth rate of the Indian IT industry with its intake of less and less qualified people to meet head-count projections, fast-track promotions, and high attrition rates had to be compensated, managed, and controlled by solid processes.

Having said this, many individuals in Indian IT companies have taken quality to their hearts; they have not only implemented quality systems in their respective companies, but have also contributed actively to further improving these systems, which leads to the development and adoption of the various CMM levels.

It is important to mention that CMM certification at the highest possible level does not give you quality deliverables; this is still the job of humans and this aspect especially holds true for the future. At one time, India's IT industry was only asked to maintain age-old legacy systems on mainframes, but now offshore providers are challenged to build new systems from scratch, implement standard packaged applications, and support mission-critical processes. All this is well beyond the software development steps required by CMM and other certifications; it requires a good deal of business process knowledge. Quality certification really only ensures that deliverables are of consistent quality, deviations are detected, and the root causes identified. They will thus continue to be an important building block to ensure quality, but they alone will not be enough for the projects and challenges in the years to come.

Government

There is a saying in India which people don't whisper, but shout: The enormous success of India's IT industry is not because of India's government, but in spite of it!

The government has certainly helped the IT industry to become competitive by giving them generous tax breaks under the scheme of software technology parks (STPs) or special economic zones (SEZs). It has also attempted to simplify some regulations of the Indian bureaucracy, but at the same time has introduced a dozen others.

What critics mull over are hard facts. First, before the worldwide recession hit India as well, the IT industry was so hungry for resources that it took in 20 per cent more new resources every year. Indian universities, on the other hand, were only able to increase their output by 4 per cent every year;[36] naturally this leads to an ever-increasing talent gap and the government is accused of not doing enough to improve the education system. Second, the public infrastructure is so bad in India's megacities that employees need to be shuffled in company buses or taxis to work; an acceptable public transport system is more or less non-existent. Traffic is so badly regulated that the rush hour turns major ring roads into parking places. Many colleagues I know waste between three and five hours on the road every day. And third, is the government doing anything to eradicate corruption and bring law and order into the country – so that employees with forged references and qualification certificates will be blacklisted, if not put behind bars for document forgery as in other developed nations?

Investment

Despite the global slowdown, India has managed to display resilience and attract good investments. The foreign direct investment (FDI) inflows during the financial year 2009 (from April 2008 to March 2009) stood at approximately USD 27.3 billion.[37] As global flows decline, India still manages to achieve substantial increases to the tune of 85 per cent in foreign direct investment flows.[38]

February 2009 saw changes of attitudes and policies towards FDI in India and some sectors are now open to 100 per cent foreign investment while financial services, insurance, retail, and telecommunication are still very much restricted.[39]

The post financial liberation era after 1991 has seen a huge influx of multinational companies (MNCs) into the subcontinent. The majority of these companies are of American origin, but in recent years more and more companies from Europe, Asia (mainly Japan, Malaysia, Singapore and South Korea), and the Middle East are showing huge investments. While they appreciate India's market potential, labour competitiveness and macro-economic stability, they keep complaining about the government's sometimes irrational policies with respect to trade barriers and tax structures, the low investment in physical and information technology infrastructure, and the slowness of political reform to improve stability, privatization, deregulation, and labour laws.

Good corporate governance, which is the system that helps firms control and direct operations, used to be one of the strongest selling points of India's IT industry. Unfortunately, it has come under a negative spotlight as a result of the Satyam and WorldBank case (see p. 24) as key parts of the governance framework, such as audit and finance functions, have failed to check the promoter-driven agendas. While the frameworks as such are mostly on a par with other developed countries, the industry will, going forward, need to implement them both in letter and in spirit. The government needs to prove not only that it does not fail to prosecute, but takes swift and severe action against culprits.

Language

Perhaps the most important aspect of British colonialism was the creation and psychological indoctrination of a new Indian quasi-caste of British sympathizers that not only picked up the English language but also supported foreign rule. As a result, English established itself as the *de facto* social and business language of the Indian upper class and this continued after independence. It helped to resolve the problem of not having one common language on the subcontinent; India has 15 officially recognized languages and more than 1,600 mother tongues and dialects. Hindi is the national language, but is the primary tongue of only about 30 per cent of the people and is only widely spoken in the North. There are even attempts in the southern states to restrict the use of Hindi.

While India can surely take pride in having a much larger English-speaking workforce compared with China and other offshoring destinations, other (especially non-native) English speakers complain about difficulties in understanding 'Indian English'. While education in India's better colleges and universities is in English, most Indians do not speak English at home, but their local language. Their English, though fluent and sometimes with a surprisingly wide vocabulary, may thus have some gaps; they tend to speak very fast, at an even pace, in a syllabic rhythm, and without much intonation. This makes Indian English initially difficult to understand. However, although thickly accented English may be annoying, at the end of the day it is not so important for most offshore development positions; technical and managerial skills are of far greater relevance.

Going forward, as the USA and UK account for less and less of the offshore delivery pie, the advantage of an English-speaking workforce in India will not be as great as it used to be. Many Europeans still prefer to be served in their local languages. Indians are multi-lingual, but only in the various languages of their own country, and foreign language education falls short in the curriculum of most schools.

Talent

India's IT industry is keen to highlight and advertise its huge number of qualified IT engineers and the quality of its colleges, universities and business schools, which are supported by private training institutions. The Indian Institutes of Technology (IITs) and Indian Institutes of Management (IIMs) are frequently mentioned as government-owned premier flagship institutions, leading one to believe that every IT engineer has a degree from one of these truly world-class schools.

Together, all universities and colleges in India annually produce around 117,000 engineers with an IT-related 4-year degree and another 76,000 with a 3-year diploma course. However, the IT industry required between 200,000 and more than 400,000 new joiners each year.[40] Here we have discovered the first gap – the industry needed to add more people annually than the whole university system would produce for the job market. The second gap is that of skill requirements. According to a study by the McKinsey Global Institute, 75 per cent of Indian engineering graduates lack fluency in English or in interpersonal skills, or demonstrate educational emphasis on theory at the expense of practical knowledge.[41] All this does not fit well with the requirements of multinational companies and the India boom. That is why the *talent shortage* is the single largest impediment to the growth of the IT industry in India.

As a consequence, companies have been forced to open up additional offices outside India's silicon valleys, the so-called tier I cities, namely Bangalore, Chennai, Hyderabad, Kolkata, Mumbai, and the New Delhi National Capital Region (NCR). These tier II and III had lower property prices and sometimes surprisingly good infrastructure to offer because the regional governments were really interested in attracting IT and BPO industries. Some 50 per cent of India's students also graduate outside the tier I cities and the industry was able to compete on the employment market with a location advantage. The salaries offered to attract talent also shot up. In 2007 and 2008, I saw consultants with some five years of programming experience being offered a team leader position at a competitor with a 90 per cent salary increase. While such were extraordinary – or lucky – cases, an average 40 per cent rise when joining a competitor was pretty much expected. Many compromises on formal educational requirements and soft skills had to be made in order to fill positions. While in 1997 and 1998, a good number of the functional consultants working in my team had first-rate educational backgrounds from IITs and IIMs, in 2007 and 2008 such people could only be found in management positions leading units of 500-odd people – if they were attracted to the IT industry at all. As a countermeasure, the IT industry had to take education and training into its own hands. Many companies built separate training campuses for inducting college graduates into the real business world. During the first three months, they go through technical and personal training in order to upgrade their competencies, then they work-shadow more experienced colleagues on a real project for another three months, and only afterwards are they allowed to work on their first client-billable project.

Especially rare were the experienced project or middle managers. New market entrants and other offshoring nations tried to lure them from established companies, offering high salaries; many were also looking to migrate to the Western world. As a result, the salary arbitrage was really only valid for entry level programmers, and not for heads of delivery. The salaries of directors and vice presidents could comfortably compare with Western salaries. Annual salary increases in these years before the recession of 2008 were around 15 per cent, not taking into account increments due to promotion.[42]

Of course this situation has also driven up attrition; employees were always ready for a job change in return for a good salary rise. In reality, no Indian IT vendor had attrition under control. But customers still always asked for attrition figures – and never got an honest answer. It has helped that there is no industry standard for calculating attrition. Many companies have thus not included new joiners who had signed the employment contract, but never showed up for work, or new joiners resigning within the first six weeks, or employees absconding from work who haven't even bothered to formally resign. Nevertheless, some project teams could show very low attrition rates because their technology and work environment was very promising for the career aspirations of their team members.

To combat the hiring pressure and at the same time keep up quality, leading IT companies have implemented stringent hiring processes designed for maximum efficiency and at the same time to filter out 'fakes' as early as possible. Figure 1.10 shows an example of this recruitment process.

India: long-term industry scenarios

India has garnered a 51 per cent market share in the global sourcing business (see Figure 1.11) and today it is one of the most competitive IT offshore locations. However, as we have seen, India cannot afford to be complacent. Unless it achieves a radical transformation in its business

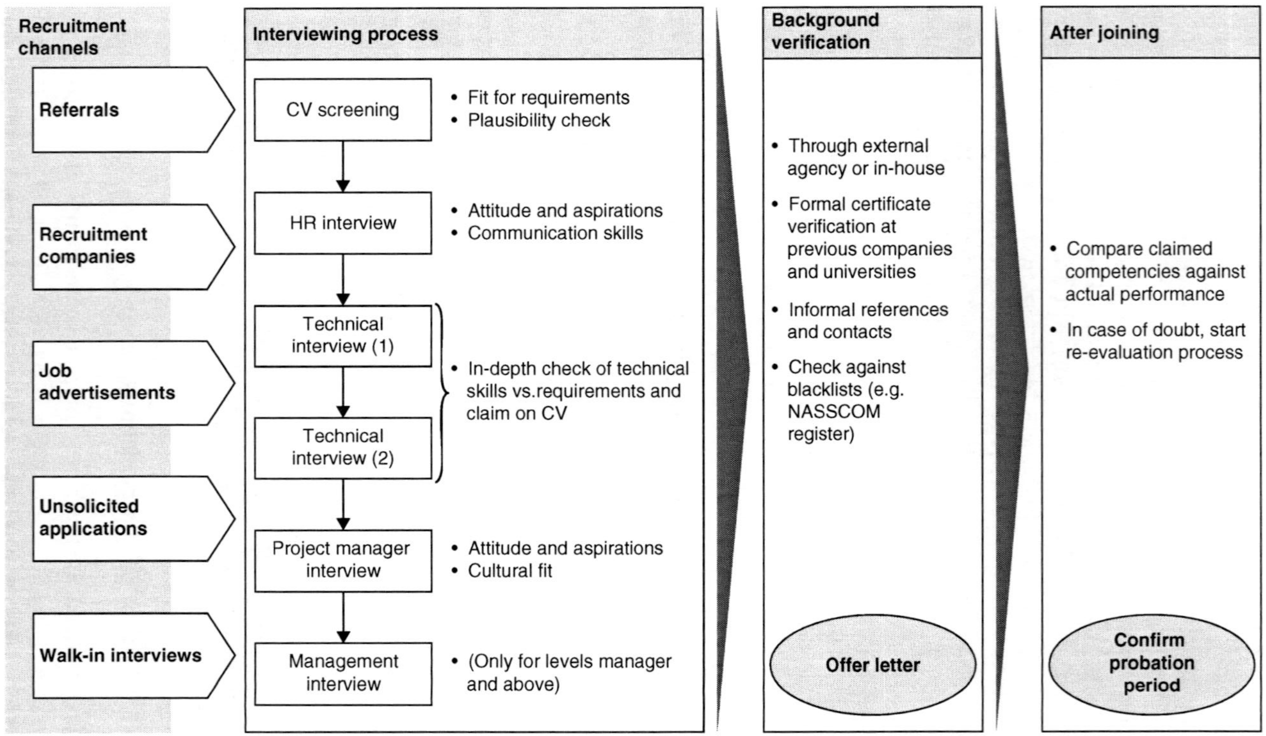

Figure 1.10 Recruitment process

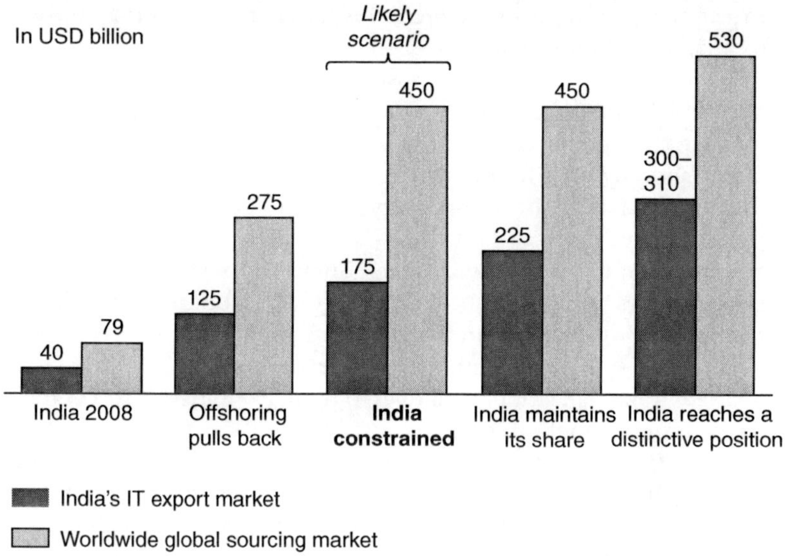

Figure 1.11 Long-term India offshore scenarios for 2020
Source: Adapted from Nasscom and McKinsey (2009), p. 23.

environment and education system, its long-term IT revenues are at stake.

The possible industry scenarios will not only be determined by the adoption of global sourcing by worldwide customers; India's competitive position in relation to other emerging low-cost nations, the actions taken by India's Government, and the conduct of India's IT industry will also shape the scenarios of the future.

A joint analysis by Nasscom and McKinsey[43] has identified the following four long-term possible scenarios for India's export-oriented IT industry:

- *Scenario 1: Offshoring pulls back*. The adoption of global sourcing slows down considerably due to protectionism by Western governments, perhaps driven by political pressure through increasing unemployment. Nearshore destinations, which are part of the same economic zone, could be favoured and promoted. This pull-back could be further exacerbated by the decreasing attractiveness of India, for example through reduced cost saving and limited productivity improvements through industrialization, or an increased threat of terrorism bringing problems for effective business continuity management (see Chapter 4).

- *Scenario 2: India constrained.* Most Western nations do not impose any restrictions on global sourcing. However, India does not manage to improve the depth of its talent pool, resulting in a severe talent shortage in the market. In addition, industrialization is not fully utilized and the IT industry remains at its current level of productivity.
- *Scenario 3: India maintains its share.* Thanks to several industry and government initiatives, India manages to counter competition from emerging markets and keeps its market share of 51 per cent. Companies sporadically improve their productivity through half-hearted industrialization initiatives, but largely remain cost-competitive through labour arbitrage.
- *Scenario 4: India reaches a distinctive position.* India's IT industry not only retains competitiveness, but fosters breakthrough innovation and industrialization. This distinctive position would largely depend on bridging the employability gap of India's graduates and fostering a high-talent employee pool.

The study by Nasscom and McKinsey identifies the most likely scenario by 2020 as 'India constrained', with the global sourcing industry being worth USD 450 billion annually and India garnering a share of 40 per cent (USD 175 billion).

If you are thinking about offshoring to India today, threats to India's competitiveness and possible future scenarios are important for you to consider, as the decision you take today should be a solid and long-term one.

2
Considering Offshoring

There are no hard and fast rules about which part of the IT value chain you can offshore and how you go for it. Unquestionably, some areas have been more popular than others, mostly the ones in well-known and mature technologies with predictability and established models. In a changing business climate, however, you may also want to explore areas off the beaten track.

Lifecycle approach to offshoring

Offshoring is most successful when managed as a lifecycle, and not as a one-off activity. In view of the sometimes unpredictable challenges that lie ahead of companies jumping onto the offshore bandwagon, managing this lifecycle is one of the real essential competencies that your IT department needs to master. There is no right way to go through the offshore lifecycle, but there is a general sequence of twenty-four activities that companies can follow. These activities are shown in Figure 2.1 and can best be separated into six distinct stages:[1]

- Evaluate
- Plan
- Select
- Transfer
- Operate
- Reconsider

A structured approach such as this can eliminate uninformed decision making, faults in the setup, and non-alignment of individual activities with your company's overall sourcing strategy. Then again, it requires

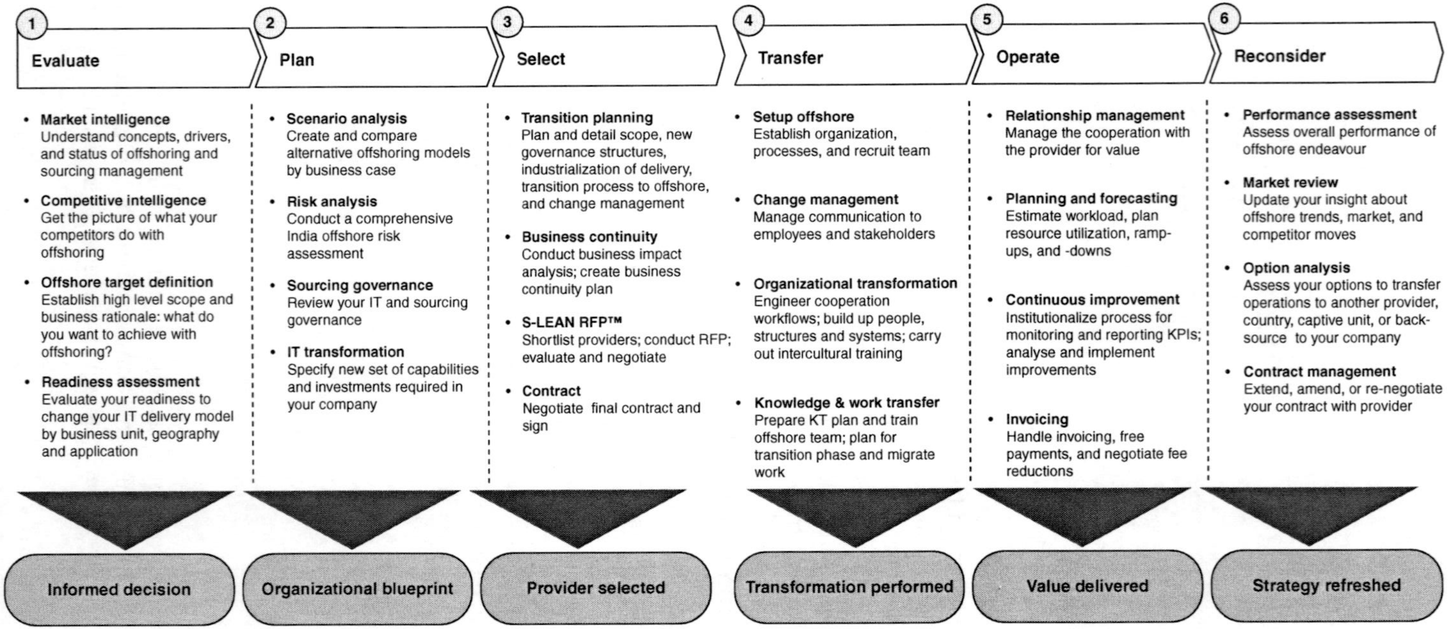

Figure 2.1 Offshore lifecycle

planning and detailed consideration of issues. This will cost you money, both in terms of internal hours spent and external support from consulting companies. However, starting the offshore journey uninformed and unaligned will cost you dear later on, albeit this may often be hidden in other cost categories. And I am sure your company does not want to become one of the many disappointing stories about outsourcing, offshoring and India in which organizations finally decide to backsource to headquarters again.

Let us devote some time to describing the activities of the six stages and twenty-four activities. The remainder of this book will provide you with content input for these phases. However, it does not operationalize the phases into an offshore project method. As I have said, there is no right way to run the offshore lifecycle wheel and a stringent method would be of mere academic interest and little hands-on value.[2]

Evaluate

In the first stage, *evaluate,* you should try to understand the concepts and drivers behind offshoring, appreciate the value of a sourcing strategy and provider governance, and identify where the market in general and your competitors in particular are heading. It is very important not to assume each and every myth about India and offshoring is true – believe me, there are many of them and they are also frequently copied and pasted into new analyst reports of reputable market research companies and publications by renowned publishers. Instead, it is essential that you do your own bit of analysis based on your own rationale for offshoring and your company's particular circumstances.

Then define the business rationale and the high level scope for offshoring, which is to answer the question: what do you really want to achieve with offshoring? It is important to acknowledge the different models of offshoring and choose the right mix. You also need to take into account your organization's strategic preferences and adopt a holistic view. Do not simply try to copy the imperfectly observed success of others, or what you have read in case studies and heard from promoters of the Indian offshore story. Nor should you allow offshoring to be ideologically driven! Inevitably, all these press announcements are flawed by the need to show success, sometimes well before the first bit of work has actually been transferred to India. Fortunately I have experienced real evidence of offshoring results and pitfalls over many years and can report on them in this book.

Critically evaluate what you want to achieve with your company's own readiness before commencing this journey; examine the preparedness at an organizational level, by business unit, geography and application area. This sets the parameters of what will happen next.

Plan

During the second stage, *plan,* you compare various alternative models from a business case perspective. First, of course, you need a base case for the *status quo* against which you will compare your options and also later the providers' offers. This requires a comprehensive and sometimes painful examination of your current IT costs as well as anticipated future costs.[3]

A risk analysis should look at the feasibility and impact of the offshore endeavour on your business and its operations. This also includes a country risk analysis in which you detail and quantify the possible threats of doing business in a country halfway round the globe to your executive management. This is often simply ignored and executives resort to panicky actions when news about flooding, terror attacks or tensions at the Pakistan border makes it to international television.

An evaluation of your IT and sourcing governance will be your first step to establish the necessary management oversight for the offshore endeavour and provide an answer to whether your IT department is ready to start talks with outside providers. Leaving this until later would mean that the first provider you talk to gets a great opportunity to drive the process. A result of this evaluation will be a list of new capabilities and structures that you will need to build up in your own organization. This will of course cost money, but please be aware that the need to spend this money does not come from the offshore project you are about to start. We are in fact talking about a potentially inherent defect in your organization which needs to be addressed for better performance, with or without offshore and outsourcing.

Select

The moment you start talking to providers in the *select* phase, the word 'India' will spread like wildfire through your organizations, with a plethora of rumours about motives and job losses. Therefore it is not only important to plan and detail the offshoring scope, new governance structures, and the transition process to an industrialized offshore IT delivery platform, but at least equally important to sketch the change management and communication process.

Now go back to your risk assessment from the previous stage. It's imperative to normalize the risks, not eliminate them, which would be either impossible or far too expensive. What you need is a plan for business continuity in case a disaster should strike your new offshore operations. With these two activities (transition planning and business continuity) you really design the future of your IT organization; it is in your own company's best interests to do this diligently, because the provider selection process will build on the outcomes created here. Entering a contract with an external provider for an unclear project is not only bad practice, but can be quite dangerous to the success of the entire offshore journey.

Finally, you are ready for the big step. Shortlist possible providers, assemble the request for proposal (RFP) documents, and follow a very lean RFP process to quickly shortlist a few select providers with which you can start the negotiation process. The five-step S-LEAN RFP™ process is introduced in Chapter 5. Spend time on drafting a good contract that both parties can live with – and sign it. Now the hands-on work will start.

Transfer

In theory, the phase *transfer* begins the day after the contract has been signed by both parties. In practice, however, it usually commences well before this point when both parties are reasonably sure that the deal is going to materialize. Sometimes the provider will ask you for a letter of intent to help cover expenses in case the contract does not go through in the end.

This phase entails setting up the organizational structure of the offshore centre, institutionalizing the processes, and recruiting the team. Your change management programme will swing into operation, reaching out to all stakeholders. Hand in hand goes the organizational transformation, which really engineers the cooperation workflows at a micro-level, building up the people, structures, and system support. During this process, you need to keep an eye on creating awareness of 'soft' differences between cultures, either in the form of intercultural training or via coaching.

You need to transfer knowledge from your own organization to the provider, plan for a transition approach, and finally shift the work to India.

Again in theory, the phase ends with successful work transfer and an acceptance document signed by both parties. Unfortunately, the sad reality is that the knowledge and work transfer phase seems to be unending in many offshore projects. Your success in the following phase and in reaping in the benefits for your company really depends on how well you have planned and executed this part of the lifecycle.

Operate

Now preparation is over and the real work starts in the phase *operate*. From a management perspective, you cannot leave the offshore endeavour alone; it needs to be continuously managed. Your organization needs to learn to manage for outputs, rather than inputs and processes. In addition, the relationship with the provider needs to be directed, run and governed for value creation on both sides.

Internally, you need to become excellent in your planning and forecasting processes; this is about being efficient and reducing the wastage caused by non-utilized bench resources. At an operational level, a close eye on important key performance indicators (KPIs) will help you to continuously improve processes and ultimately deliver more value at reduced costs.

A very operational perspective, and yet of importance to the management, is the verification of invoices, the processing of payments, and the negotiation of possible fee reductions based on KPI measurements.

Reconsider

Last in the lifecycle comes a phase where the past is reviewed and future options are assessed. During the lifecycle of an offshoring contract, your organization and the market environment can change. You should therefore critically assess your contract and your provider's performance, update yourself with the latest developments in the market, and question your offshoring decision. Based on an analysis of your options and whether the contract is to be renegotiated, retendered, or even backsourced to headquarters, there are different re-entry points into the lifecycle.

Changing business priorities in a downturn

I have already provided some India offshore market intelligence in Chapter 1; let us now demarcate our offshore target and discuss what you want to face up to, do and solve with offshoring.

There are surely no greater business challenges than an economic downturn. What started with a financial liquidity crisis in September 2008 quickly spread to businesses and consumers all around the globe. This is different from previous recessions. By November 2008, virtually every developed economy was already suffering a recession or at least noticing a wrenching slowdown. By March 2009, most banks accepted government money to keep them afloat and many manufacturing companies were begging for a bail-out package, too.

Even India's fantastic GDP growth rate of nine per cent suddenly had to be corrected – to a still very enviable seven per cent for the financial year 2009/10. However, it very much became clear that this world is now global and connected as it never was before. The so far booming IT sector was hit by several corporate scandals. The World Bank blacklisted both Wipro and Satyam for inappropriate behaviour in bids, meaning attempts to bribe their customers' decision makers. For Satyam this was the least of its troubles, its founder and chairman B Ramalinga Raju having been found to have manipulated not only the balance sheet to make it carry fictitious cash, but also employee numbers, and to have transferred salary income of imaginary employees to his own account.[4] These events have thrown a grim light on the governance structures of India's most beloved industry – and have left everyone dealing with India in a state of shock.

If you are a CEO, by now you will most likely have taken action on reshaping your company to carry it through whatever the economy will continue to throw at you in the months and years to come. Some say it will take at least a year – or maybe three years? – for the global economy to normalize again. Your job is now to not only initiate changes that will allow your business survival, but also to ensure that your company will emerge from this downturn in better shape than it was before. There will be a tomorrow after the crisis, but its economic context will be different from the past; nonetheless, it will be no less rich in possibilities for those who are well prepared.

For now, here are at least seven significant efforts you will need to manage in order to cope with this downturn (see Figure 2.2): cost and cash; supply chain and partners; products and services; customer focus and sales; workforce planning and human resources; trust and transparency; and – last but not least – getting prepared for rising in the recovery.[5]

(1) Cost and cash

You will have to adjust your most fundamental thoughts about how to run a company; your focus will need to shift from the income statement to the balance sheet. In the good times, your company's indicators of success were increasing earnings per share, growing revenues and gaining market share in comparison with competitors. Now the most critical factor is cash. You need to understand the cash implications of everything you do: of the earnings you get from your customers via your service operations and/or sales of products, of development you undertake in order to introduce new and better products onto the market or increase operational efficiency in the future, and of your

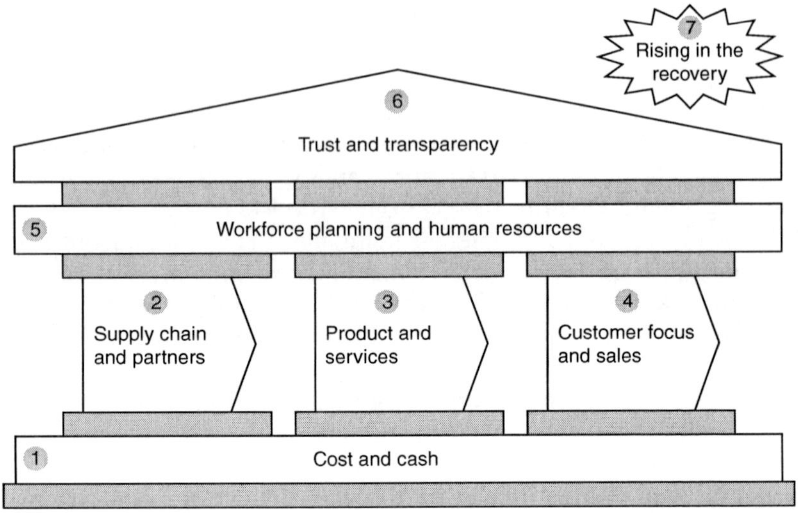

Figure 2.2 Business priorities in a downturn
Source: Adapted from Capgemini (2009), p. 5.

internal operations. Operations are at the heart of the business; this is where the work gets done – and where cash is spent every day (and sometimes also burnt) to fulfil these five well-known goals: keep the operating costs low; put your resources to the best use possible; keep your working capital low; conserve cash; and exceed both your internal and external customers' expectations with respect to quality and delivery on time. You will also probably have told your CIO already that his IT budget will be cut. The IT department also has to make its contribution in a downturn by watching every dollar spent. Application portfolio rationalization, server virtualization, and labour costs are specific areas to look into. Research by consulting companies shows that if an enterprise can reduce application costs by forty per cent, it can generate as much as one per cent increase in operating income.[6]

(2) Supply chain partners

Your supply chains need to become very lean, cost-effective and agile; inventory often ties up unnecessary capital. Sourcing from India and other low-cost countries may be an option. But even more important, planning and forecasting is now key to swiftly respond to sudden changes in market demand. The concept of 'just in time' (JIT) may see a new revival. Please try to understand the position of your partners as well; it is not only your company which needs to manage for cash, but the situation is the same for your partners. Together you will need to collaborate and solve this challenge; a hitherto reliable partner now running out of cash and going bankrupt does not help you manage and survive the downturn.

(3) Products and services

It is time to fully analyse your products and service offerings – where do we make money and where do we lose it? Which ones add to the margin and which ones dilute it? In a downturn, a tight grip on the product and services portfolio and its cost structure is important. Outsourcing or offshoring of business processes may help to reduce the cost pain. Of course you know from the past that product profitability analysis alone is not sufficient, but needs to be viewed in conjunction with customer profitability analysis.

(4) Customer focus and sales

The customer, his experience with your company and finally his willingness and ability to purchase from you is key to defending your market share. Any cuts should not be at the expense of customer experience. Often activities and projects around customer relationship management are the first to get cut in a downturn. But this is wrong! Selling goods and services at the right price is now a key capability; price and revenue optimization become crucial means. Many customers will substitute goods or services in a downturn to save cash themselves; understanding the customer and predicting such fast changing preferences will be crucial to survival.

(5) Workforce planning and human resources

Headcount reductions are sometimes unavoidable in challenging times; they need to be carried out as part of your overall plan to reshape the company. Always remember that it is the job which is to be cut and not the person holding it. Maybe someone whose job is becoming redundant can do something else much better than another person still holding a position. You can't afford to dismiss the wrong people – or your company loses force and you will struggle to replace the people later. All this should be bold, the process may only occur once, several rounds of job losses will only create an atmosphere of distrust and demoralization.

(6) Trust and transparency

Corporate corruption scandals have seriously harmed companies like the American energy company Enron together with their accounting firm Arthur Andersen, in 2001,[7] the American banana producer Chiquita which was charged with financing Colombian terrorist organizations to protect their employees, in 2007,[8] and India's Satyam Computers for corporate fraud, in 2008; a lack of trust and transparency in 2008 almost brought the entire worldwide financial system to a standstill. Trust and transparency are key attributes for employees identifying themselves with their employer, for clients, regulators and the broader community.

(7) Rising in the recovery

At the end of the long dark tunnel, there is going to be a recovery. As mentioned before, there will be opportunities for the strong and thrifty. For now you need to keep an eye on what to do when things turn around: how to expand your market share again, scale up when opportunities arise, and when and where to invest again. 'And finally, among the survivors, the winners will be those that keep an eye on what to do when things turn around' (Capgemini, 2009, p. 5).

Downturn IT requirements

In managing the economic crisis of 2008/09 from an IT perspective, there is obviously very little use in referring back to the Great Depression of the 1930s. But even the burst of the Internet bubble just a few years ago is hardly comparable.

Most IT organizations these days do not have as much fat as they had during the eCommerce boom. Back then, there was a portfolio of experimental projects without a solid business case, a pile of legacy systems combined with heterogeneous infrastructure solutions. It then proved very rewarding to stop fancy projects, consolidate applications and infrastructure, and move into outsourcing or offshoring.

If you are the CIO, simply cutting IT costs won't work this time. Where would you start cutting in order to achieve a remarkable saving, not just a few percentage points here and there? You need to stay focused by having a strong viewpoint on the prioritization of your department's work and projects.

Your first priority has to remain with projects related to compliance and regulatory requirements in order to avoid any legal trouble which could paralyse the company in tough times. Government scrutiny of business and IT systems is likely to further intensify in developed countries. Already today, Sarbanes-Oxley drives decisions about accounting systems across industries, the resilience of banking systems is under close scrutiny by central banks and other government offices, and the Food and Drug Administration (FDA) in the USA requires many IT systems in the pharmaceutical industry to be validated. Management information systems (MIS) and processes directly interacting with the CEO and the board also need to be fully supported; the company's business management needs to be informed fully and on time about possible deterioration of key health indicators; only this will allow them to navigate the business through this downturn unharmed. Your second priority is with 'keep-the-lights-burning' projects, which will keep operational processes up and running. At times of budget cuts, after taking care of these two non-discretionary priorities, your reduced budget may already be almost fully depleted. Now you still need to look into value-creating discretionary projects. It is a difficult decision to sacrifice projects which eat up a lot of cash today, but promise to deliver huge returns later. However, you will also be required to manage for cash and you may have to slow down expenditures on such projects. You know that you cannot give up on them or sacrifice one for the sake of another, because your company will need these value-generating activities when it wants to come out of the economic slump fresh and eager to beat the competition. It is a good idea to sort these projects by their linkage to the CEO's business priorities, providing a bridge from IT to tangible business value, a much needed foundation for prioritization and business cases – and for your discussion with the CEO. You will need to position yourself as an honest broker evaluating IT investments in a fact-based way, yet at the same time avoiding any perception of favouring one business unit over another.

How can you arrive at this overview in practice? If you look into the systems, products, and solutions that make up your information technology landscape, you can identify six clusters which address the business drivers of your organization:[9]

- *User interface.* Capabilities in this uppermost cluster drastically improve user friendliness by personalization and individualization. Rich Internet Applications (RIAs) are executed through a simple Internet browser, yet they are highly interactive and media-rich. Role-based applications transform content to the specific, situation-based need of the user. Mashup architecture allows assembly of virtual solutions from multiple internal and external sources. Simple yet powerful mobile devices allow different access channels to the system for the end user.

- *Business networks*. Capabilities around business networks enable companies to connect to the outside world and build up networked relationships with clients and partners. Customer and supplier processes are connected through a continuous flow of information to enable a just-in-time fine-tuning of events like delivery time, type and number of products and so on.
- *Business process and rules engines*. Responding to business-critical events just in time, business processes are adapted, improved and changed, thereby taking an organization's policies and various internal or market constraints into account.
- *Business intelligence*. The value of organization-internal data is amplified once it is processed, enriched with external data sources, analysed and applied to business operations and customer interaction.
- *Industrialization*. Business services can be identified through simplification and rationalization of the business situation. Such service solutions can then be encapsulated, supported with standard systems (and not bespoke custom-made legacy systems) and maybe even outsourced.
- *Service-oriented architecture (SOA)*. Underlying infrastructure, such as servers, storage, network facilities, middleware and interfaces, is to be presented to upper-level business solutions as nearly invisible. SOA provides the necessary framework to manage all elements in a uniform and complexity-reducing way.

For your discussion with the CEO, you can now build up a matrix comparing your six IT clusters against the business priorities in a downturn, which are discussed on page 60. Differentiate the importance of the technology for a business priority by marking the pivot point with high, medium, and low. Figure 2.3 shows an example which can help you as a starting point; of course you will need to adapt it to your own industry vertical and to the specifics of your organization. While IT competence is critical in most industries, returns on technology investments vary drastically. Nonetheless, we can already derive from this generalized value equation matrix that the business priority of cost and cash is heavily influenced by the IT clusters and that business networks, business process and rules engine, and business intelligence are the most important IT clusters to focus on in a downturn. Activities and projects in these clusters should receive generous funding even in a downturn as they support the company's downturn business priorities.

Nevertheless, the CEO will continue to tell you to reduce the IT department's operating costs. If you are not already doing so on your own

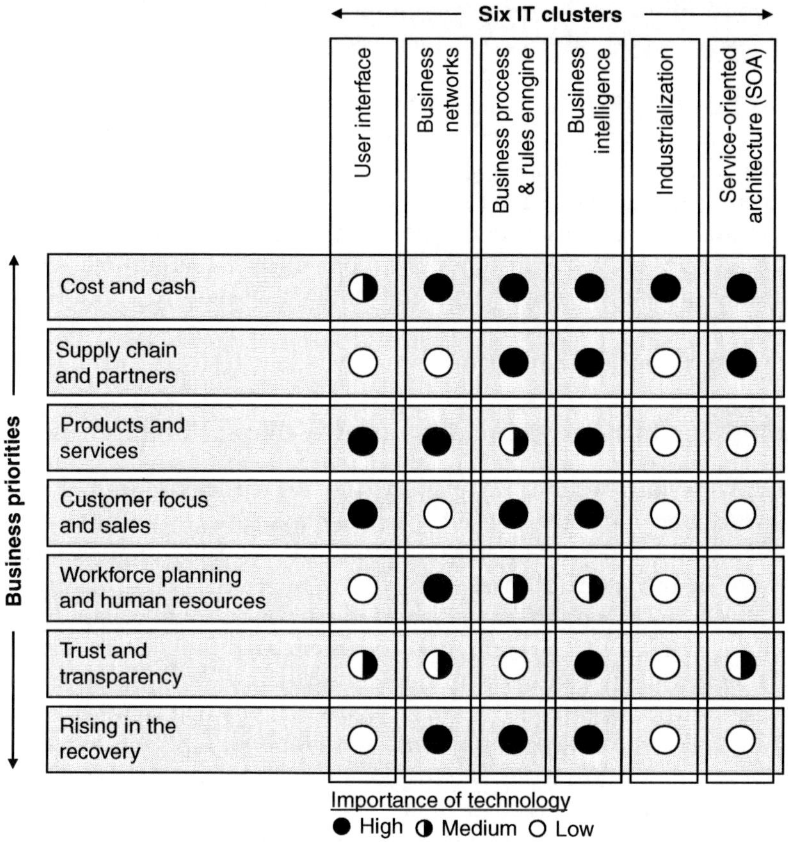

Figure 2.3 Value equation matrix: business priorities and IT clusters

account, he will demand you get rid of your expensive but knowledgeable and specialized freelancers, and he will throw the words 'offshoring' and 'India' at you. And he will ask you to analyse which of your IT operations and projects can be offshored and how substantial the cost savings are.

At the same time, and adding to the pressures, IT service providers from India, often referred to as firms of Indian origin (FIOs) or simply pure players, are knocking at your door offering temptingly cheap rates for their employees. Multinational companies with India operations advertise their blended project teams, combining the best of home country onsite consultants and offshore teams. They, of course, paint a dark picture of pure offshore delivery and praise their one team approach distributed over two continents. Still you continue to read newspaper reports about companies backsourcing work from India to the Western world, cases of data theft in India, a worsening relationship with Pakistan after the shocking Mumbai terror attacks of November 2008, and corporate scandals like the Satyam case. Other offshoring nations like China launch government-sponsored initiatives to grab some of the lucrative market share.

Naturally, you will wonder if offshoring to India is now the answer to beat your budget crunch. Or is it your miracle solution to receive applause as a cost-cutter, which not only allows you to continue to deliver the same service, but at the same time helps you to strengthen the core of your IT department?

Achieving business priorities with the help of offshoring

In the previous section, I explained how the business priorities of a downturn are supported by IT clusters to varying degrees. The IT clusters in turn are further leveraged through the modality of IT delivery, offshoring being one of these.

As a CIO, at this point you will need to ask your team to collate applications, systems and projects, and sort them according to IT clusters. In a second step, you can compare them against the business priorities, and using the weightings defined in Figure 2.3, you will arrive at a first estimate on which of your applications, systems and projects are really helping your CEO to withstand the downturn. You can take this matrix with you to the CEO in order to talk about the funding of your activities and which ones should be supported even more, halted, or put on hold.

Watch out: huge chunks, but not everything, can be offshored to India. Let us look at the IT value chain in Figure 2.4; it illustrates a sequence of tasks from strategy and design through development and testing to maintenance and support. All IT-related work in your company can be seen as falling into this structure. Analysis of the cost base along the value chain is a helpful instrument for decision making on changes of the delivery model. Today, realization, testing, application management, infrastructure management and support together make up almost 90 per cent of the total IT spend. Only 13 per cent of the IT budget is allocated to strategy, planning and the design phase. In order to optimize the delivery model, companies are currently trying to shift IT budget from the later to the earlier parts of the value chain. The use of offshoring in the later phases can help you to free such

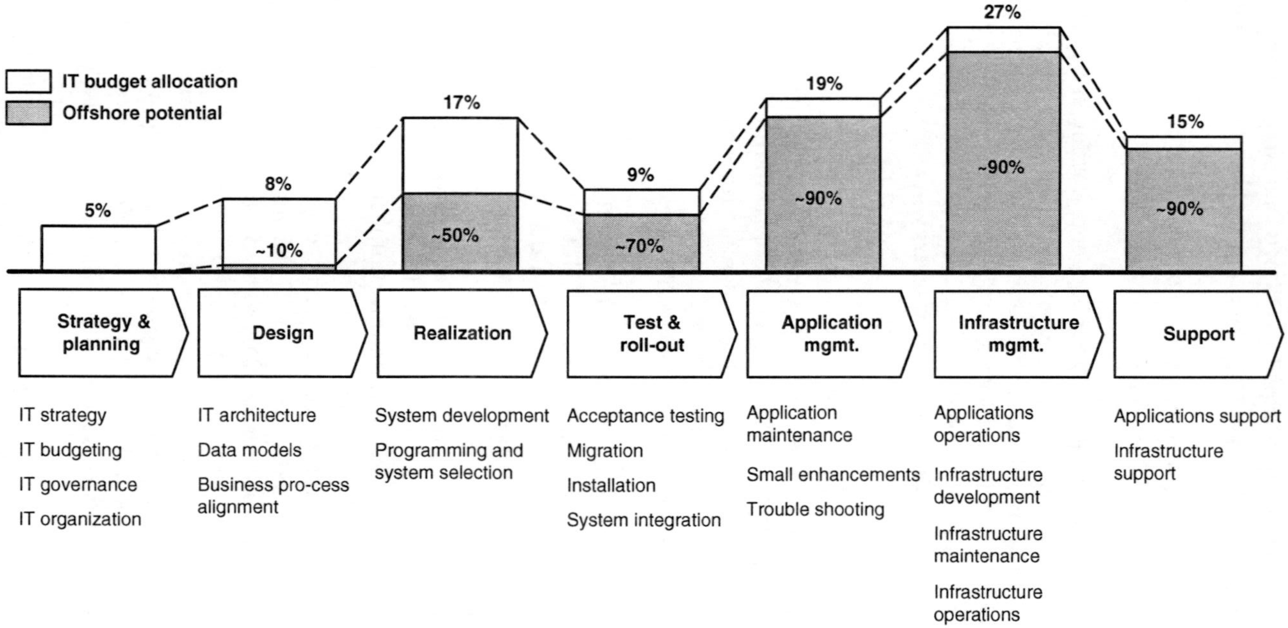

Figure 2.4 Average IT budget allocation and offshore potential
Source: Concept of IT delivery chain and percentages for IT budget allocation based on Capgemini (2006), p. 12; offshore potential based on project experience.

funds. Going forward, project experience shows that around 50 per cent of costs in the realization phase can be taken out of onsite or in-country delivery and executed from offshore. The percentage is even higher for test and rollout with 70 per cent; up to 90 per cent of costs can be taken out of the last three phases, application management, infrastructure management,[10] and support.

All this is only a preparation for your budget discussion and does not really help you to answer your CEO's question as to whether offshoring can help you financially. At this point you should think about the three levels of offshoring: tactical, strategic, and transformational (see p. 4) – and translate them into hands-on terms. Let us look at it from a very simple perspective and identify common levers where you may want to use offshoring.

- *Replacing freelancers with offshore resources*. Across all your activities, you may have freelancers working in your IT department. They may be highly specialized, relatively expensive, easy to throw out from a contractual point of view, but they may sometimes have worked for many years in your organization and have very skillfully protected their area of work from your own employees and, of course, the competition. Replacing freelancers with Indian IT engineers falls in almost all cases into the category of tactical offshoring.
- *Replacing freelancers with landed resources*. If the new Indian resources do not work from offshore in an Indian delivery centre, but apply for a work permit, pack their bags and work in your company from onshore, this is commonly referred to as 'landed resources'. It was very popular during good economic times, as it provided direct control over Indian colleagues, but still offered a cost saving as compared to home country freelancers. In a downturn, however, immigration departments are tightening their rules and applications for long-term work permits will be much more difficult. Also, this lever loses out on any industrialization potentials of the IT delivery chain.
- *Getting new things done cheaper*. For some of the business priorities, the CEO will request additional IT support and it is not unlikely that you will need to start new initiatives even in a downturn. However, you will not be able to run these new initiatives as you used to before the economic crisis and this is where offshoring can help you to reduce delivery costs. Such projects will be mostly of a tactical or strategic nature.
- *Replacing a function with offshore*. Finally, you might consider replacing an entire part of your IT organization and moving it to India.

This is either a strategic or transformational initiative, depending on how you are going to use the offshore unit.

Watch out: do not fall for a patchwork approach trying to solve your own resource constraints, realize cost savings, and simultaneously fix some end-user support issues or network management problems. You need a clear perspective to guide which functions and roles to include in it. Once you have identified in which area or project one of these offshore levers can be applied, you have to analyse the business case. And in a downturn you always need to keep in mind that a best return on investment which will only come in after a lot of initial spending, is not going to go down very well with the CEO.

The offshore business case

All offshore business cases that I have seen are based on just two positive leverages: the factor cost difference of an individual Indian resource versus a home country employee, and the clever use of industrialization experience.

- *Factor cost difference*
  When all is said and done, it is really the labour arbitrage that drives the offshoring business case – and it is the foremost reason why anyone would ever think about going through the hassle of moving work to a distant country like India. Typical charge-out rates for a consultant or senior consultant working from an Indian delivery centre with a standard workplace and software configuration today range from 170 USD to 300 USD per day.[11] Internal cost rates[12] of employees in developed Western countries are around 700 to 1,000 USD per day, freelancers would charge anything from 700 USD per day upwards, and professional IT service providers would charge anything from 1,100 USD per day upwards. Of course, during an economic downturn and its higher bench rates with home country IT service providers, these rates will fall, but even in the long run and worst case, they will typically remain at least three times the Indian charge-out rates.
- *Industrialization experience*
  The sheer size and many years of India's IT delivery experience have created best practices, standardized methods and sophisticated tools. This drives productivity, increases quality through a highly specialized workforce and is further leveraged through scaling across

various clients. This means in simple terms that commodity work is not only done for your company, but the same people will work with the same methods for other companies as well (see p. 9). There is a substantial saving of about 25 per cent of the original effort[13] through experience and industrialized delivery approaches in various areas of the IT delivery chain.

These are the business benefits which have an immediate financial impact. Sometimes outsourcing or offshoring creates *flexibility options* to accelerate other initiatives at a later date. Examples are the ability to expand into other areas with reduced costs and time and to scale quickly to meet increased demand at lower incremental costs. These options may not produce any immediate return, but will see that your organization is set up for future growth or adaptation. The value of these flexibility options needs to be understood and compared with the incremental cost of making them available. While there are no universally accepted methods for specifying this value, options pricing models from financial markets, such as the Nobel Prize-winning Black–Scholes Call Option Formula, can be adapted to help quantify the flexibility inherent in outsourcing or offshoring.[14] It is important to show the mathematical approximation of the flexibility value to management, because the inclusion of flexibility and scalability within IT projects is often the first to be cut in times of budget pressures.

On the other hand, the business case is weakened by the time it takes to make the knowledge transfer to India, the additional overhead for managing distributed delivery, the productivity loss through using remote resources, and maybe even redundancy costs for laying off employees in your own company. Let us look at these negative cost levers one by one.

- *Knowledge transfer*. This is the time and effort it takes to bring the India offshore team up to speed. It may also include a certain handover time where the India offshore team is working in parallel. Knowledge transfer to the other part of the world is not a once-only effort; in fact, it has to be a continuous process, which also includes training new team members to counterbalance the effect of attrition.
- *Additional overhead*. Managing teams distributed across the globe means an additional management and communication overhead. Specifications, test cases and many more documents need to be written, agreed on and reviewed more carefully as they form the basis for offshore work.

- *Productivity loss*. Despite the fantastic news about the quality of India's IT engineers, in real life all India projects I have seen experienced an average productivity loss of between ten and twenty per cent – as compared to running the project with American or European IT developers. Where does this phenomenon come from? India has seen a tremendous demand-driven overheating of the employee market in the past few years; the industry had to absorb people who are no longer on a par with international standards and the known quality of Indian software engineers at the turn of this century.[15] Notwithstanding all these changes at the macro level, if the productivity loss goes beyond twenty per cent, there is mostly something fundamentally wrong in the project setup, communication structures, expectation setting and knowledge transfer. A countermeasure to this productivity loss is industrialization of offshore IT delivery, as discussed on page 9.
- *Redundancy costs*. This category summarizes all costs for moving work away from your own employees and making them redundant in one form or another. This can range from simply assigning them different work areas, to re-training, and finally laying them off. The costs associated with these options depend largely on the legal framework in your home country and the position of the workers' council in your own organization; the legal frameworks in some European countries require you to pay huge amounts of severance pay on dismissing employees.
- *Other one-off setup costs*. Depending on the scenario, you may need to cater for some other one-off costs, for example, special infrastructure, software licences, and business continuity management in order to normalize country risk (see Chapter 4). If you plan to establish your own company's captive centre in India (see Chapter 5), you will need to allow for a lot of different one-off costs.

Any number associated with costs and benefits is an estimate based on the available knowledge at the time of calculating the business case. While the offshore endeavour is being implemented, unknowns and changes will cause the costs and benefits to diverge from the original estimates. Hence, you should build in a level of uncertainty and quantify risks on the estimates to arrive at a more realistic projection. While there are an endless number of risks to any project, you should focus on five core categories: implementation risk; impact risk; provider risk; measurement risk; and business continuity risk. Their typical characteristics are shown in Figure 2.5. Implementation and impact risk are applied to individual cost and benefit estimates, provider and measurement risk are calculated at the investment level, and business continuity risk is estimated at the business level.

Now that we have analysed the origin and effect of the positive and negative levers in the business case, they can be related to the different offshoring options. Figure 2.6 serves as a rough overview and starting point. The factor cost difference is important for all options unless you want to replace home country resources with Indian landed resources; the additional travel, hotel and salary component expenses usually eat substantially into the factor cost savings. Also, in this case, industrialization experience does not apply. Indians work in a team atmosphere and if a single consultant is sent onsite, he loses contact with his delivery centre and needs to work alone – just like a freelancer.

Unless your company has worked extensively with offshore projects before, it is difficult to estimate the impact of these levers correctly. It may be advisable to get expert external support; this book can only

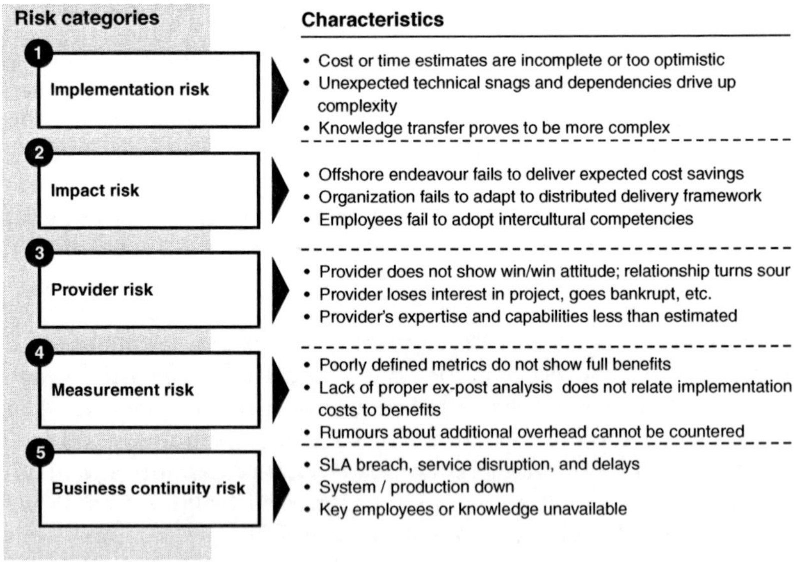

Figure 2.5 Offshore risk categories and characteristics

	Positive levers		Negative levers				
	Factor cost difference	Industrialization experience	Knowledge transfer	Additional overhead	Productivity loss	Redundancy costs	Other one-off setup costs
Replacing freelancers with offshore resources	High	Medium	Medium	Medium	High	Low	Low
Replacing freelancers with landed resources	Medium	Low	Medium	Low	Medium	Low	Low
Getting new things done cheaper	High	Medium	Low	High	High	Low	Medium
Replacing a function with offshore	High	High	High	High	High	High	High

Relative impact of a lever on offshoring area
● High ◑ Medium ○ Low

Figure 2.6 Levers for the offshore business case

help you to understand and critically question the India business case. In short, it will help you not to blindly fall for the glossy slide decks and promises of IT providers. Most likely, however, it will not provide you with enough information to independently build a waterproof business case.

After careful consideration of the levers affecting the business case, you will get a diagram similar to Figure 2.7 out of your calculations. You can see an initial investment period which generates a negative cash flow. At some point the promised cost savings will kick in and due to positive cash flows, the cumulative cash flow curves upward. However, this is not yet an offshore success – the cumulative cash flow curve merely remains below zero. Only when the project has generated enough positive cash flow will the cumulative cash flow curve cross the *x*-axis: the endeavour's ROI (return on investment) is achieved. From then on you can start to make real money and reap the benefits of your investment.

As mentioned earlier, during an economic downturn your CEO will ask you to keep investment as small as possible in both absolute

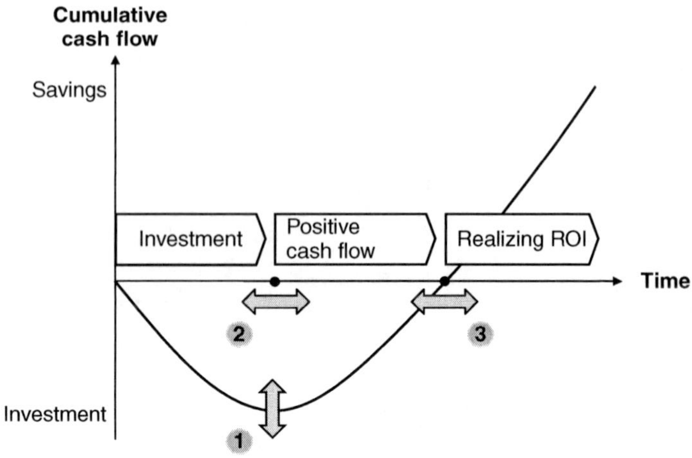

Figure 2.7 Offshore business case

terms (point 1) and also with respect to the investment time (point 2). In addition, and this is no different from better economic times, an early ROI (point 3) should also be achieved.

The levers have various influences on these points. Point 1 is majorly impacted by the amount of one-off costs, for instance the necessary knowledge transfer, payouts to redundant employees, and infrastructure setup costs. Long investment periods of these cost categories adversely influence point 2. In short, during these testing times your job is to move point 1 upwards by reducing the amount of investment necessary and point 2 as far to the left as possible by limiting the set-up time of the offshore endeavour. How early the ROI can be reached and how far to the left point 3 is positioned, depends on one hand, of course, on the position of points 1 and 2. On the other hand, a best possible arbitrage from factor cost difference, industrialization experience, and a minimization of productivity losses and additional overhead, moves it further to the left.

Economic effects of offshoring on the home country

The debate around offshoring and the creation or destruction of wealth and employment in the Western world is very controversial. As a responsible CEO or CIO, you may want to have some background information on this topic as well.[16] But be aware: you do not have the

Case Study 2: Business case for an offshore support centre in India[17]

An international company with headquarters in Europe, let us call it Comp AG, was forced to increase the size of its IT support team from 12 staff to 90. It was in the process of a global roll-out of its ERP system, based on a template containing scenarios and configurations. In order to keep the template consolidated, it was decided to support the ERP system from Comp AG's headquarters. However, hiring almost 80 IT experts proved to be challenging, not only because of high workforce costs, but also because Comp AG is headquartered in a rather remote area, which does not attract much IT talent.

Comp AG therefore looked at the option of building a support centre in Bangalore, India, not as a captive unit, but as part of an external IT provider. Figure 2.8 shows the intended organizational layout. The overall management responsibility of the support centre was to lie with the support centre manager and remain at headquarters. One of Comp AG's staff would be given the job of development coordinator and tasked to 'wheel and deal' between the business areas and the development teams. An employee of the Indian IT provider was to go on a long-term onsite assignment to headquarters, to report directly to the support centre manager, and as distributed delivery coordinator, to manage the day-to-day interactions, deliverables and the relationship with the India back-office team. In Bangalore, between 84 and 90 consultants were to form the dedicated staff of the support centre. In case of more workload or special technical requirements, of course, additional resources from the provider could be added to this team on an *ad hoc* basis allowing flexibility and easy scalability. In addition to the distributed delivery coordinator, one Indian functional developer would be stationed onsite to ensure knowledge transfer by working closely together with two European functional specialists.

The ramp-up plan in Figure 2.9 (top) shows that the provider selection phase was planned to take about three months and the transition of the existing work to the Indian provider about six months. During this time, no new work with respect to global template maintenance would be performed, but the newly formed support centre would concentrate on establishing cooperation processes to headquarters and to the worldwide locations of Comp AG. The baseline services would continue to be conducted by Comp AG's old internal team. In the next two quarters, the ramp-up was scheduled to happen and knowledge to be transferred to Bangalore. The Bangalore centre was to be in charge of the IT support from the fourth quarter, but still backed up by a slightly reduced team at headquarters. The sixth quarter was to see the highest number of employees in India. It is envisaged that subsequently development and support processes would mature, leveraged through the re-use of methods from other projects run for other clients by the Indian IT provider; this was conservatively estimated at six per cent headcount reductions.

The business case in Figure 2.9 (bottom) initially sees internal costs rising due to the required setup of infrastructure and implementation of a business continuity plan. The transfer of the support centre already promises to be profitable after three quarters of initiating the transition to India, as compared to the alternative of internally ramping up the support centre at Comp AG's headquarters. The total savings after two years are estimated to be in the range of EUR 4.7 million. Based on these encouraging business case results, Comp AG started the provider evaluation process.

luxury of putting your strategies on hold to await the outcome of this debate. You need to achieve your business priorities now – or you will fall behind those competitors who do make changes.

The general fear is that offshoring leads to redundancies on a large scale, spelling trouble for the wealth and social stability of Western countries. Or in simple terms, that Indians take away the jobs of Americans, Europeans, and so on.

We need to enter this debate with extreme caution. First, official authorities do not provide any statistics on the impact of offshoring. Not even the volume of work going offshore is clear; different agencies project a different trend. For example, Bureau of Economic Analysis (BEA) data on US imports of software from India between 1998 and 2002 shows much lower levels and a different trend (slightly declining) than data provided by NASSCOM, the Indian trade association.[18] Second, offshoring can either belong in the category of cross-border trade for service offshoring, or be classified as foreign direct investment (FDI) for captive offshoring. Hence we need to talk about tendencies.

There is a difference between jobs at risk and jobs actually gone offshore. Studies estimate that between eleven and twenty per cent of jobs are going to be relocated; this would be the first category. Less

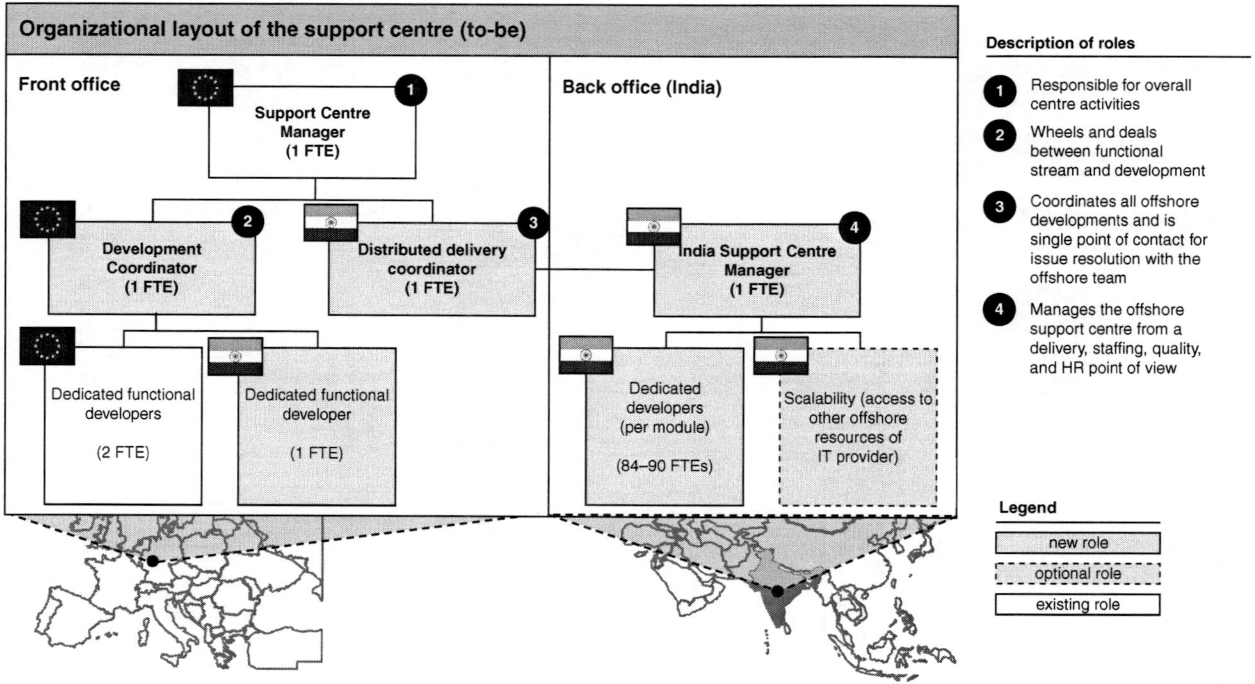

Figure 2.8 Organizational layout of the support centre (case study 2)

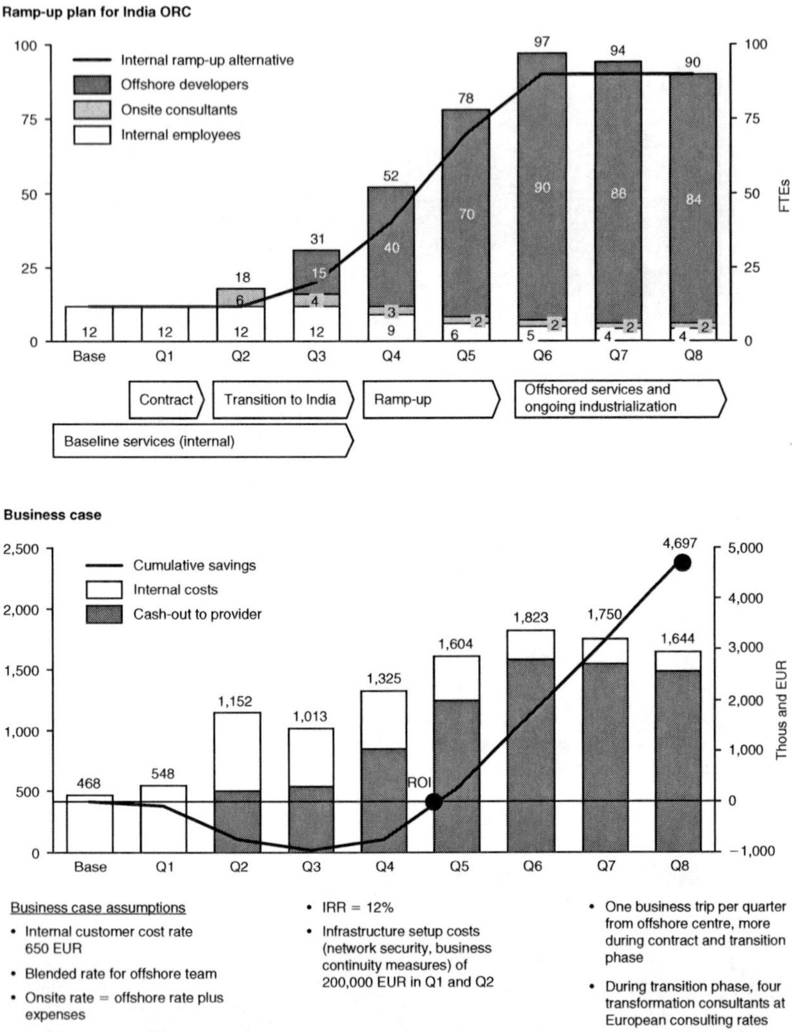

Figure 2.9 Offshore business case (case study 2)

threatening is the actual picture. In the USA, offshoring-related unemployment is estimated to account for 250,000 layoffs per year, which is less than two per cent. Considering, further, that the re-employment rate for jobs outside manufacturing is around 69 per cent, the overall impact of offshoring on Western labour markets should be rather limited.

The ability of laid-off employees to secure re-employment within a short period of time is key to measuring the effects on the economy as a whole. For one, it is the employees' responsibility to upgrade skills in order to secure more complex and higher value jobs which are more difficult to move to an offshore location. In addition, respective governments need to provide flexible labour market regulations to provide incentives for companies to take on employees even during tough times. Findings of the McKinsey Global Institute suggest that for every dollar of costs moved offshore from the USA, a net gain of USD 0.12 to 0.14 flows back to the home economy. Inhibiting offshoring thus only reduces long-term incomes. For countries with more rigid labour market regulations, like Germany and France, on the contrary, offshoring means a net loss.[19] These studies show that politicians need to solve the puzzle of creating the right conditions and that labour market regulations have to be sufficiently flexible to provide incentives for recruiting. You will also need to contribute by reinvesting profits saved through offshoring in your own domestic markets. Only if you create different new jobs will laid-off employees actually be able to secure new employment.

Even though Western politicians frequently start anti-offshoring campaigns during elections with the sole purpose of collecting votes, regulating offshoring will not work for a very practical reason. The migration of IT jobs is too difficult for anyone to spot. It is not only the IT departments which close down and make 200-plus people redundant in one go; it is much more the slow movement of several jobs which mostly goes unnoticed. How can you ask multi-national companies to stop recruiting software engineers in India and check availability in New York, London, or Frankfurt first? Can you really tell software providers which location they should deliver their fixed price contracts from?

In the current changing business climate, companies are under extreme pressure to save their margins (see p. 41) and, as I have shown, offshoring can offer such substantial cost benefits that companies have little choice but to go for these opportunities.

3
Readiness for India

The word 'offshoring', useful as it is, draws attention away from the central issue. It is not simply a story of moving jobs to India; instead, it is about a fundamental reorganization of work, in which different tasks are carried out by different individuals and groups in different locations.[1] Many CEOs and CIOs have unrealistic expectations of how quickly and easily they can ramp up for offshore and realize savings. The obstacles are not only in India; many retarding elements are also found in the customer companies. Therefore, before embracing an India offshore project, you need to make realistic assessments of your organization's readiness for change and develop a rational strategy for change.

Assessing offshore readiness

Tough questions need to be asked around your company's ability to deal with aspects of offshore IT development work. This is one of the most difficult exercises to undergo; an honest assessment will expose gaps in how your IT department works and how qualified its employees are. Such criticism can be political and painful; however, without an honest appraisal at an early stage, the potential for later disaster is great. An offshore readiness assessment therefore requires a firm commitment from executive management and the outcome should be seen less as about who is right or wrong, and more about spotting what needs to be done to get offshoring right in the first place.

As a result of my work with many companies, I have developed a structure for a two-step internal readiness assessment. It looks at the two vectors that organizations need to consider: *organizational* and *technical application* offshore readiness.

Organizational offshore readiness

Organizational offshore readiness is made up of two dimensions (see Figure 3.1): *IT processes* for managing the collaboration with the provider and *cultural readiness* for commencing the India journey.

IT process readiness

You need to carry out your own due diligence on your internal IT processes before you do anything else. Without effective processes for IT governance, provider management and IT lifecycle management, and without adequate standards and tools in place, it can be difficult to manage projects half a world away. An IT process readiness assessment must confirm that all pieces are in place to effectively manage, communicate and collaborate with the offshore partner.

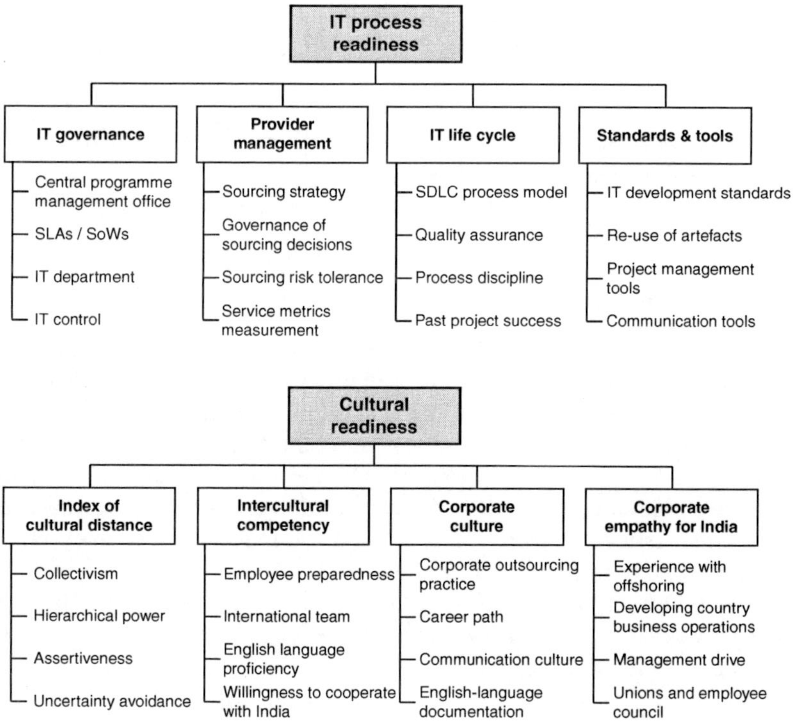

Figure 3.1 The two dimensions of organizational offshore readiness

IT governance

- *Central programme management office.* Do you have a central programme management office in place and do you manage your IT project portfolio through this office? How many of your IT projects and investments are measured comparatively in terms of costs and value?
- *SLAs and SoWs.* Does your organization rely on service level agreements (SLAs) to establish a meaningful level of mutual responsibility between the business and IT department? Are internal and external work packages defined in statements of work (SoWs)? Do you have standardized requirement definitions and control over change request procedures? Is your goal-setting and are your key performance indicators (KPIs) realistic?
- *IT department.* What is the business importance of the IT function in your company? Are its responsibilities and tasks growing or shrinking? How much does your company spend on IT compared to total revenues? How cost-competitive is your IT department compared to your top three competitors? Is your IT department distributed or centralized?
- *IT control.* Do you conduct (internal or independent) audits of divisional processes? Do you have strong and documented escalation procedures in place? Does your organization invest in process discipline? Are IT investments and ongoing expenditure governed by strict business cases?

Provider management

- *Sourcing strategy.* Is outsourcing or offshoring compulsory as per the order of the board, the CEO, or any other party in the organization? Or does it follow a careful consideration with the right questions being asked? Do you outsource only commodity functions or only when outsourcing is more effective than internal operations? Do you have a sourcing action plan for each and every service to guide you in the offshore venture? How often is your sourcing strategy reassessed in dynamic market times?
- *Governance of sourcing decisions.* How are decisions made, who has the right to make them, and who is accountable for the decisions? How good are such decisions?
- *Sourcing risk tolerance.* Are you aware of your organization's risk profile and tolerance? Did you go through a process of risk discovery? How much budget do you keep aside for managing risk? Do you

include the costs of managing risks and the benefits of avoiding disaster in your business plan?

- *Service metrics measurement.* Do you have a framework for measuring both quantitative metrics (service levels, cost and value) as well as the quality of your offshore relationship? Do you regularly assess the performance of your relationship? Do you ensure objectivity, for instance by engaging a third party in this process?

IT lifecycle

- *SDLC process model.* Does your organization have a standardized software development process (SDLC)? Do you have clear handover points and processes? Do you follow a formal sign-off procedure between business and IT for specifications and delivery?
- *Quality assurance.* Does your company have a quality management system (QMS) in place? Do you have regular internal and external quality audits? What do you do with audit findings – do you really act on them?
- *Process discipline.* Is your organization's IT maturity independently assessed, for example by the Software Engineering Institute (SEI), and rated at least as level 1 on the Capability Maturity Model CMM?[2] Do you have processes and controls in place which ensure that defined processes are always followed?
- *Past project success.* Do your IT projects generally come in on time and on budget? What are the typical sizes and durations of your IT projects?

Standards and tools

- *IT development standards.* Do you have prescribed and documented development standards? What is your approach to software testing? Do you use tools for testing? How do you document your test cases? How do you manage version management in the development and production environment?
- *Re-use of artefacts.* Do you have a central/global programming library? How is it maintained and used? What is your maturity in industrialized software delivery?
- *Project management tools.* What percentage of your staff hold a certification in project management? Do you have standard tools to support project planning, work assignment, and time reporting? Are such tools mandatory and actually used by projects? Are your employees sufficiently trained and conversant with these tools?

- *Communication tools.* Do you have established real-time communication, workflow and content-sharing tools? What is the usage of these tools in your IT team? Does the business also connect with such tools?

Cultural readiness

Culture can have a significant impact on the ability to achieve success in offshore. And by culture I do not only mean the difference between your home country and India, which can be measured along intercultural dimensions, but also the cultural preparedness of your employees, the corporate culture and a general corporate empathy to work with India. If your company does not fully embrace the rationale for the change, the tendency will be to view the India offshore partner as 'them', rather than as a remote 'us'.

Index of cultural distance

Cultural distance can be described by cultural dimensions, which have an effect on the functioning of societies, groups, individuals, and thus also businesses. The GLOBE study[3] identifies nine such dimensions and ranks countries on a scale of one to seven. Out of these intercultural dimensions, I have selected the four most important ones for offshoring, namely collectivism, hierarchical power, assertiveness, and uncertainty avoidance. Chapter 7 provides more in depth information on how to navigate such cultural differences.

- *Collectivism.* Whether employees are integrated into strong groups and the company organization (collectivism) – or whether they share loose ties among themselves and consider themselves as largely independent from their organization (individualism).
- *Hierarchical power.* The extent to which less powerful employees accept that power is distributed unequally, how they are obedient to their superiors, or whether they take control of their own affairs.
- *Assertiveness.* It reflects beliefs as to whether people should be assertive, tough and aggressive (of course, within the boundaries of social acceptability) – or rather modest, non-aggressive and gentle in social and business relationships.
- *Uncertainty avoidance.* The ways people deal with a diffuse feeling caused by ambiguous or unknown situations; whether they prefer rules and order to manage them, or whether they can tolerate uncertainty in their projects and personal lives.

When analysing the index of cultural distance, it is important to look at the relative distances of two countries in these dimensions, because these show the real differences which can potentially lead to friction in global project teams; the absolute values are of far less importance.[4] Table 3.1 shows the cultural distances for selected countries which typically offshore their IT work to India.

Sometimes, of course, project teams are distributed across various Western countries and its members are made up of several nationalities and cultural backgrounds. Depending on the setup, you can either take a weighted average (based on the strength of the sub-teams) or take the maximum distance for the score calculation.

Intercultural competence

- *Employee preparedness*. How many of your employees have attended intercultural sensitization programmes? How many have lived and worked abroad? How many have worked in offshore projects before?
- *International team*. How diverse, internationally and culturally, is your IT and business team? Are your employees used to working with other cultures, especially nations outside the developed world?
- *English language proficiency*. How many native or near-native speakers of English do you have in your organization? And how many employees are not conversant with English?
- *Willingness to cooperate with India*. How open-minded are your employees? Can they put themselves into the shoes of an Indian IT engineer, and do they respect people from another (very different) culture as equal to themselves?[5] Are your employees willing to go on several weeks of business trips to India or maybe even take up an expatriate assignment to coordinate the activities from India? Are time zone differences regarded as an advantage or disadvantage?

Corporate culture

- *Corporate outsourcing practice*. What percentage of your IT budget is handled by an outsourced provider as compared to in-house development? Is confidentiality of knowledge and data regarded as an issue when outsourcing or offshoring?
- *Career path*. How do your own employees feel if they give away technical system responsibility to India? Are they ready to take up functional, consulting and management roles? Does your company promote this type of IT career? Or are your employees evaluated against their technical competence only?

Table 3.1 Cultural distance to India, selected countries

	Collectivism			Hierarchial power			Assertiveness			Uncertainty avoidance			Index of cultural distance
	GLOBE	Delta	Scale	GLOBE	Delta	Scale	GLOBE	Delta	Scale	GLOBE	Delta	Scale	
India	5.92	–	–	5.47	–	–	3.73	–	–	4.15	–	–	
Australia	4.17	1.75	4	4.74	0.73	6	4.28	–0.55	6	4.39	–0.24	9	6
Austria	4.85	1.07	6	4.95	0.52	7	4.62	–0.89	4	5.16	–1.01	6	6
Canada (EN)	4.26	1.66	4	4.82	0.65	7	4.05	–0.32	8	4.58	–0.43	8	7
Denmark	3.53	2.39	2	3.89	1.58	2	3.80	–0.07	10	5.22	–1.07	6	5
Finland	4.07	1.85	3	4.89	0.58	7	3.81	–0.08	9	5.06	–0.91	6	7
France	4.37	1.55	5	5.28	0.19	9	4.13	–0.40	7	4.43	–0.28	9	7
Germany (West)	4.02	1.90	3	5.25	0.22	9	4.73	–1.00	3	5.22	–1.07	6	5
Italy	4.94	0.98	7	5.43	0.04	10	4.07	–0.34	8	3.79	0.36	9	8
Japan	4.63	1.29	5	5.11	0.36	8	3.59	0.14	9	4.07	0.08	10	8
Netherlands	3.70	2.22	2	4.11	1.36	3	4.32	–0.59	6	4.70	–0.55	8	5
Sweden	3.66	2.26	2	4.85	0.62	7	3.38	0.35	8	5.32	–1.17	5	5
Switzerland (GE)	3.97	1.95	3	4.90	0.57	7	4.51	–0.78	5	5.37	–1.22	5	5
UK	4.08	1.84	3	5.15	0.32	8	4.15	–0.42	7	4.65	–0.50	8	7
USA	4.25	1.67	4	4.88	0.59	7	4.55	–0.82	5	4.15	0.00	10	6
Max (worldwide)	**6.36**			**5.80**			**4.89**			**5.37**			
Min (worldwide)	**3.53**	**2.83**		**3.89**	**1.91**		**3.38**	**1.51**		**2.88**	**2.49**		

GLOBE: Value as per the GLOBE study; higher scores indicate more pronounced characteristics on a scale of 1 to 7.
Delta: difference between India's GLOBE value and the respective country.
Scale: normalized level of difference between India and the respective country on a scale of 1 to 10; higher scores signify greater similarity.

- *Communication culture.* How is information currently transferred – as written documentation or in face-to-face meetings? Are employees set to easily share knowledge with an offshore provider?
- *English language documentation.* Is English your corporate language, that is, is every essential communication and item of documentation in English? Or are local projects conducted in local languages?

Corporate empathy with India

- *Experience with offshoring.* Looking at the past five years in your company, what experiences of offshoring have you had as a company? And what experiences have your employees had (possibly in other companies as well)?
- *Developing country business operations.* Do you have business operations or customers outside countries of the developed world? Is your company experienced in dealing with other cultures?
- *Management drive.* Are business sponsors interested in going offshore? To what extent are your business processes regulated? How important is business knowledge at an outsourced (or offshored) provider location (reverse scored)?
- *Unions and employee council (reverse scored).* What percentage of your employees are unionized? What is the employee's council opinion about offshoring to India? How strong and influential are the employee's council or unions in your organization?

Evaluating IT process and cultural readiness

Most companies fall into three distinct groups, which have an effect on the choice of and the relationship with the supplier, the scope of and the way to start the journey, and lastly also the expected savings (see Figure 3.2).[6]

- *Ready IT processes and culture.* These companies have a long history of outsourcing and know how to moderate the risks, they also have IT processes in place which can manage the work of an offshore provider or connect with the provider's processes. A ramp-up for offshore requires little preparation. You are pretty much free to choose between multi-national providers with India operations, the big firms of Indian origin and specialist Indian players.
- *Inconsistent IT processes and global culture gaps.* These firms need to carefully select the kind of projects that they send offshore and they

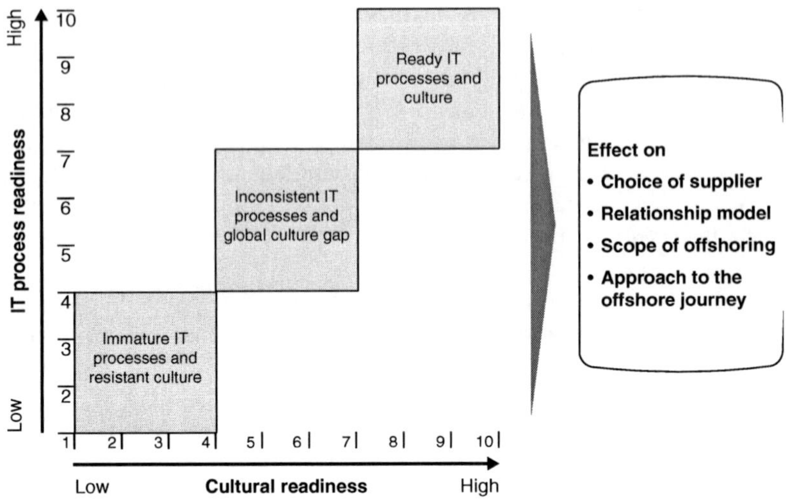

Figure 3.2 Distinct groups of offshore readiness

also need to select a provider which helps them to improve their own internal processes along with making the first steps on the India journey. Typically, these will be multi-national providers or one of the best Indian pure players.

- *Immature IT processes and resistive culture*. It is unlikely that these companies can fully realize all offshore benefits right from the beginning; they need to embark on a long and sometimes painful journey, first investing in bringing their own IT department up to speed. Such firms are best served by multi-national providers which have an offshore arm in India, because of their cultural closeness and their experience with similar scenarios. They can offer a blend of onsite, nearshore, and India offshore.

Although the two dimensions of organizational offshore readiness are not correlated, it is still very rare to find companies which excel in one dimension, but trail behind in the other. A global corporate culture usually brings with it the necessity for mature IT processes. However, for instance, an SME which acts purely at a national level may have highly matured IT processes, but can trail behind on a global cultural perspective.

Technical application offshore readiness

Most companies that I have seen do not use a formal process for deciding which part of their IT portfolio they should offshore; it is all based on management decisions and – hopefully – common sense. Such an informal approach imposes many risks; it may not only affect the savings you generate from offshoring, but it can also cause you to lose money on the offshore endeavour. Instead, you should use a standardized approach and examine your IT portfolio, area by area, application by application, for offshore-ability. Only then will you arrive at a set of applications and activities which are safe to be touched by India – and economically beneficial.

As a first step, eliminate your 'untouchable' applications quickly. These are applications which either demand a very high level of data security, whose business requirements constantly change, or which require expert business domain knowledge. Some firms also include core applications which help them to differentiate themselves from competitors. However, this criterion should not be used too light-heartedly and especially not as an excuse; just think about the number of interfaces in today's IT landscapes and you will see that most applications are contextual rather than core.

As a second step, examine the remaining applications according to technical criteria. I suggest applying the following six criteria:[7]

- *Size and lifespan.* Is the application big enough to warrant all the effort of giving work offshore? Consider the necessary effort for knowledge transfer and the ongoing management overhead, which needs to be offset against the cost savings. Also, applications should not be too close to their decommissioning date so that there is still a realistic chance of recovering the ramp-up costs.
- *Documentation.*[8] Applications with up-to-date and complete documentation are easier to offshore, as it is easier for Indian colleagues to pick up the context. In addition, past and new documentation should always be in English.
- *Business criticality (reverse scored).* The offshoring of high business-critical applications increases the application or project risk, which might impact business operations. This can be countered by additional efforts to ensure a smooth delivery; however, it will negatively affect the offshore cost savings generated.
- *Mainstream technology.* Applications or projects with common technology, that is, not too proprietary, neither too old nor too new, and not too exotic, are the best candidates for offshoring because

of easier resource availability in India. It takes a while before new technology becomes part of the curriculum in India; on the other hand, work on outdated technology is hardly inspiring for Indian software developers and this will lead to motivational problems in the offshore team.

- *Business domain knowledge (reverse scored).*[9] Proprietary business knowledge needs to be passed on to India during the knowledge transfer, adding costs to the ramp-up phase. Therefore, applications with a lesser degree of inherent domain knowledge are more suitable for offshoring.
- *Complexity (reverse scored).* An application's complexity can be measured in terms of number of interfaces, number of users, its geographical spread, and the characteristics of its inputs and outputs. Again, a high degree of complexity requires more effort during the knowledge transfer leading to more costs during the ramp-up time. Very modular applications with a high degree of separability are more suitable for offshoring.

And as a third step, score and rate your applications and projects. You should start with selecting a smaller area, but scale quickly in order to reap the financial benefits. Of course, the decision on what to offshore is not complete without calculating a detailed business case. Please refer back to Chapter 2, p. 51.

A note on self-assessments

Some authors, consulting companies and market research firms have designed offshore readiness assessments as self-assessment questionnaires;[10] you tick some boxes for about twenty key questions and the replies nicely add up to a score which is supposed to describe your company's readiness to engage with an offshore vendor. I believe this approach falls short of its purpose for two reasons. First, these questionnaires are designed to be self-assessments and this would require you to be fully conversant with the subtleties of offshoring, and if you were, you would probably not be reading this book right now. Self-assessments typically lack impartiality. In order to objectively assess a company's readiness, one needs to have an idea of the offshore world in India; one should have seen a few leading and also not so good cases and should have a feeling why things have gone well and badly in real life. Second, the depth of a standard questionnaire is hardly sufficient to argue and justify the implementation of measures, which basically means the initiation of IT process realignment projects. Such projects mean taking cash into your hands – and do you really want to do it based on a twenty minute online assessment?

Don't misunderstand me: questionnaires have their place in assessments. However, they need to be embedded in a small assessment project, consisting of scoping, interviews, data and evidence collection, scoring and packaging of implementable measures. This is serious work and my advice is to give it to an external advisory company. Put together with an offshore business case study, it means a small project of eight to ten weeks, two to four consultants depending on the size of your internal IT department and your application portfolio. Figure 3.3 shows this kind of approach.

One more word of advice: acknowledge that this is serious work, be willing to pay for it, assign it to an independent and experienced consulting company. If one of your shortlisted providers is willing to do it for free, avoid it; think about why the provider would want to do it for free and what outcome he would preferably see from the study. The offshore readiness assessment is too important to be biased.

Developing an IT offshore sourcing strategy

Has your company taken on more and more IT providers, have you entered into an increasing number of outsourcing or offshoring

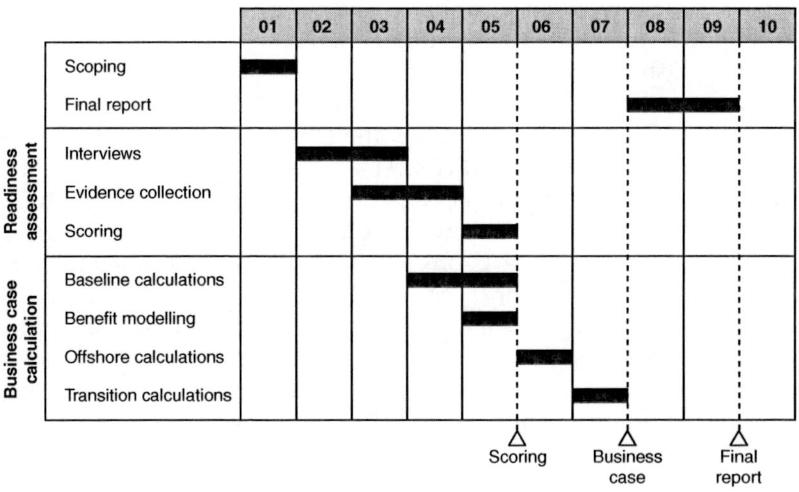

Figure 3.3 A possible readiness assessment approach

deals – and all this without a strategy? Giving work from your internal IT department to the outside world has become pervasive; offshoring it to India is no longer restricted to some 'niche' areas, in fact, for many companies today it is already encompassing critical business areas. Offshored projects are no longer standalone, instead they need to interact with internal operations, other outsourced or offshored projects to a hitherto unknown extent. Without a strategy to guide you in this process, you can only fix things here and there, thereby achieving some limited success, but your company will increasingly face difficulties achieving business priorities (see Chapter 2). Or as the American writer and futurist Alvin Toffler puts it:

> There is a slightly odd notion in business today that things are moving so fast that strategy becomes an obsolete idea. That all you need is to be flexible or adaptable. Or as the current vocabulary puts it, 'agile'. This is a mistake. You cannot substitute agility for strategy. If you do not develop a strategy of your own, you become a part of someone else's strategy. You, in fact, become reactive to external circumstances. The absence of strategy is fine if you don't care where you are going. (Toffler, 2000)

And I don't think anyone would be happy to let the Indian offshore provider take the lead in the offshoring initiative; instead this should stay with you in your own company. And that is exactly why you need to develop a stringent sourcing strategy and adhere to it.

An IT offshore sourcing strategy helps you to describe how your organization will achieve its goals by taking a long-term and holistic approach. Starting with a map of current sourcing operations, it provides and blends business and IT services in an optimal way from both internal and external providers, from onshore, nearshore, and offshore locations, thereby always following business goals.[11] In short, a well-honed and communicated IT offshore strategy prevents sourcing decisions being made at random.

You should start by defining a set of meaningful key business principles, and identifying what they mean for offshoring decisions. These principles will provide further direction in the decision-making process. You can arrive at these principles by examining your current strategies (or decisions), competencies, services and existing sourcing contracts. Combine these findings with a good overview of the Indian offshore market, which I aim to provide with this book, and you can carve out a set of principles and get them agreed by both your business and IT leaders. Some of the areas you need to look into are:

- *Organizational readiness*. Your own organizational offshore readiness (as analysed on pp. 63–6) influences how bold or careful your offshore approach can be; and it gives you an idea of the investment you need to make in your own company.
- *Competitive stance*. Are your current IT services meeting the business needs? How is the annual expenditure in relation to your top competitors?
- *Human and knowledge capital*. What is your IT staff good at today? Are your team leaders able to manage relationships for results rather than control the process of delivering results? What you need here is a competence profile of your own IT department and the providers that you are already using. Over time companies have built best practice operational processes and ways of delivering value to the customer. You have to judge how business-critical this organizational knowledge is and whether you can afford to have a provider participating in it.
- *Politics*. In some enterprises, offshoring decisions will spark a number of controversial and emotional discussions about job losses, risk through loss of control and cultural animosities. You need to know what implications these discussions will have on all stakeholders of your company and judge honestly if you can defend them.
- *Risk tolerance*. Finally and most importantly, you have to evaluate what is at risk when offshoring to India and compare it against your company's risk tolerance. This is really important and in this book, I have dedicated the whole of Chapter 4 to the risk of doing IT business in India.

Now you can go back to your business case (p. 51) for individual applications, projects or services and develop your offshore options. Consider the following dimensions:

- *Global options*. Your global options span a matrix from in-house to outsourced and from domestic to offshore. It is important to note that these choices are not necessarily exclusive; instead, a global delivery model can include a combination of locations.
- *Type of delivery*. Describe how the service is delivered, whether it is completely customized to the idiosyncrasies of your organization, that is, the company's unique products, its workflows, and maybe historical ways of doing things; or whether it is a standard service,

in other words, something in which the organization adapts itself to given best practice processes of software packages. Typically, standard services are more suited to industrialized offshore delivery than heavily customized services.

- *Level*. Third comes the level of offshoring: tactical, strategic or transformational (see p. 4).

Map all your applications, projects, and services along these three dimensions, always taking the offshoring principles into account, and you have a pretty good idea where the offshoring journey can take you. This path is really your IT offshoring sourcing strategy.

Take your sourcing strategy one step further: look at the providers you want to work with and integrate their deliverables to offset or minimize your risk exposure, improve value through collaborative innovation, and keep prices low. This is called real *multisourcing*. Your competitors are currently evaluating multisourcing and their providers' ability to integrate their services with other competing providers, they are weighing up who can truly partner with them to deliver outcome and business value – without the usual discussions around whose fault it was, finger-pointing and quoting the exact wordings of the contract.

Are India's IT companies ready to actively participate in multisourcing? To put it bluntly, in many cases Indian executives, managers, and their organizations need to go through a huge cultural shift to move away from the finger-pointing game. Especially with firms of Indian origin (FIOs, see Chapter 5), the service integration mechanisms are often not yet developed and executives are not yet clear about the revenue opportunity coming in through multisourcing. In order to drive this change, you as a customer can make the first step by offering a *quid pro quo*, such as greater project opportunities or a wider range of locations to support.[12] Providers need to see where they can work together with you and how this collaboration will enhance their revenue stream.

Case Study 3: Guardian's global sourcing concept[13]

The Guardian Life Insurance Company of America (Guardian) was founded in 1860 and is today one of the largest mutual life insurance companies in the USA. As of 2007, Guardian and its subsidiaries had USD 41.3 billion in assets. With close to 3,000 financial representatives and 80 agencies nationwide, Guardian and its subsidiaries protect individuals, small business owners, and their employees with life, disability, health, long-term care, and dental insurance products, and offer the 401(k) pension plan, annuities and other financial products and trust services. Specializing in the small to midsize business market, Guardian's business unit serves more than 120,000 employers, 6 million employees and their families.

In 2001, its sourcing principles were pretty simple: replace high-priced local consultants, increase quality, expand the resource pool and retain control through vendor aggregation. However, its CIO Dennis Callahan did not go for a project-by-project approach; after a short pilot installation and a careful provider selection process, Guardian immediately set up a 100-people dedicated resource centre with an Indian provider in Mumbai (Patni Computer Systems). Believing firmly in avoiding concentrating risk on one location and one provider, Callahan signed up with another two providers: one with headquarters in New Delhi (NIIT), but with multiple locations outside India, and the other an American-based company with Indian subsidiaries (Covansys). When tensions flared between Pakistan and India over Kashmir in 2002,[14] Guardian had enough global fall-back options.

The initial employee ratio between offshore work in India and onsite work in the USA was 50/50, moving to 70/30 within two years. The return on investment with respect to provider selection, people, process and system transitioning was reached within the first year. Annual savings are estimated at USD 12.5 million.

The offshore providers have incorporated their best practice development standards and processes, but operate under the standards put forward by Guardian. During steering committee meetings, offshore project status and relationship metrics are reviewed with representatives from each provider. Important metrics are customer satisfaction measured through quarterly satisfaction studies on provider consultant level, quality metrics, provider consultant retention for the account, offshore leverage, quality and productivity.

Case Study 4: Offshore IT partner strategy

Sports Co. is a pseudonym for a market leader in the global sporting goods industry. It is headquartered in Europe and offers a broad portfolio of products. The IT department includes close to 900 staff and operates with a global budget of not more than 2 per cent of net sales. IT is seen as an important service function and as a key enabler supporting the corporate strategy. The aim is to develop and support applications centrally and standardize the currently close to 500 applications across business functions. The challenge to deliver more, faster and at better quality directly affects the relationship management with IT providers. As well as efforts to consolidate the provider portfolio into less, but stronger partners, there is a focus on total cost of partner contribution (measured by cost and quality) and a demand for fixed price projects.

Sports Co. has therefore introduced a partner model with four classifications:

- *Preferred suppliers* have a global account manager mandate and are administered through steering committees which have the CIO's personal attention. Such suppliers have access to the company's internal resources, such as databases and subject matter specialists, and become familiar with the business processes of Sports Co. Therefore, the list of preferred suppliers needs to be stable and is only reviewed every twelve months.
- *Special suppliers* are preferred suppliers, but limited to one competence centre or department. They are not actively managed as partners through an account manager mandate or by steering boards.
- *Qualified suppliers* have an assigned account manager and when required are managed through a steering committee.
- All *other suppliers* are indirectly managed by third parties.

Over the past few years, Sports Co. has gained experience with offshoring work to India, both to an Indian pure player and a multi-national company with India operations. On this journey, the offshore ratio has increased from initially 20 per cent to now 40 per cent, allowing an overall project cost reduction of 10 to 40 per cent depending on the complexity, project size and the required coordination effort. Sports Co. works with the concept of dedicated offshore delivery pools, allowing a long-term partnership to build up, which makes the most of India offshoring in terms of quality, agility and cost. Indian offshore programmers switch between different projects for Sports Co., thereby leveraging company-specific process know-how while at the same time enabling job rotation and providing the Indian employees with a career path within the Sports Co. account. Tight management allows a fast switch of resources between projects to cover peaks, increase utilization and bring down overhead costs.

And when should I refrain from offshoring?

Much as an IT offshore sourcing strategy is about how your organization can achieve its long-term goals through offshoring, it also needs to provide answers for cases where India is not an option. The offshore readiness assessment (see pp. 62–72) helps to substantiate claims of not being ready for embarking on the offshore journey. So what are these key factors which can hinder you from going offshore?

First, if the readiness assessment shows that your *organization is fundamentally not ready* for India on both the organizational as well as the technical preparedness fronts, introducing offshoring is probably not a good idea. Having said this, the outcome of the readiness assessment not only means that you are not ready for India, but offshoring aside, your organization is in such a mess that you need to take immediate action. Maybe 'India' can be an ultimate goal and incentive to fix your processes and application landscape.

Second, there is a problem around *languages* other than English. If you are from the USA, UK, or Australia you will probably shrug this obstacle away. However, the many local languages of Europe can be a real hindrance. It is not that employees in European companies cannot read or write in English; historically, a lot of software was developed locally with specifications, program documentation and code comments in languages other than English. Continental European international banks still run mainframe programs from the 1960s – and all the documentation around them is neither in a nicely formatted document nor in English. Sometimes the front end needs to support users in various countries in different languages. IT managers often ask if they can get French- or German-speaking Indian developers and Indian IT providers tend to overpromise by highlighting the number of language courses they offer and advertising cheap translation services. True, Indians are good at languages, but only conversant with their own native languages; foreign languages other than English are not really taught at school and very few Indians have attended sufficient language classes to be able to speak foreign languages. Translation services vary in quality, but they usually struggle with technical or business English. In short, if you are dependent on language support other than English, consider a mixed-bag combination of onsite, nearshore, and offshore support for core delivery; but don't rely on India to solve this problem.

Third, India is not for the faint-hearted; there is considerable risk involved doing business on the subcontinent, mainly in terms of *risk for business continuity*. If your organization is hundred per cent dependent on 24×7×365 support, you need to have very good back-up options in your portfolio in order to include India. As I will show later in Chapter 4, the threat exposure through terror attacks, internal unrest, cross-border tensions, natural disasters, inadequate handling of infectious diseases and infrastructure breakdowns is real – even though the IT industry was fairly lucky in the past and operations remained functional. Other risk categories (see pp. 25–31) may also provide an obstacle; however, it is easier to come up with a risk mitigation plan for them.

Fourth, if your *IT managers are control freaks* who cannot imagine changing their working model when working with a team halfway around the globe rather than working with freelancers who are sitting two doors away, the offshore endeavour will fail for cultural reasons. If you cannot train or replace them, it is better to stay away from the investment that comes along with starting the offshore journey; at least with the current management team, the offshore endeavour will not get off to a good start.

To summarize: yes, there are cases where India offshore is not the right solution to meet your company's business priorities. However, this is a decision which should not be taken too quickly as there are also competitive risks involved in not utilizing offshore; your competition will do it and reap the benefits, and you will be left behind in the game with an outdated cost structure. In some cases, a balanced distributed delivery model utilizing both onsite, nearshore, and offshore resources may be a good way to start.

4
Normalizing India's Country Risk

Moving organizational activities outside your firm and outside your country's national boundaries exposes you to risks which were previously more or less non-existent or even unknown to you. The terror attacks on Mumbai in November 2008 put India's country risk under the limelight for a few days, companies imposed travel restrictions on India and quickly examined their business continuity plan, should the situation escalate. Such reactions were interesting to see and showed a complete misinterpretation of the security situation on the subcontinent; in fact the threat had been there for a long time, the threat has not changed since the events, and the security concern does not only come from terrorist attacks or Pakistan. It is critical that you understand these risks, measure the potential impact on your business and come up with a plan to mitigate the risks. You will never be able to eliminate the risks on the subcontinent, but you should at least normalize them – and this is the term I will use in this chapter.

At the same time, I re-iterate that it is also risky for your business to stay away from offshoring because of its inherent risks. These are different risks though; they are about losing cost advantage to competitors.

Correctly judging India's country risk

Before countering risks with mitigation plans, you should get a flavour of possible causes of disruption and understand the odds that you are up against. Let us organize the discussion around six broad categories:

- Terror attacks
- Internal unrest
- Cross-border tensions

- Natural disasters
- Infectious diseases
- Infrastructure breakdown

Of course, there are other risks that you need to consider when embarking on an offshore journey, such as risks of migration and delay, employee capability and attrition; last but not least your market reputation can also be at stake. These risks have nothing in particular to do with India as an offshore location, they will surface even if you are outsourcing to a provider within your own national boundaries.

Terror attacks

The spectre of domestic and international terrorism raises its ugly head every now and then, leaving violence in its wake. Islamic radicalism now seems to be becoming an increasingly serious threat to India. The most recent attacks came on 26 November 2008, when terrorists took hostages in some of Mumbai's most famous hotels, hospitals and other landmark buildings. Mumbai's streets emptied out and the country watched in horror as the hostage incident in the Taj Mahal Palace hotel played out on live TV for almost four full days before the gunmen were overpowered.

During the years before, bomb blasts in public areas took place with alarming frequency across the country, affecting Ahmedabad, Bangalore, Mumbai, New Delhi and other cities. However, their magnitude, the business disruptions caused by them and the worldwide attention was never as big as in the November 2008 attacks on Mumbai. The international media first named this incident 'Mumbai's 9/11', a reference to the attack on the World Trade Centre in New York, but as the scale became known, soon referred to it as 'Mumbai 26/11'.

Where does all the terror come from? Many terror attacks, including Mumbai 26/11, are attributed to the two terror organizations Lashkar-e-Tayaaba (LeT) and the Students' Islamic Movement of India (SIMI), which are believed to be directed from certain elements within Pakistan. LeT was founded in Afghanistan and is one of South Asia's largest and most active Islamic militant organizations. SIMI was started in India in 1977 and aims to 'liberate' India from Western materialistic cultural influences, thereby converting the country to an Islamic society; it is feared to be infiltrated by Al-Qaeda.

Notwithstanding the terror threats of the past, India's government, police and military is only now waking up to the need to put effective anti-terror measures in place. After Mumbai 26/11, the anti-terror readiness was heavily criticized by the world press, India's media and foreign intelligence agencies. Just look at a few facts and you can judge for yourself how well prepared India is to handle an attack of around ten terrorists. It took the NSG squad commandos ten hours to reach the terrorists from their base in New Delhi; their dedicated plane had gone to another city and first had to fly back to New Delhi to pick them up. Upon reaching Mumbai, they were stuck at the airport once more waiting for the police to arrange for local city buses to pick them up and drive them to the site of the terrorist attacks. Mumbai's fire brigade did not have sufficient bullet-proof vests and the firemen had to do their job without any protection. Not only this, Mumbai's fishermen had witnessed the arrival of armed terrorists in inflatable rubber speedboats and reported the sighting to a nearby police post, but the tip-off failed to rouse the police.[1]

India's corporate sector and IT providers revised their security procedures but also raised concerns that CCTVs, metal detectors, and unarmed security guards are not effective against trained terrorists with machine guns.

Internal unrest

In addition to terror attacks, India faces internal unrest and violence caused by minority subgroups. Hindus and Muslims frequently clash, leading to widespread riots. The worst incident happened in Mumbai in 1992/93 when tensions between Hindus and Muslims rose to the extent that 900 people died in riots and some 200,000 fled the city. In addition, members of different castes and communities sporadically clash. In June 2007, differences about quota benefits led to a full-blown caste conflict in Rajasthan; the Jaipur-Agra highway very much resembled a war zone. Migrant workers occasionally come into the spotlight of racial conflicts. In February 2008, the cities of Mumbai and Pune saw vitriol-laced campaigns against north Indian migrant workers and as a result, some 10,000 people in Mumbai and 25,000 in Pune left their work at construction sites behind and fled to their homes in other states.[2]

Naxalites are insurgents with communist or Maoist ideology operating mostly within the rural parts of India for the past 30 years and responsible for at least 6,000 deaths. It is estimated that at least 40 per cent of India's territory is under Naxal control and unpoliced by the government; 20,000 Naxalites are believed to be operating underground and armed – with many more overground members and sympathizers. The frequency and magnitude of Naxalite attacks in India is growing at an alarming rate, prompting Prime Minister Manmohan Singh to declare them as the most serious threat to India's national security. Despite this and some 130,000 military forces engaged in keeping the Naxals under control, there does not seem to be a clear government strategy or policy to deal with the Naxal guerillas; they get paid by construction companies to let the government build roads in their territory, and they get wooed (and paid again) by political parties, because on election day all votes count.[3] For a fair and complete picture, I need to mention that the Naxal threat has not (yet) made it to the big cities and IT operations are pretty much unaffected by this threat.

Some parts of India are prone to being affected by strikes, which can result in a whole city shutting down. Sometimes it is the transport sector calling its members out on strike against a rise of gas prices or against a mandatory installation of speed delimiters in taxis. Sometimes it is a political opposition party calling for a general strike. While the IT industry is in most parts of the country declared an essential industry and as such exempted from the obligation to strike, employees' ability to commute to work is disturbed and attendance in offices can be adversely affected. Owing to inadequate public transport systems, most Indian IT companies run their own arrangements with a transport vendor to bring employees in to work. These transport vendors employ drivers who form a loose union prone to calling strikes whenever they feel that their demands are not being met. Employees then have to rely on private transport or otherwise manage to get in to work. This is all very well during normal business hours. However, a female employee working the night-shift for American operations will not find it as easy to get home from work in the small hours. Some companies therefore have prior arrangements with hotels or supplies inside their building to meet such situations.

Cross-border tensions

The November 2008 terror attacks have further strained India's already tense relationship with Pakistan. While the attacks should make it clear to India, Pakistan, and indeed the entire world, that it is essential for the two countries to work together to combat extremist threats before everything derails and throws both countries back into a dangerous border game in which they view themselves as natural and mortal enemies, unfortunately Pakistan still views India and its military as a living threat and perhaps as a greater menace than the Taliban and other extremist groups.

Pakistan and India have fought a number of wars over the disputed territory of Kashmir, in 1947–8, in 1965, in 1971, and most recently the Kargil War in 1999. Many small border incidents happen every year, but the region saw its last real big stand-off in 2002 when India and Pakistan built up 500,000 and 120,000 troops respectively at the border. Concerns about a nuclear exchange returned and probably restrained both parties. The USA had then recommended all its non-essential citizens to leave India.[4]

Relations between India and Pakistan thereafter continued to improve again and full diplomatic relations were restored in 2003. However, the recent upward spiral in terrorist activities culminating in Mumbai's 26/11 and unrest in Pakistan raise concerns for the future, both in India and the Western world. Depending on the political parties in power and the state of rule (military versus democratic) in Pakistan, the Pakistan–India relationship can swing from one extreme to another very quickly.

Unfortunately it is not only the border between India and Pakistan which is problematic on the subcontinent. Other borders are also disputed, occasionally flaring up into public consciousness. India's eastern states of Assam and Meghalaya saw violent skirmishes at the border with Bangladesh in April 2001. And while the long-running border dispute with China on the frontier with the Indian Himalaya state of Sikkim was finally peacefully resolved in July 2003, the line of border control in Ladakh remains partly unclear, and Indian defence experts continue to see China as a real long-term military threat. Both countries are competing for the same strategic space in the Indian Ocean region. China is hugely dependent on the oil shipping lanes passing through this area and appears to be actively helping Pakistan with its missile and nuclear programmes, possibly intending to checkmate India. The Indian defence establishment goes as far as to believe that it will not be long before the Chinese navy begins to make active forays into the Indian Ocean region.[5]

Natural disasters

Cyclones, monsoons, and other weather extremes can leave behind floods that cause havoc in people's daily lives and subsequently also affect their ability to commute to work. The Mumbai monsoons in 2005 brought life to a standstill in the city; for some of those people who ventured out unwarned (and there was no weather warning at all), a daily commute of one or two hours turned into a 14-hour trudge back home wading through waist-high water and corpses of dead animals. Mumbai's international airport had to be closed for 30 hours and many offices remained closed for several days till the waters finally receded.

Some major cities and also IT hotspots lie in zones with seismic activity and are therefore prone to earthquakes. Cities in high damage risk zones are Chandigarh and New Delhi; Bhubaneshwar, Kolkata, Lucknow, Mumbai and Trivandrum are in moderate damage risk zones.[6]

Infectious diseases

India has had its share of panic in the form of the 2003 outbreak of severe acute respiratory syndrome (SARS), avian influenza and swine flu in 2009. So far, the country has always escaped lightly. Even during the swine flu scare, India only counted a few thousand confirmed cases as of mid 2009. The government was swift to react with checks at international airports for inbound passengers and facilities for quarantine. But consider the government's stockpile of 10 million antiviral tablets (as of mid 2009, raised from an initial 1 million stock)[7] for a population of more than 1 billion and you realize the country's good fortune in not having to deal with a deadlier and faster-spreading virus.

Infrastructure breakdown

IT offshore operations are very reliant on communication links with the onshore location including broadband access, phone lines and so on. While most operations are well served by dedicated communication lines, breakdowns occur every so often. A major disruption in 2008 came from an underwater cable line being brought down by a ship which had strayed off the coast of Egypt, affecting Internet availability in parts of India.

Power supply in India still trails behind demand and most offshore operators have their own private arrangements with back-up diesel generators keeping the power supply going when the main lines go down. These arrangements are very much dependent on the availability of fuel (diesel). July 2008 saw weak rainfall lowering water reserves in most of the hydro-electric power stations in the southern state of Karnataka. This led to a general weakening of electricity supply and greater dependency on back-up power options – generators running on diesel. The resulting scarcity of diesel in parts of the country, including the IT hotspot of Bangalore, had companies scrambling to shore up storage capacity so that they could run on back-up power for longer than 5 to 8 hours at a stretch.

On top of this, infrastructure arrangements are also thrown into disarray at times by strikes or other forms of internal unrest.

How to conduct your business impact analysis

Your offshore outsourcing contract should not be seen as an insurance policy against all possible risks. Unless a particular risk is specified in the contract, the providers will not price it into their cost model, and they will not compensate you for it when it happens.[8] Most of the country risks are in any case generally considered as falling under *force majeure* and the Indian provider would not be responsible for a delivery failure under international contract law.

Obviously, you cannot expect the Indian service provider to bear all the risks and uncertainties around your offshore project. Many of the country risks are speculative in nature, unpredictable and lacking in any sort of reliable estimates of their financial or strategic impact. So, what can you do?

Figure 4.1 outlines the overall business continuity planning process in four phases: assessment, strategy, implementation, and quality assurance. In the first phase, assessment, *disaster scenario planning* can help you to create specific situations, consider likely possibilities and develop reaction or mitigation plans. Such situations cannot be handled through normal management procedures, but they require considerable and company-wide support through business continuity management (BCM). In plain language, BCM procedures help you to stay in business in the unlikely event of a disaster. It is preferable to plan for very far-reaching disasters rather than for small problems, since most smaller problems are partial elements of a bigger disaster. Figure 4.2 shows a possible high-level threat scenario analysis.

One of the first steps towards business continuity management is to understand the impact of the disruption. This is called the *business*

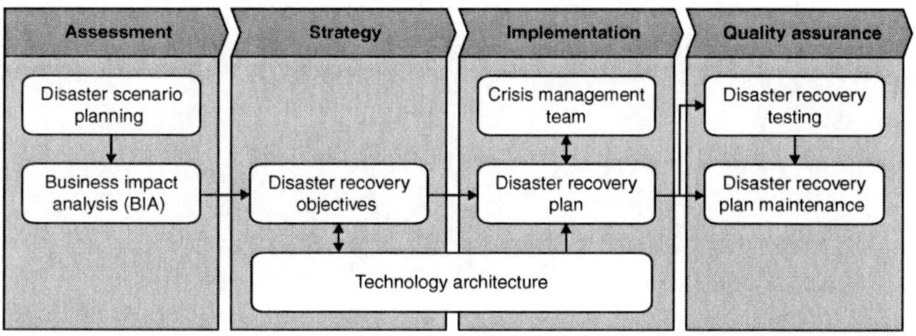

Figure 4.1 Business continuity management

Threat scenarios	Possible causes	Business impact	Recovery measures
1 Operational disruption at location	• Connectivity (WAN, telephone) down • Prolonged power outage with shortage of diesel supply	• Project / ticket delays • SLA breach • System/production down	• Prioritize work • Takeover by backup team at another location / in another city
2 Low employee attendance at location	• Transport disruption or road blockages (strike, riots) • Sick leave due to pandemic or food poisoning from office canteen	• Key employees and know-how not available • Project/ ticket delays • SLA breach	• Prioritize work • Remote access from home • Takeover by backup team at another location / in another city
3 Location outage	• Building inaccessible due to riots, police blockage • Building destroyed (fire terror attack); flooding	• See (1)	• Shift employees to backup location • Remote access from home • Takeover by backup team at another location
4 City outage	• Serial terror attacks • Flooding, earthquake • Local riots	• See (1)	• Takeover by backup team in another city • Minimal support from location in affected city may be possible
5 Country (or region) outage	• Country-wide riots • War	• See (1)	• Takeover by backup team in another geography • Minimal support may be possible from India

Figure 4.2 Scenario analysis for business continuity management

impact analysis (BIA), which tries to identify answers to the following key questions:

- How does it affect you financially?
- How does it affect your customers?
- How does it affect your suppliers?
- How does it affect your relationship with the authorities, for example, regulators?
- How does it affect your reputation?

India's country risk carries certain implications. However, it should be remembered that so far none of the scenarios described earlier have affected the IT industry in a big way. Even during the Mumbai 26/11 attacks, Mumbai's IT firms managed to continue operating to some extent. Hence you should not overreact at this point and look closely at the cost implications of countermeasures. Even if you are doing business in the Western world, there is also a business continuity risk. Just think about the terror attacks in London, Madrid, or New York in recent years.

Based on this analysis, in the second phase you will need to build your strategy and prioritize your *disaster recovery objectives*.

- How quickly do you need to recover? The *recovery time objective* (RTO) is the acceptable amount of time till your operations should be up and running again.
- How much do you need to recover? This is the *recovery point objective* (RPO), which is a measure of the acceptable latency of data, development work, and so on.
- What do you really need to do during a disaster? Identify the minimum you need to do (with respect to project team members, application configuration and so on) in order to support your business during a disaster; this is called the *minimum acceptable recovery configuration* (MARC).

In parallel, you need to examine your *technology architecture*, the development platform and communication infrastructure with your Indian IT provider, for robustness in case of disasters.

Implementation of business continuity management

As part of the business impact analysis you have identified the recovery objectives, which will help you pin down the logistics for business continuity management in the third phase: how do you intend to recover from the disruption? This is the *disaster recovery plan*, which identifies concrete activities for the following questions:

- Will you pass back the work to your company's home location?
- Will you relocate to a back-up site in the local vicinity around your Indian main delivery site?
- Will you relocate employees to another city within India?

Since modern technology makes it possible for employees to remotely log onto the company's systems, other decisions will need to follow.

- Should you source all back-up arrangements and infrastructure, for example the recovery building, workplaces, desktops, phones and govern them by appropriate contracts?
- Should you keep these arrangements in-house with the provider? Based on your recovery objectives, you will need to decide whether to evacuate to a back-up site in time of need or keep a dedicated site ready to be used at a moment's notice?
- Who forms part of the recovery team? Do all members of the recovery team relocate to the back-up location or do you have a split recovery strategy, that is, some relocate, some work from home, and some come back when the situation is back to normal?
- What contact numbers are important in the event of a disruption? How do you reach your employees (call tree) should there be an event outside office hours? How do you ensure that your customers and suppliers are informed appropriately?

Documenting all the above is the final step towards a plan for business continuity management. This should be discussed with your IT provider and be built into your offshoring contract. It is best to already be aware of your requirements during the vendor selection phase (see Chapter 5).

Of course, the next big task is to set up a *crisis management team* and ensure that everybody knows about the plan and has an idea of what is required in the event of a disruption. You will find it useful to hold brief sessions with all employees walking them through the plan.

The last and fourth phase of the business continuity planning process is about quality assurance. Physically testing the effectiveness of the plan (*disaster recovery testing*) is essential, especially in cases where you need to recover IT operations in a couple of hours. Needless to say, the plan needs to be kept up to date and revisited at regular intervals or whenever there is a material change in the project setup (*disaster recovery plan maintenance*).

5
Selecting the Service Provider

You may have picked up this book looking for advice in the middle of an offshore provider selection process and jumped directly to this chapter. Please do sit back for a few minutes and go back to the section in Chapter 3 (pp. 73–6) which is dedicated to the sourcing concept. Many companies struggle to identify the right offshore partner simply because they attempt *ad hoc* sourcing and do not have any IT sourcing strategy and/or governance in place. For many CEOs and CIOs, offshoring gets attention only during the selection and contract negotiation process. Deciding whether to do it alone in a captive offshore model, selecting the best offshore provider, choosing between multi-national companies or firms of Indian origin, and agreeing on a contract, are tasks doomed to fail without a proper IT sourcing strategy in place. You simply will not know what to scrutinize, what weightings to assign to the criteria, and what content to put into the contract. Naturally you will begin to view the offshore provider as kind of an untrustworthy enemy, who does not tell you the truth and tries to suck too much money out of you, while not understanding and supporting your company goals. This view has no place in offshoring. Both you and the offshore service provider will need to work together to control risks and build a lasting win–win relationship, which starts with your sourcing and governance strategy, and is then implemented in the evaluation, selection, and negotiation process.

In this chapter, let us sit back for a moment and compare the two general operating models: whether to run your own captive unit in India or engage the services of external providers. We begin with a look at India's highly fragmented IT provider landscape and review the myths and truths about Indian pure players and multi-national companies with operations in India. I will go on to explain why the traditional RFI/RFP process, as you may know it, adds little value to selecting the right provider and building a long-lasting value-creating relationship. Instead, I will introduce a five-step S-LEAN RFP™ procedure which briskly walks you through this process, makes the offerings of the service providers easier to compare and helps to get the expectations right in order to build lasting relationships. The chapter ends with advice on the Indian legal system and designing the offshore outsourcing contract.

Captive centre

An offshore captive centre is set up as a subsidiary of the parent company and hence the overall management responsibility of the captive centre in India lies with the parent company in the West. Why would you do this and not entrust the work to an established provider? The reasons for setting up your own facility in a low-cost destination are typically fourfold:

- The *management drive* to go the captive offshore way is usually given impetus by the activities of competitors (who might already have set up something in India), pressure by investors or analysts and a general intention of leveraging offshore to the fullest possible extent.
- *Intellectual property concerns* and the belief that having your own facility helps to protect your knowledge assets further drives the decision to mistrust external vendors and instead open your own facility.
- There is a belief that a fully-owned subsidiary not only allows for *better end-to-end process control*, but also for tighter general management control. For many it also means better access to senior employees (instead of having to utilize an army of junior consultants) and the flexibility to offshore all kinds of different business functions to India.
- The stunning profitability figures of Indian IT providers make senior management believe that they can hold on to this profit as *additional savings*.

This kind of reasoning has sent a large number of companies down the captive do-it-yourself route. However, according to Forrester, the research company, more than 60 per cent of captives fail to meet expectations.[1] Their delivery track record is poor, the delivery efforts in person days are much higher than initially estimated, employees' morale is down, attrition rates are skyrocketing, and the whole thing is not profitable any more. Why is this so? What has happened?

Captive centres do not usually succeed unless they acquire a certain critical volume, referred to as the captive critical mass (CCM). Gartner, the market research firm, recommends a CCM of 500 people for general IT operation consisting of a mixture of application development and maintenance.[2] As the talent pool tightens further in India and industrialization of IT delivery becomes part of the mainstream (see page 9), the CCM will go up even further. In some cases, initial senior management support for the India initiative dwindles and control freak operations managers in your company take over and refrain from giving work to the new offshore location. The captive centre stops growing, employees already recruited sit idle, get bored and leave the company. In order to be successful, you should have a very detailed plan of how to be confident of reaching the CCM within a maximum of 18 months after the centre's inception. Otherwise your chances of achieving steady state with respect to productivity and employee retention will become very slim.

Managing the brand of the offshore captive centre is also essential to its success in recruiting and retaining the right employees. Working for a good and recognized brand is important for employee motivation and is viewed as an additional prerequisite, carrying good standing in society. This process is by no means intuitive: a strong (customer) brand in your home market does not necessarily translate to a strong (employee) brand in India. There is a widespread prejudice in India that work done out of captive centres is generally boring and on old legacy systems. To counter this perception, you need to get your marketing department involved very early in the process – and also make sure that the captive centre receives the right mix of standard and 'exciting' jobs. Be aware, your standard (customer) brand promotion activities may not work in this case, you have to invent new approaches to talk with employees and finally attract them to your company.

In many cases, a feeling of unity between the headquarters and the offshore unit does not exist. It is not just that processes are not integrated; the entire captive centre is often not formally woven into your company's global fabric. This results in demotivation of your Indian employees; they feel like second- or third-class employees. And finally this leads to quality issues and loss of productivity due to low motivation and necessary rework.

Your Indian employees' expectations regarding salary are not necessarily aligned with your global compensation framework, but they are shaped according to industry standards and tax laws in India. You need to be flexible in adjusting to such requirements and create a fair

India compensation framework even if it means introducing some inconsistency in your global policies. The same holds true for corporate titles and career plans. Career advancement goes much faster in India – and is also expected to do so; you need to live with the fact that your global corporate titles are not comparable with the ones in India.[3]

If you still plan to set up a captive centre in India after all these concerns (and there are many successful examples), you can choose between three principal options. First, and this is the most common approach, you can found your own subsidiary in India. Second, you can enter into an equity partnership with a local company (joint venture). Third, an Indian IT provider or any other specialized third party can help you to set up, start, and ramp up the centre with the intention of transferring ownership to you after an agreed period of time. This is referred to as the build–operate–transfer (BOT) model.

And if you are already running your own captive centre, you may or may not experience some of the issues mentioned above. In any case you should accept that a captive centre can be a stage in the offshore evolution lifecycle, so you may want to reset your captive offshore strategy at some point in time. You have the following four options:[4]

- *Shut down the captive unit and offshore to external providers simultaneously*. This strategy may be applicable if your captive unit is so small that the closure will hardly be recognized internally (service disruption) or externally (negative media coverage). An example is Apple's customer support facility (Apple Services India), which was established in April 2006 with 30 employees, but with plans to ramp up to 600 within less than a year. However, it was shut down only two months later and most of the work handed over to an external Indian provider.[5]
- *Embrace third parties to augment captive work*. In this alternative, third party external providers are used to take over some of the captive's work, usually the part which is less strategic or innovative. The driver behind this is the recognition that development on established software platforms and maintenance-related work can be done more efficiently with external offshore IT providers. Many large high-tech firms follow this approach (see Case Studies 5, Texas Instruments, and 6, HSBC) and reap the benefits of industrialized IT delivery (see Chapter 1, p. 9, and Chapter 2, p. 51).
- *Get hollowed out*. If you are struggling with your captive centre and the recruitment and retention of skills, but there is no prospective buyer in sight – what do you do? Indian IT providers have become

interested in hollowing out captive centres by gradually augmenting your staff with their own employees. You are left with an 'India oversight office', which allows senior managers in your company to keep their reputation and at the same time provides an interesting way of combining a close watch on offshore activities with efficient execution.

- *Sell the captive unit and offshore instead.* Early market entrants were able to build up their captive centres to an attractive size and capability that IT providers became interested in purchasing. Companies like Deutsche Bank are now customers of the IT providers who have bought their captive centres (see Case Study 7).

Case Study 5: Texas Instruments' hybrid captive approach in India[6]

Texas Instruments (TI), a world leader in analogue, microcontroller and signal processing technologies, commenced operations in India in 1985, becoming the first multinational to set up an R&D facility in Bangalore. Texas Instruments India Pvt. Ltd. started with the development and support of proprietary Electronic Design Automation (EDA) software systems used for Integrated Circuit (IC) design by TI's semiconductor design centres worldwide. In 2004 TI combined its two facilities in Bangalore into one new development centre and in July 2006, it expanded its local presence in India by announcing the second R&D centre in Chennai.

Since early 2001, TI India has actively promoted its partner programme and now has approximately 50 Indian partners working under its global Third Party Program. It also enables Indian companies to reach out to international customers through TI marketing channels.

Case Study 6: HSBC's IT captive cooperation with Capgemini[7]

With headquarters in London, HSBC Holdings plc is one of the world's largest banking and financial services organizations. It serves over 128 million customers worldwide through around 10,000 offices in 83 countries. HSBC is marketed worldwide as 'the world's local bank'.

In 2002, HSBC opened its captive software centre in Pune, with initially just 30 people working on software maintenance, rising in only four years to 2,500 developing software for the company's operations worldwide. Although HSBC's offshore centre is captive and in-house, it operates like an independent provider, getting paid market rates for whatever it does for the bank. Initially, of course, the centre ran into problems. The bank's business departments would sketch out ambitious jobs, which Pune would accept knowing they had the technical skills, but not quite the domain expertise to deliver successfully. HSBC recognized the problem and solved it by asking business experts within the bank to sit alongside the technical consultants during the development projects.

In 2003, HSBC acquired US financier Household Finance, which had had an offshore development partnership with Kanbay for developing consumer-lending software since 1990. Kanbay is a US listed offshore company. HSBC suddenly found itself operating its own captive centre, as well as collaborating with an external IT provider. Right from the beginning, HSBC did not consider Kanbay as a competitive threat to their own captive centre, but collaborated and jointly devised a plan to partner on projects in a commercial relationship. At the end of 2003, a venture capital shareholder exited Kanbay and gave HSBC the opportunity to acquire a 20 per cent stake in Kanbay for USD 26 million.

By 2006, Kanbay employed 6,900 people, 80 per cent of them in India; it produced revenues of around USD 400 million annually, of which 79% were in the financial services domain. However, it was very little diversified, depending largely on its business with HSBC; 2,400 of Kanbay's employees were interwoven with HSBC's global IT organization, bringing in 34% of the company's revenues. Capgemini, the consulting, technology and outsourcing services company with headquarters in France and at that time 16,000 employees in India, acquired Kanbay in order to increase its presence in India, focusing not only on staff augmentation, but on domain expertise, thereby building a competitive proposition in offshore provisioning compared to its European peers.

In June 2008, HSBC and Capgemini extended their strategic relationship till the end of 2010 and agreed about 4,500 person years of resources. According to Ken Harvey, Group Managing Director HSBC, this cooperation between HSBC and Capgemini and between its respective on- and offshore teams works extremely well in aggressive project schedules. The provider and captive teams are very tightly intertwined so that software code can be turned around twenty-four hours a day. Development is concentrated in standardized Centres of Excellences (CoEs) in India, where Capgemini as a provider contributes best practices, standards and knowledge, thereby also leveraging HSBC's own captive units to deliver superior performance.

Case Study 7: Deutsche Bank's captive IT centre in India[8]

Deutsche Bank, founded in 1870 and with headquarters in Frankfurt (Germany), is a leading global investment bank with a strong private client franchise. It has more than 80,000 employees in 72 countries.

Deutsche Bank established its captive IT centre in April 1992 in Bangalore, initially serving its regional Asian headquarters in Singapore with projects around core banking implementations, groupware solutions and electronic banking. The unit was named Deutsche Software India Pvt Ltd and steadily expanded its reach to other worldwide locations of Deutsche Bank. For most projects, senior consultants were sent to an onsite location to work and interact with colleagues for a period of three months up to a year, then take the knowledge back to India and guide the delivery team. Right from the company's inception, an employee of Deutsche Bank Germany was sent on a three to five year expatriate assignment to Deutsche Software to support the management team. Deutsche Software offered the best salaries in Bangalore's IT industry and could choose between candidates for employment.

By 2000 and 2001, the 450 employees of Deutsche Software were delivering commercial value of USD 25 to 30 million annually within the Deutsche Bank group out of its 6,400 square metre office in the heart of Bangalore. Its employees were also working onsite at Deutsche Bank's locations in Singapore, Frankfurt, New York and London. At the beginning of 2001 it began its transformation into a profit centre, building a sales and marketing team to cater to the financial sector.

In September 2001, HCL Technologies formed a joint venture with Deutsche Bank AG and acquired a 51 per cent stake in the holding company of Deutsche Software. HCL had close to 4,000 employees and gross revenues of USD 298 million in 2001; it was mainly interested in combining the domain knowledge and consultancy expertise of Deutsche Software with its own technological and offshore project management skills. Deutsche Bank's move to sell a major stake in its captive unit reflected the trend among international banks to outsource their IT development and thereby reduce their technology service costs.

Until HCL's new financial services unit was able to establish its client base outside the Deutsche Bank group, an agreement granted HCL the right of first refusal for all business that Deutsche Bank was to source from India over a period of seven years, creating a comfortable income cushion for HCL.

Within five years of selling its captive unit, Deutsche Bank managed to cut its IT costs by 30 per cent through outsourcing and offshoring, while doubling its performance.

By July 2004 Deutsche Software Ltd, now known as DSL, covering the Deutsche Bank heritage in order to gain more external business, had grown to 1,500 employees. HCL acquired the remaining 49 per cent stake in Deutsche Software from Deutsche Bank through a share swap. In 2009, HCL numbers approximately 58,000 employees.

Case Study 8: Allianz Insurance's captive subsidiary ACIS in India[9]

Allianz Insurance plc is the UK subsidiary of Allianz AG, which is Germany's largest insurance company and one of the world's leading financial service providers. The net written premium (NWP) of Allianz Insurance (UK) is around GBP 1.4 billion (2008).

In 2003, Allianz Insurance was looking into cost-effective growth of its IT function and decided to set up a software offshore development operation as a captive subsidiary in the Technopark in Thiruvananthapuram, Kerala: Allianz Cornhill Information Services Pvt Ltd (ACIS). John Knowles, CIO of Allianz Insurance, consciously decided on a tier II location on the subcontinent, against the advice of consulting companies and the trend to go to established locations in the Indian IT triangles. He was interested in attracting employees seeking a long-term, in-depth career in the insurance business, not the quick job-hoppers who would soon begin to emerge in India's IT hotspots in the years to come. He also did not want to compete with the industry giants for talent and growth, but being a smaller company, wanted a smaller pond to play in. Thiruvananthapuram offers an established infrastructure, a good university system, and a quality of life that is probably unique among India's state capitals. At the same time, John Knowles knew that his UK employees would need to go on frequent business trips to India in order to continuously build up and expand ACIS. He wanted to make these visits attractive and Thiruvananthapuram's beach location definitely helped in this regard. Another pillar of success was the hiring of an experienced Indian management team with Rakesh Kumar Gupta as chief operating officer (COO).

The ramp-up of ACIS built on the principle of steady growth and non-mandatory offshoring, so Allianz Insurance did not stimulate demand for its offshore services by dictating which functions should send which percentage of work to India. Instead, various parts of Allianz Insurance worked with ACIS to develop the required services at very attractive internal cost rates. The quality of its deliverables then did the internal marketing. Allianz Insurance in the UK seeks to work with ACIS in a very integrated way – in the so-called one-team approach. As a part of it, ACIS took responsibility for the IT knowledge transfer process. The standard way of Westerners teaching Indians about an IT application was found not to work too well. Hence, ACIS took the lead and introduced the knowledge acquisition process (KAP), which puts the Indian team entirely in charge of it. Now motivation and responsibility were aligned properly.

What started with application development and maintenance (AD&M) services was soon complemented by sales and back-office processing support (BPO) in summer 2004, and later by infrastructure maintenance (IM). The venture into new areas was made successful by starting a small number of separate seed projects in parallel. Allianz Insurance was ready to give them time to be successful, even let some fail if necessary, but most importantly, collected the learning from different business areas to inform the next stages of development.

By mid-2009, ACIS had 400 employees in BPO, 150 in AD&M, and 50 in IM. All application maintenance work from Allianz Insurance UK is already offshored to India, the quality management function is well established, and ACIS is accredited at CMMi-Level 5. ACIS is already starting to extend its reach into the wider Allianz Group, including the start of SAP application development and maintenance in India as well.

External service providers

The external IT provider market in India is very fragmented. At a very high level, the players can be segmented into:

- Firms of Indian origin (FIOs) or so-called Indian pure players; and
- Multinational companies (MNCs) with operations in India.

Firms of Indian origin

Indian-owned IT service providers (with headquarters in India) are commonly referred to as firms of Indian origin (FIOs) or Indian pure players. They were the first to pioneer global distributed delivery models and even today own the biggest slice of the offshore IT delivery cake.[10]

FIOs are consistently ranked high by analysts for the depth and breadth of their technical skills and project management resulting in delivery on time. However, only the top players have pockets of specific process and industry skills; most FIOs cannot be rated very highly on their transformation programmes as business solution leaders.[11] They are generally very cautious about exploring market opportunities other than outsourced application development, maintenance and business process outsourcing (BPO).

For many years, FIOs have built on cost advantages through labour arbitrage as their unique selling proposition. However, this lead is quickly diminishing as foreign IT providers continue to grab a foothold in the Indian market space, ramp up their facilities, and make offshore the centre of their activities. The differentiation of 'being offshore' has already evaporated.[12] FIOs therefore attempt to counter this invasion by invading the Western markets themselves; recent years have seen an increasing number of Indian firms buying Western brands and companies. Through such inorganic growth, Indian IT providers try to move up the IT services value pyramid.

As utilizing the offshore option for IT delivery continues to move into the mainstream, in other words as it spreads from huge international conglomerates to more and more small- and medium-sized enterprises (SMEs), the FIOs begin to face two challenges. First, the SMEs are less sophisticated in their IT management and use of IT. Second, IT is not as important to them as it was to the early offshore adopters in industry verticals like financial services, insurance or telecommunications.[13]

One would think that FIOs would primarily concentrate on the domestic Indian market and other less developed countries as it is commonly accepted that success in the domestic market is a prerequisite for global success. Very surprisingly however, for many years and while the Indian domestic IT market was evolving steadily, it was not a target for its own service providers at all. In fact, they appeared to have less success with them than their global competitors.[14] The reasons are twofold. First, the government of India wanted to promote export-oriented software development as a driver to create employment and wealth in the country; in 1999 it established a scheme called Software Technology Park (STP), under which export-oriented IT service providers were exempted from paying tax on their export revenue. This scheme was originally planned for 10 years and scheduled to end in 2009, but was subsequently extended till March 2010, driven by the heavy profit concerns of India's IT industry; a second extension was announced in July 2009 as part of the new government's budget up to 2011. The second reason for less commercial interest in the domestic market is its extreme price sensitivity on top of the loss of tax exemptions.

Multinational companies

Established multinational IT providers have by now fully replicated the offshore delivery model, their delivery centres in India are comparable in size, methodology, and quality with the Indian pure players. However, they still trail behind them in terms of growth and profitability. Let us examine the statistics. The five largest multinational companies together account for less than nine per cent of the Indian IT workforce and together are just a little bigger than the two largest Indian pure players combined.[15] Nonetheless, they certainly have a better reputation for transformational projects because of their experience with the needs of global clients, a well-educated force of Western consultants complementing the Indian delivery teams, and strong client relationships at executive level.

Deciding between FIOs and MNCs

If you are in the process of conducting an RFP and doing a vendor evaluation, you will certainly have spent some time wondering whether an Indian pure player or a multi-national company is the better option for you. While you should not actually ponder this question and should shortlist providers based on other capabilities as I will show you in the following two sections of this chapter, one can generalize a few points where FIOs and MNCs differ.

The *experience of working together* with a multinational offshore IT provider is probably culturally closer to home than the one of working together with an FIO. MNCs will staff a mixture of home country and

Indian consultants onto the project, your executives, the project managers and the business analysts will mainly interact with colleagues from your own culture.

On the other hand, FIOs are usually more *cost-competitive* compared with MNCs. The reason is that they try to staff everything and everyone from India, because that is where their main employee base lies. MNCs tend to offer less aggressive offshore versus onsite ratios, making your life as a customer a little easier, but of course also driving up the costs. Many FIOs have fantastic showcase offices where they take their customers on visits, but try to lower the infrastructure costs of offices where the real work is done, or they move project teams to tier II or tier III cities (see Chapter 1, p. 30) where property is cheaper, attrition less, and employees command lower salaries. MNCs tend to be clustered in the big tier I cities and have the same kind of offices in all their locations.

While FIOs are comfortable handling tactical and strategic offshoring deals, which reduce costs and improve operations (see Chapter 1, p. 4), they still struggle with the requirements of *transformational offshoring* deals, which target improvements in the client's business. MNCs will be most comfortable with strategic and transformation offshoring, while in most cases they can't offer the same cost benefits as FIOs in tactical deals.

Your *legal department* will find it easier putting their signature on a contract with an MNC in their own home country than endorsing an agreement with a party in another part of the world. I come back to the legal implications of signing a contract with FIOs at the end of this chapter.

And last but not least, *corporate governance* is usually more strict in MNCs; in plain words, the Satyam disaster of 2008 (see Chapter 1, p. 24) with all its effects on client projects is very unlikely to be repeated in an offshore provider which is controlled from and has its headquarters outside India.

Why the traditional RFI/RFP selection process fails

Traditionally, the provider evaluation begins with an RFI (request for information) and is followed by an RFP (request for proposal). The company puts together a team of people fairly familiar with the job to be offshored. Very often these people are handling outsourcing deals for the first time and rather desperately assemble a long questionnaire – sometimes referred to as the 'laundry list'[16] – by borrowing parts from other RFPs in the organization, checking what is available on the Internet, and including standard questions from the purchasing department. This typically pretty long laundry list is then sent to an arbitrary number of service providers. On receiving the RFI, the providers calculate their chance of pocketing the deal at the end of the evaluation process. How serious you appear to be about the RFI is one of the factors they take into account for calculating the probability of winning. As a result, some providers may choose not to invest the time and may not respond. Most others will assign low-level consultants to put some vague answers together; again these answers will be borrowed from other RFIs and will just be marketing boilerplate language. After the evaluation team receives these responses, they have the unenviable task of drilling down to some three or four candidates who will receive the more detailed RFP. In this round, they attempt to make available more detailed information on how the service is to be delivered and question the provider on the ability and *modus operandi* of delivery. In turn, the offshore providers selected to participate in the RFP will make another calculated guess as to their chances and try to answer the questions asked. The selection team again needs to spend hour after hour looking through the answers and consolidating them in order to try and decide with which provider to enter negotiations. Typically, at this stage, some three to six precious months have been spent on rather meaningless paperwork. Neither party has entered a relationship, neither has any idea of each other's capabilities, needs and expectations for a future relationship. The actual scope of work is still up in the air, the service levels are not detailed enough, and the provider has not been able to openly communicate his own concerns regarding resource availability, knowledge transfer and ramp-up time. It is a recipe for disappointment, if not disaster.

Sometimes, and this is a little different from the normal RFI/RFP process, clients start negotiations directly with a single offshore service provider. There may be an existing business relationship with this lucky candidate, or an executive from the client site has a 'special' relationship with the provider. The underlying idea is to reduce the lengthy evaluation process and invest in negotiation time instead. However, this approach does not help to foster an exchange between the two parties and it also takes away most of the negotiating power. Typically this results in substantially higher contract costs.[17]

There is something else that I have noticed in many provider selection processes, 'beauty contests', and especially exploratory client visits to India. Organizations and their representatives tend to focus on the highly visible and tangible things: they compare headcount figures, the architecture of office buildings, the fitness gyms, the equipment of training rooms, methods and tools, relevant references, and the quality of employee resumés. Reading this from a distance, you may smile about this naïve approach to provider evaluation. But when companies commence the process of a provider evaluation and travel to India on their first visit to potential supplier facilities, this is what strikes everyone first and what can be compared rather easily and objectively. Even then, the job remains mostly incomplete. Are you sure that exactly the same people are going to join your project as you have seen resumés of? Can you distinguish between (Indian) degrees in commerce and engineering? Do you know the ranking of India's colleges or universities? Did you visit the office building that your team is actually going to work out of – or was it just a showpiece which the provider has cleverly arranged all the meeting rooms in? Did you have your lunch catered from an outside five-star hotel – or did you really eat in the pantry with all the thousands of local employees?

If you cannot attach a specific focus to these exploratory trips, please do cancel them. They come at a significant cost to your company, and without a clear focus they will leave you no wiser. In the worst case, you will be even more confused by all the impressions carefully orchestrated by the service providers you are visiting.

Practical implementation of an S-LEAN RFP™ process

Let us now look at how you can improve the provider selection process and practically implement it in your organization. Difficult economic times usually require you to react quickly and as I have outlined before, the traditional RFI/RFP process with its long laundry lists adds little value to the provider selection process anyhow. This new RFP process, let us call it S-LEAN RFP™, consists of five distinct steps:[18]

- Set up the evaluation governance
- List and pre-qualify suppliers
- Establish RFP documents
- Analyse and evaluate
- Negotiate contract

Figure 5.1 summarizes the main activities in these five steps; in the following sections, what really needs to be done and watched out for will be discussed in much more detail.

Step one (S): Set up the evaluation governance

Before you even begin the provider evaluation process, or instigate communication within your own organization, you need to get the interaction

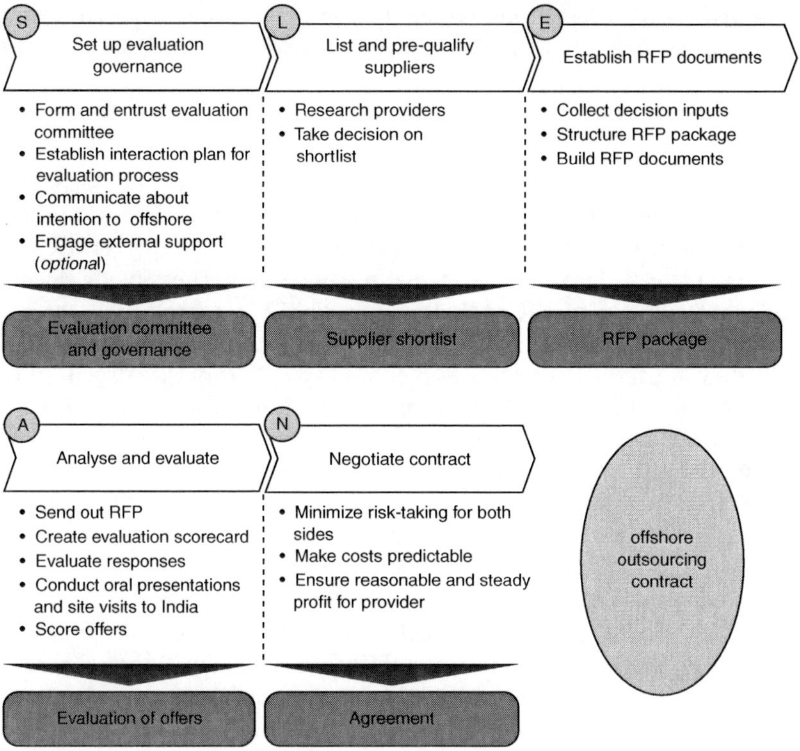

Figure 5.1 The five steps of the S-LEAN RFP™ process

plan for the evaluation process right. This plan will set out how your company is going to communicate with the providers during the evaluation process and up to the point when the contract is signed. This is crucial to the success of the entire evaluation, because without such a plan, you can be sure that the providers' account managers will try to make contact with members of your evaluation committee, other employees and especially the top of your organization, and to throw their weight around. If this process is not put in place right from the beginning, you can also be sure that later on any governance structures or relationship management processes will be taken seriously neither by the provider nor by your own employees. In the interaction plan, you need to set out the following:

- Point(s) of contact in the evaluation team
- Media to be used for any information exchange (email, phone, meetings)

- Schedule of interactions (when to send documents, receive questions, provide answers, conduct oral provider presentations, take a final decision)
- Penalties for not adhering to this plan

The final point about penalties is really crucial. Service providers will try to circumvent the evaluation committee and access the top of your organization. You have to communicate to them right at the very beginning that this will not be tolerated and will result in them being relentlessly thrown out of the evaluation process. These are tough threats which need to be backed up right from the very top of your company so that they are actually credible and enforceable. Empty threats will only weaken your position in the relationship with the provider. It is so very important to make the providers adhere to some basic communication processes right from the beginning, as otherwise you can be sure they will circumvent any such processes later on as well and will not take your dedicated staff seriously. Later on they will go right to the top even over minor issues and undermine the credibility and responsibility of your dedicated staff.

As a CEO or CIO you may not feel too comfortable delegating this responsibility; but I can only advise you to trust the evaluation committee completely, support them fully in this process, and back their decision. If you are not comfortable delegating responsibility and authority to the evaluation team, you will need to get personally involved, become part of the evaluation committee, and be very visible in this process.

At this point, and before you even begin to form the evaluation team, you will need to communicate about your intention to offshore. It is no longer possible to keep anything under wraps. You need to communicate to the board of directors, the executive management team, business unit management, users of IT services in the business units, employees of the IT department, current external providers, employee unions, shareholders, and the press. This segmentation will help you to get your message right and find the right way of communicating – through town hall meetings, typed press releases, press interviews, or via the corporate intranet. The management layers may require more detailed information; at all costs you should prevent them from having to answer too many of their subordinates' questions with 'I don't know'. So, what are your key messages?

- Why is a change necessary?
- Why was offshoring chosen?

- What is the scope and who will be affected?
- Who will *not* be affected?
- Who is supporting this decision?
- What is the timeframe for implementation?

If your company has a powerful employee union, you may want to include them early in the decision process to start offshoring. In any case, you will need to have a specific communication plan for union employees.

Once you have formalized the communication plan, it is time to form the evaluation committee. This group will carry the S-LEAN RFP™ through the process, right from pre-qualifying providers to assembling the RFP package, to evaluating, and negotiating the contract. Naturally, not all its members will be part of every part of the process and they will not do everything themselves, but they will also identify sub-tasks and delegate them to other units within and outside your company. I would recommend defining the ten roles below and assigning people to them; the complexity and size of the deal should of course be appropriate to the number of people directly involved. For less complex or smaller deals, one person may take up two or three roles.

- Corporate sponsor
- Evaluation project manager, supported by a PMO
- Experts from the affected IT areas
- Representatives from affected business areas
- Employee union representative
- India country expert
- Provider relationship manager
- Negotiator
- Legal expert
- Communicator

In many scenarios, most of your own employees will not have dealt with Indians or Indian service partners before. On the other hand, account managers from the Indian service provider are well versed in the offshoring business and interact on a day-to-day basis with Western companies and their business and negotiation behaviour may be uncomfortably astute. This can put your evaluation team on the defensive right from the beginning and you may want to consider external help in order to level the playing field. These days many companies, and also freelancers, pride themselves on being offshore sourcing experts; unfortunately you will need to do some due diligence on them to establish this. In my opinion, the company name, references and methods of supporting such evaluations are of far less importance than the experience of the individual consultant you are going to hire. If you have decided that you want external support, and again this is not always necessary and completely depends on the experience of your own evaluation team, you should try to hire someone with extensive India experience, someone who knows the rules of the game, the negotiation strategies of the Indian service partners, the employee market in India, and especially their business needs. The last point is particularly important as you are not only negotiating a price, but a sustainable relationship which is supposed to cater to the needs of both sides. Such experts are very rare; just having conducted two or three India projects or having travelled to India on some short business trips is not the magic answer for you. You may want to look into the freelancing market or ask a big international consulting company, which you deliberately are not going to include in your shortlist; you will need to be very clear with them on this point. Naturally, this is not going to get you the experienced consultant for a cheap rate, but your focus should be on getting competency and value. The role of evaluation project manager, supported by a PMO, would be the ideal role for this candidate.

Step two (L): List and pre-qualify suppliers

My recommendation is to scrap the RFI part of the evaluation process, and instead thoroughly pre-qualify possible suppliers. This requires very extensive market knowledge and also the courage to make decisions. If you have hired external support, as outlined before, this can come in handy now. Otherwise, you need to build on the experience of your own employees, use your contacts with competitors in the same market space and see what they are doing, or look into reports by market research companies. In my experience, an offshore deal will not really go wrong because one supplier has more in-depth technical knowledge than another. At the end of the day, every Indian company accesses the same talent pool with slight variations on how much salary they are paying their employees. Having said this, you should not confuse employees' technical knowledge of programming systems with methods, tools, and processes, which are at the core of the provider and are useful for reaping benefits through industrialized delivery (see p. 9).

The real difference, however, is how two corporate cultures match and how much each party is going to invest in building a successful relationship. Briefly examining one supplier more or less during an RFI process is not going to make much difference to the success of your endeavour.

On the other hand, limiting the number of participants has a number of advantages for you as well. Make sure you communicate your lean approach to the suppliers and inform them whom you are aiming to reach. Every pre-selected provider then stands a much greater chance of successfully concluding the deal and therefore will put in more effort to respond to your RFP, leading to a more detailed response, which results in more certainty for you and less clarification effort.

Step three (E): Establish RFP documents

Before you start creating the RFP documents, you will need to collect all the decision inputs: the business strategies, sourcing guidelines, IT guidelines and everything which you have used to arrive at the decision to offshore. You may have to review or update some of the information to make sure that the RFP documents will be based on up-to-date information.

The RFP documents are a critical part of the provider evaluation process and you need to be very honest in describing your setup and requirements. Some organizations feel uncomfortable revealing too much and maybe sensitive information at this point in time. However, you are about to start a – hopefully – long and mutually beneficial offshoring relationship; and how else is the service partner going to be able to design his delivery model other than based on complete and honest information?

A good RFP consists of a number of separate documents in individual sections:

- Company business and IT project description
- Project schedule
- Governance schedule
- Human resources schedule
- General contract conditions
- Pricing framework
- Transition, innovation, and exit plan

These documents should be as detailed as possible so that you and the offshore service provider can actually sign them at the end of the discussion with a short addendum based on the outcome of the negotiation process.

This is where the S-LEAN RFP™ process is a real improvement on the traditional laundry lists. Providers receive sufficient information to estimate their effort and costs correctly, respond directly without marketing boilerplates, and judge their chance of securing the deal. As a customer, you will receive more useful responses that are targeted to your needs and are comparable with responses from other suppliers.

Company business and IT project description

The first part of the RFP is a high-level description of the business your company is in, the market drivers and the business strategy. It also covers your sourcing guidelines, touches on the reasons why you are looking for an offshore service provider and outlines your internal process which has led to this RFP. By providing this internal insight, you create credibility with the suppliers; they will take your RFP more seriously, commit more resources to the reply, and you will benefit from better and more accurate information, which in turn not only speeds up your evaluation and negotiation process, but also puts it on a much more solid foundation.

Project schedule

This is the core part of the RFP as it details all your requirements. You should provide information about the scope of the project: the baseline, the approach to be taken and the desired outcomes. A portfolio analysis of other current or planned projects potentially affecting the RFP's baseline should be included so that the provider can factor uncertainty into the offering. It is better to talk about possible deviations now than pay for them later in the form of expensive requests for change.

Go one level below the project description; be very specific about expected outcomes of the project and the input that goes into achieving it. In maintenance deals, the project descriptions are in fact the service levels of your project, and the framework is referred to as service level agreements (SLAs).

Break down the project plan (for application development deals) or the organizational structure (for maintenance deals) into detailed roles and responsibilities. This will help the supplier to estimate correctly, substantially reduce the number of assumptions and exclusions, and avoid later finger-pointing which only results in hard feelings and additional costs. It should be clear right from the beginning who owns which part of the project or service delivery.

Do not forget to define how and when the achievement of the SLAs will be measured, who will collect the data, and how it will be verified to eliminate any manipulation. There are a number of things you need to consider when making your offshore endeavour measurable and this is covered in greater detail on p. 139. If you do not have the qualified staff to monitor measurement, a third party may be included to audit the measures. In any case and solely for risk mitigation purposes, you should build a clause into the agreement that at any time you may want to use external services to verify measurements and benchmark them against industry standards.

After measurement come incentives and fee reductions. You need to specify thresholds for service levels which will attract lower or higher fees. You should avoid talking about penalties; this creates a negative atmosphere right from the beginning and furthermore, in some countries, penalties in service contracts are not allowed by law[19] and are hence unenforceable. As a rule of thumb, fee reductions should be between ten and twenty per cent, maximum thirty per cent, of the remuneration associated with the measured service. Reductions of less than ten per cent fail to work as they are simply not significant enough to provide any incentive; reductions of more than thirty per cent are sometimes proposed by companies and internally seen as proof of aggressive due diligence. However, such reductions are too dramatic, scare off the provider during the RFP process, make him build in too much buffer because they eat too drastically into the margins, and, if applied, force the provider to react with extreme cost-cutting, rather than with measures to rectify the problem. As a result, most providers have around 10 per cent of their monthly revenues at risk. However, very few penalties are ever paid out. For one, there is the burden of measurement, root cause analysis, and negotiation to prove an SLA slippage. Second, many offshoring contracts include an earn-back provision, which allow the provider to recover some or all of the sums accrued in earlier fee reductions by delivering above par performance in other reporting periods.[20] Although this sounds like a good idea, striking the balance between reductions and earn-back provisions is difficult in practice. With too generous earn-back provisions, the fee reductions lose their grip. In general, incentives should only be provided for exceeding service levels that really add value to the business objectives of your project or organization.

Governance schedule

The governance structure of your project largely depends on the kind of offshoring endeavour you are going to start: tactical, strategic, or transformational offshoring (see p. 4). It defines the kind of relationship you are going to enter into and the governance schedule should make your assumptions and expectations of the provider's engagement management crystal clear.

There are five governance areas:

- *Responsibilities*. Who is responsible for which delivery task and how do handovers between tasks happen? Who identifies gaps in services and skills – and rectifies them? Leaving such questions unanswered or not drawing lines clearly enough will later cause friction in the service delivery and result in an underperforming offshoring contract.
- *Day-to-day interactions*. This area breaks down the statute of responsibilities into actionable communication streams, which ensure that everything gets done on a day-to-day basis. You will want to define specific 'go to' people from your own organization that the provider can address; and you can reasonably expect the same on the other side.
- *Adapt to change*. An offshore endeavour is not static, company strategies change and innovation occurs. Both parties need to understand this fundamental fact, communicate about it, align themselves and lastly, implement changes in processes and measures.
- *Audit*. Audit is not only about verification of facts and measures, but also about managing risks, learning from findings and implementing continuous improvement. Reporting schedules, schemes and distribution lists need to be defined together with people who are responsible for following up audit findings and implementing changes.
- *Commercials*. It is a false belief that commercials are fixed once the contract has been signed. In reality, the financial engineering behind the deal needs to be constantly revisited. Is value delivered? Is the provider fairly compensated? Does the provider fund the project according to prioritized business needs? Both parties will regularly need to revisit these items during the lifecycle of the contract to adjust to changes in market conditions, in the business environment and the availability of new industrialized delivery innovations.

Later on (see p. 136), I will give you recommendations for an offshore governance structure covering the first two bullet points above.

Human resources schedule

The human resource schedule covers two important points. First, it documents your decision on which of your internal staff should be retained in which positions and which will be laid off. You need to make sure that your internal communication is fully consistent with the information you provide in this part of the RFP. In normal outsourcing deals, the human resource schedule needs to include the fate of your own staff and whether the service provider should take on any of them. However, this is only very rarely the case in offshoring deals with Indian service providers.

Second, it lists your expectations of your involvement in staffing the India offshore team. Most Indian providers try to argue that staffing should be entirely their responsibility and that they take the risk of having to replace someone in case of poor performance. It is true that most client companies do not have the necessary insight into the Indian IT market to define hierarchy structures, necessary qualifications and experience levels. Some Indian providers take full advantage of this fact and try to sell their unutilized bench resources to upcoming projects, regardless of the fit. This risk is especially high in an economic downturn. In my opinion it is therefore very necessary for your representatives to be involved in the interviewing of key personnel, especially during the entry transition period and until you have established enough trust with your selected provider. At this point in the RFP process, you should outline your requirements and provide a score card which you are later going to use to evaluate individual candidates and the composition of the India team. Most likely you are not fully aware of how the Indian IT market functions and how offshore teams are typically staffed to ensure maximum performance while also catering for the needs of individuals. You may need to use consultants for expert support on this. You should also offer the Indian vendor the opportunity to refine this scorecard during the negotiation process, thereby incorporating the provider's know-how to ensure that it is a realistic one.

General contract conditions

You will need to check whether your company's standard contract conditions fit the service under consideration for offshoring. Data access issues, confidentiality and regulatory clauses should be removed and covered under the SoW section. However, the following topics should be covered in the general contract conditions:[21]

- Invoicing and payment terms
- Record keeping and right of audit
- Intellectual and data ownership
- Confidentiality, security and data back-up
- Regulatory compliance requirements
- Warranties, liabilities, insurance and indemnification

- Termination clauses
- Governing jurisdiction

Three points from the list are worth highlighting. First, you should specify the expected frequency, form and content of invoices very clearly. Some Indian providers have a strange habit of sending unchecked invoices directly from their time reporting systems; you may end up getting hundreds of invoices every month, separated by sub-type, resource or internal cost centre code. This is not only irrelevant for you, but involves an additional overhead in invoice processing. Second, it is important for you to agree on full transparency with your provider; that includes your right to audit the project, its measures and people at any point of time. Third, governing jurisdiction is not only about the country and place of jurisdiction, but also whether you want to sign the contract directly with the Indian vendor or with their subsidiary in your own country. Multi-national companies with Indian operations offer a significant advantage as they are mostly your direct legal contract partners; in turn they subcontract their Indian subsidiaries (see p. 128).

Pricing framework

Naturally you cannot tell the providers what price they should offer you. What you should do is lay out a framework for pricing which is appropriate to the type of work you are planning to offshore. The provider then knows about your risk profile and you are able to compare different offers from different providers.

The following three pricing frameworks are common for IT offshoring deals:

- *Charge-out rate pricing*. The Indian provider charges you a fixed cost per resource, the charge-out rate (COR), which is basically the employee's cost to the Indian company plus a mark-up. It is important to document clearly which provider costs are included in the charge-out rates and which are to be charged extra, for example, taking on new resources during a scheduled ramp-up, replacement of resources due to attrition, training costs and time and employee sick leave. As a customer, you face a relatively high risk as service levels or project outcomes are not guaranteed.
- *Fee-for-service pricing*. The pricing is variable and based on the work delivered, which is measured in terms of amount, quality, or adherence to agreed measures. While you only pay if the service is delivered successfully, costs are not entirely predictable in your

business forecast. The Indian offshore provider needs to factor in a risk margin as his costs are not covered unless the agreed measures are satisfactorily met.

- *Fixed price.* Based on a specific project result or service level, a price is set to compensate the provider for the delivery. The number of resources required to meet the defined outcome is the responsibility and risk of the provider and hence a risk margin is added to the estimated person days. This framework encompasses a very low risk for you as a client. However, you are also not able to participate in cost reductions should the project scope become smaller or the need for services decrease. As you will need to pay in addition for any enhancements to the originally agreed scope, you should make sure you agree on a pricing framework for requested changes as well.

Other pricing frameworks include client compensation based on business outcome achievements. However, this type of incentive framework is not commonly used at present when offshoring work to India; it is also not understood by many Indian service providers. Notwithstanding, it can be applied if you are outsourcing an entire process to a multinational provider, who in turn will offshore work to its India subsidiaries.

Transition, innovation, and exit plan

For some offshore endeavours, the transition stage is of tremendous importance and entirely different from the active stage; I therefore recommend dedicating a separate section in the RFP documents to it. For other projects, and these are mainly to be found in the application development sector, the transition phase is part of the project setup and can be included in the earlier section on the project SoW. During the transition, different service levels and methods of measuring them, roles and responsibilities, knowledge transfer processes, and meeting structures apply. The transition time-frame should be clearly defined so that both you and the provider have a clear understanding of when normal expectations will begin to apply.

A big mistake in most long-running contracts is the assumption of a steady state. Be it an offshore resource centre (ORC) for application development or a maintenance deal, there is always room for learning and innovation, followed by improvement. Factor costs of Indian IT engineers may still go up in the long term, but industrialization should more than counterbalance this trend and add to delivery efficiency. Without setting such expectations, the offshore provider will either pocket all the innovation savings in fixed-price deals, or, if it is a headcount deal, simply not be interested in rolling out new methods, applying experience from other projects and incentivizing employees to come up with improvements. Some leading corporations clearly expect their offshore providers to reduce their prices (or efforts for the same delivery) year by year and they incorporate these same expectations in the contract.

Your deal will either end at the time specified under the contract and come up for prolongation and renegotiation, or either party may have invoked the exit clause. You need to plan for four possible different processes:

- *Renegotiation.* Of course there is nothing to preclude you from renewing the contract under the same conditions or accepting the provider's nominal increase. However, in real-life scenarios the business context changes and the contract will need to be amended, if not renegotiated. You should plan enough time and outline a fixed timetable for renegotiation, failing which you will need to have sufficient time to start a new RFP process, terminate the contract, and disentangle the project from the old vendor.
- *Partial disentanglement.* Plan for the possibility that some of the services will be shifted from one provider to the next. Planning for this transfer mode helps to keep the relationship with the old provider intact.
- *Termination.* If you decide to terminate your contractual relationship with the service provider, you need to either bring services back to your own organization or completely take them out of the old provider's processes and shift them to another provider. Document what support the provider needs to provide in order to ensure a smooth transition.
- *Natural end.* Some projects come to a natural end, for example when a system has been decommissioned and the maintenance contract is over, or an application has been developed successfully. Even then, a planned exit transition should take place and this involves documentation, handover of any documents, and ramp-down of resources.

It is inevitable that your contract will end at some point and it is almost certain that some parts of it will be assigned to a different provider. However, the exit plan, disengagement, and disentanglement of services are very often neglected in contracts. Unless you want to suffer a painful experience a few years down the line, it is imperative that you think about it right now and build exit provisions into the RFP package:

- *Duty to continue*. Once the intent to disengage has been expressed, the uncoupling of the client–provider relationship has to be conducted in such a way that your business is not affected. The provider is required to continue operations as if the contract termination has not occurred. However, if you wish, you have the right to remove services from the provider and hand them over to another party or perform them yourself.
- *Exit plan*. If you cannot set out or foresee exit procedures and responsibilities at this point in time, you need to include provision for the termination date, or simply demand that the provider, given notice, should come up with the necessary plan. You also have to reserve your right to audit the provider's compliance with the exit agreement and plan an appropriate enforcement strategy, if it should become necessary.
- *Exit and handover support*. When you want to transfer the contract to another provider, you should include provision for the old provider to give access and hand over to, and review all processes, documentation, and deliverables with, the successor. A major issue, if it is not arranged now, is always ensuring access for the new provider's employees to the old provider's building for a proper handover. For onsite assignments, the provider needs to be required to vacate your premises and remove all equipment.
- *Staff, assets, and subcontract transfer*. You may want to hire some of the provider's staff for your own organization and you should make careful provision for all aspects of the offer of employment process (right to interview employees, right of employees to reject, payments to provider, period in which such transfers are allowed). You may also be interested in taking over other assets which you have either transferred to the provider at the start of the assignment or which the provider has generated in the course of the contract. Newly generated assets can be leaner processes, improved systems and other innovative approaches. You therefore need to talk about access rights to such assets and their pricing. In some cases, even subcontracts or software licences need to be transferred to the new provider. Of course, there will also be services which are not going to be taken over and it is important to assign the responsibility for cancellation to the provider.
- *Handover delivery*. The provider needs to surrender all access rights to your systems, return assets to you and hand over back-ups, documents and all other confidential material. Anything else needs to be destroyed.

- *Post-exit assistance*. Once the disengagement period is over, you should reserve the right to request your old provider to give follow-up assistance on demand, for example, answering questions or providing training. You need to specify this post-exit period and preferably agree rates for such services.

If you are reading this book while you are in the middle of an offshore engagement and you are unfortunate enough not to have included such provisions in your contract, I can only advise you to take your chance and try to secure such an agreement in addition to the existing contract. A good time is when you switch offshore governance responsibilities in your company, but definitely well before you consider terminating the contract. Of course, it will be entirely up to the provider to agree to such a deal, but if he does not, you have a real relationship issue and you may be well advised to start looking for back-ups and alternatives right away.

Step four (A): Analyse and evaluate

This step of the S-LEAN RFP™ process is focused on sending out the RFP documents to the Indian service providers, developing a scorecard to evaluate the providers' capabilities, and evaluating the RFP responses.

Sending out the RFP

At this point, please turn to step two of the S-LEAN RFP™ process and the list of pre-qualified suppliers. Send your RFP documents strictly to this list only. By now the word will have gone out that you are planning to offshore and many account managers of other reputable service providers will try to get a foot in the door. If this S-LEAN RFP™ process is going to work, you need to stick with your earlier decision and limit the number of providers who are going to participate in the process. Don't be afraid of losing out on the best Indian provider; your project is not going to fail because you have not considered a player who has marginally better technical skills, resources, or references. Building the relationship and agreeing on all its parts and processes is far more important. Having said that, of course you should not neglect to look at the competencies; however root causes for possible failure are rarely found in a lack of competencies, but much more often in problems with the relationship.

Providers should now respond to your RFP by accepting, modifying or rejecting all individual statements in the RFP. In addition they are expected to provide you with a financial offering.

Create the evaluation scorecard

While the providers are busy preparing their answers to your RFP, you need to work out how you are going to evaluate them. It is important that you agree who in your team is going to evaluate which part, what the criteria are, and what their relative importance is. You may want to restrict the scoring of certain criteria to your experts, while these experts in turn will not be allowed to score other criteria.

What to focus on during the evaluation? You should be less concerned about rating the physical and human assets of the provider, but should evaluate how they can build up to capabilities which in turn create client-facing competencies, ultimately generating value for your company. Figure 5.2 illustrates this journey.

Which client-facing competencies you eventually need depends on your current situation and strategic plan with the offshore provider. Three important competencies can be identified.[22] The *delivery competency* is the offshore provider's ability and willingness to deliver your project successfully on a day-to-day operational basis. This competency is important if you want to maintain or slightly amend a legacy application system, operate a data centre or maintain the current service levels in your call centre. However, when you are seeking more than minimal improvements in the service levels and cost structures, you should focus on the vendor's *transformation competency*. This is the ability to deliver radically improved services, both in terms of quality and cost, through process improvement, project management, technology exploitation and consulting capabilities.

Finally, when you seek a long-term commitment from the offshore provider, the *relationship competencies* need to be closely evaluated. They rely on the supplier's governance and programme management, but also on how experienced the provider is in developing business with customers. Everyone in India wants to grow big fast. However, proper customer planning and contracting capabilities are rarely to be found as they entail building a trusting partnership and bridging the conflict between two different performance and success indicators.

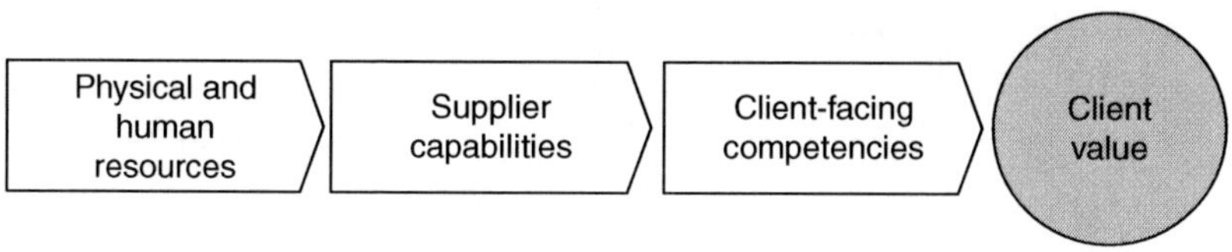

Figure 5.2 The path from supplier resources to client value

These three competencies are leveraged through twelve offshore capabilities (see Figure 5.3):

- *Leadership* is the provider's resourcefulness, competence, and aptitude for making the endeavour successful throughout its lifespan.
- *Programme management* is the capability to coordinate, oversee and deliver a portfolio of inter-related projects.
- *Governance* is the ability to define key performance measures, both with respect to commercials and delivery, subsequently track them consistently, analyse the figures, and initiate the implementation of continuous improvements together with you.
- *Customer development* relates to the provider's qualification and interest in helping you in your decision about project structures, technology, service levels, and – last but not least – how much money you need to invest up front to achieve optimal results.
- *Resourcing* is the provider's capability to attract the right people to join your project, at the right salary and seniority mix. Through their capabilities, these employees will ultimately deliver value for you.

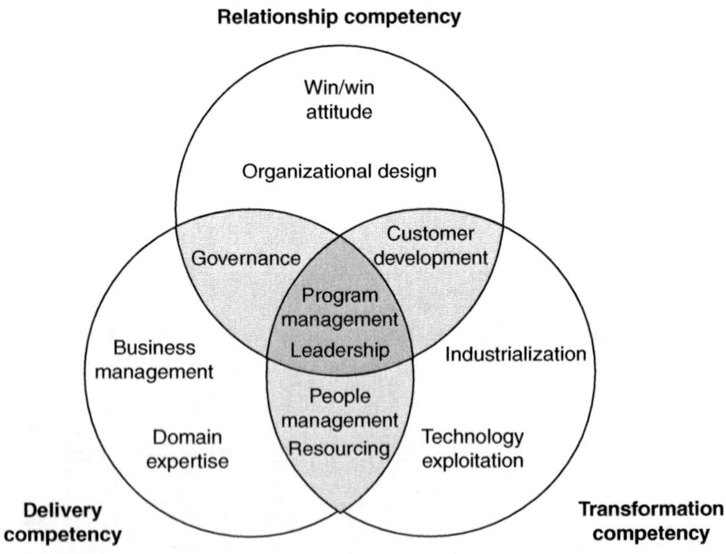

Figure 5.3 Twelve offshore provider capabilities
Sources: Adapted from Cullen *et al.* (2009), p. 283, and Willcocks *et al.* (2009), p. 6.

This capability is founded on the provider's standing and reputation in the Indian market.

- *People management* goes beyond resourcing. It is the art of inspiring, motivating and retaining the right employees, who are already doing the job for you and whom you need to keep on board to avoid service disruption.
- *Win/win attitude* is about the provider's competence to design and negotiate contracts which create an advantageous win/win atmosphere in which both parties can thrive and reach their commercial targets.
- *Organizational design* as a capability challenges the provider to implement best practice and sometimes also highly customized organizational structures to successfully run your specific projects.
- *Industrialization* has two aspects. On one side, it is the provider's capability to design and/or improve the delivery or service process so that it meets business targets. On the other side, and this is where the provider's experience really comes in, it is about not having to re-invent the wheel for each and every client (see p. 9).
- *Technology exploitation* is the provider's potential to quickly adapt to new or hitherto unused technologies, recruit or train such resources and effectively deliver results for your projects.
- *Business management* is the provider's capacity to deliver according to the contract, the service level agreements and the business plan – on time and of the expected quality. A part of this capability is to reduce delivery risk by having a compelling business continuity plan in place, in case the provider's office should be out of production for one of the reasons highlighted in Chapter 4.
- *Domain expertise,* at the end of the list but still very important as it forms the basis of each and every delivery, is about the provider's technical expertise, industry knowledge and experience with the business environment and/or technology setup of your company. It also includes the ability to normalize attrition rates of the project team thereby retaining professional expertise and securing investment in knowledge transfer and training (see p. 154).

Clearly, these capabilities and competencies are also linked to the level of offshoring (see page 4) that you plan to engage in. Not every business context requires the provider to excel in all twelve capabilities and three competencies. If you want to go for tactical offshoring, the delivery competency will be most important to you. For transformational and strategic offshoring, a mix of transformation and relationship competencies are required. You really do not need outstanding relationship competency from your Indian partner for the offshoring of application maintenance services based on an incident tracking system! This is where the weighing up of criteria comes into the picture. I recommend that you group the twelve capabilities into two hierarchy levels: capabilities and competencies. Some capabilities in Figure 5.3 are in the grey shaded overlapping areas and can be aligned with more than one competency; it is really up to you to best match them to one or more competencies according to your project needs and priorities. At each hierarchy level, the capability criteria are weighed against each other. I further recommend keeping the price comparison separate from the evaluation scorecard, so as not to mix quality and quantity. Keeping the pricing apart will enable you to compare the various vendors from a quality perspective and subsequently match the pricing scheme to it.

You also need to come up with a scoring scheme, scoring ranges and especially the meanings of each score. It is important that all members of the evaluation team fully understand the meaning of the different scores. The scoring range should not be too narrow. I have seen many evaluations offering only five choices. It is human nature never to tick the best or worst scores, which leaves the evaluator with only three possible choices. Summing up such limited choices and calculating an overall score is then pretty meaningless; it simply lacks enough differentiation. Just try to change one score, for instance, from three to four, and watch what happens with the overall score and, more importantly, with the position in the ranking of the different providers. Instead, you should use at least a 10-point scale and count nine and ten as fully satisfactory. Only then will average calculations and rankings begin to make sense.[23]

Never forget to check the provider's health, either as part of the leadership category or as a separate assessment. Especially in a time of recession you need to avoid struggling providers and carefully look into the provider's strategies for fighting and overcoming adverse economic conditions. Figure 5.4 suggests some questions to ask on four dimensions of 'recession readiness'. Try to get as much information as possible from publicly available resources; don't trust your account manager too much. First, the information will surely be biased and second, the account manager will most likely not have enough background information to give you truthful and complete answers.

To summarize, evaluating Indian suppliers according to these capabilities and focusing on the competencies that you actually need for your offshore project helps you to conduct a fair, target-oriented, and lean vendor evaluation without the ubiquitous, little useful, and – on the supplier side – much hated 'laundry lists'.

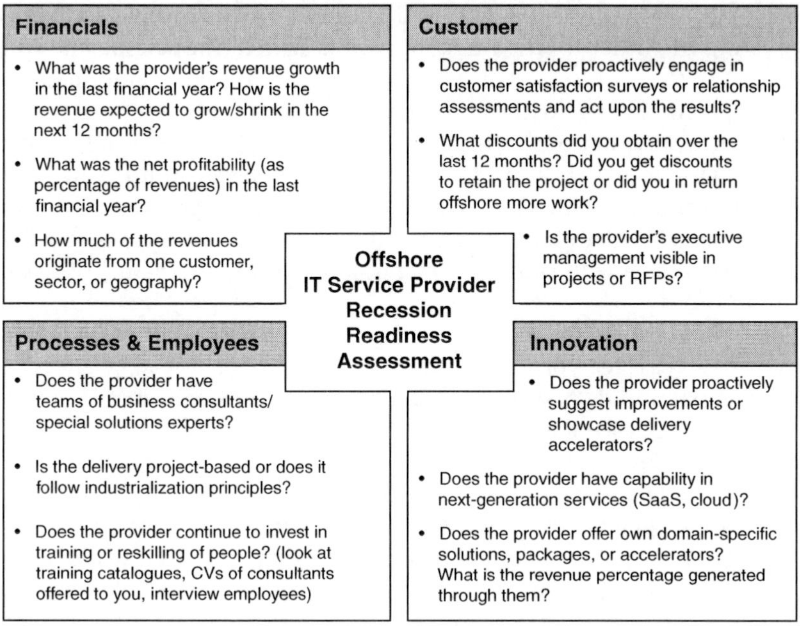

Figure 5.4 Offshore IT provider recession readiness check
Note: The checklist has been kept simple and it avoids questions which are not likely to be answered, such as around attrition rates or percentage of near-bankrupt customers. A scoring mechanism has deliberately not been included as the scales and thresholds would be completely arbitrary.

Evaluation of responses

While your evaluation team examines the providers' responses according to the evaluation scorecard you have just created, they need to create a list of questions on the responses which require further clarification. This list will be your starting point in driving the oral presentations from your side. Without it, the provider is likely to take over and be in the driving seat – and you will not get sufficient information out of this exercise. The evaluations of different team members should not be shared till after the last presentation; every interaction with a provider will produce a new perspective, new learning, and probably a slight updating of the score. The oral presentation is your first chance to really assess the competency and cultural fit of the various providers. Do not let the provider's salespeople take over this presentation, but insist on the account or relationship manager heading the presentation, and on subject matter experts, who will later be part of the delivery team, covering the other topics. After the deal is signed, the salespeople will be out of the picture and it is important that you are comfortable in dealing with the real delivery personnel. It is good practice to conduct these oral presentations in India itself. At this point, you should never miss a visit to the location of actual service delivery unless you have a long working relationship with a specific Indian provider and you exactly know what you can expect. If you cannot arrange for the site visit to coincide with the oral presentation, you need to plan a separate trip to India.

For guidance on the market situation and dynamics of the Indian IT industry, please read pp. 17–34 carefully. For help on how to be effective in meetings and discussions, see Chapter 7. In India, you should watch out for the following evaluation points:

- *Office culture*. Indian offices in the IT industry are of near-to international quality; this 'near-to' bit is where the real difference lies and you should have a careful look at it. In the Western world, a lot of effort has been put into designing offices and workplaces so that employees not only feel well and motivated, but are also enabled to perform more efficiently. In India, it is usually all about saving costs and providing the minimum acceptable equipment. Check out the quality of office chairs, the size of screens, the size of workspace cubicles, the number of meeting rooms, cafeteria areas and so on.
- *Employee retention*. The quality of office space has a direct impact on the willingness of employees to 'stay back' on a job; Indian software engineers come from varied backgrounds and are usually excited to be working in a top-notch environment. However, a lot more needs to be done to retain employees. The quality of food and beverages provided, relaxation areas, sports facilities and regular events are some other indicators.
- *Security*. Most reputable Indian service providers have invested quite a lot in the security of their IT infrastructure and these days this topic no longer requires detailed scrutiny. Where Indian providers differ a lot is in building and access security and background checks for hiring new employees.

Scrutinize everything you see and hear with a pinch of doubt; otherwise your site visit will do more harm than good to your evaluation process. It is a good idea to engage India experts to accompany you on these visits and help to independently open your eyes.

After the presentations and visits, every evaluation team member has to incorporate the new learning into the evaluation scorecard, maybe change some ratings, and share it with the team. According to the previously agreed mechanism, the final score is created and can now be compared with the offered pricing scheme.

Step five (N): Negotiate contract

Before you start negotiating with Indians for the first time, you have to understand the meeting, discussion, and negotiation culture of the subcontinent and preferably engage expert support. Please refer to Chapter 7 of this book for more details. If you fail to do this, you will be overwhelmed by new and hitherto unknown tactics and you will sooner or later lose control over the negotiation process and fall prey to the Indian provider's perspective and motivations.

The offshore provider's view of your RFP can be completely different from yours. Do not falsely assume that the Indian provider is willing to deliver on all the twelve capabilities and 'go the extra mile' for you.[24] This depends largely on the provider's perception of how desirable you as a customer are to him, driven by the following factors:

- Your prestige as a customer, both for the provider's reference list and to attract and retain employees
- The duration and size of the contract
- The potential for good profit margins versus the perceived risks
- The potential for a contract extension, for getting more business from you, or from other clients because of the relationship with you
- The opportunity to build up competency in new technologies or market domains – again as a motivator for the provider's employees and as a chance to enter new markets.

Having said that, the negotiation should be around balancing interests on both sides:

- Minimizing risk-taking for both sides
- Making costs predictable for the client
- Ensuring a reasonable profit and a continuous revenue stream for the provider

There is a dichotomy around risk and costs; a high perceived risk by the Indian providers needs to be built into the margins and will finally result in higher costs for you. Sometimes, of course, providers will offer or agree to rock bottom prices that obviously cannot provide much profit. I can only warn you against entering this kind of deal; it will inevitably result in the provider trying to cut costs and corners during the relationship. Not surprisingly, you will not get the best resources and the quality and efficiency of your work will suffer. Why do providers offer these deals? Mostly, they are trying to buy themselves into a new market or a new technology for which they need you as a credible reference. However, a rock bottom price does not always have only negative implications for you. Being the guinea pig can temporarily also give you extra management attention and greater service levels. However, even these advantages will fade over time and the provider will need to adjust the rates – or start cutting corners.

During the past five years, Indian service providers' costs have been spiralling through wage inflation, property prices, employee retention programmes and fluctuations of the rupee. Through industrialization, re-use of programming artefacts, methods, and the employment of non-IT graduates, they have managed to insulate you as a client from these cost pressures. Now that the recession of 2009 is beginning to affect the number of projects coming to India and also, as a result, the billable utilization rate of the employee base, Indian providers are trying to introduce indirect price increases. You should watch out for the following common tactics:[25]

- *Definition of work time.* Indian IT providers used to charge for a set number of days and hours per week, mostly five days and eight to nine hours per day, regardless of how many hours their staff actually worked. Recently, providers have been making their employees work six days a week and increasing the number of mandatory daily office hours. The provider's cost base remains the same, Indian salaried employees not usually being paid overtime. However, through this practice, the cost of a time and material project to you as a customer can easily go up by 20 per cent. Another 'trick' which I have seen used by an Indian pure player is to charge annual rates per head, thereby completely transferring the risk of sick leave, vacation, and attrition to the customer. You can protect yourself against such practices by agreeing on outcome-based contracts or fixed price deals, as opposed to paying for the number of hours worked in time and material contracts.
- *Travel and onsite staff.* During the knowledge transition phase, Indian offshore consultants are temporarily deployed onsite and it was customary in the past for customers to pick up the travel expenses and

daily allowances for these employees. Indian pure players in particular now try to cover some of their cost increases by building these expenses into hourly rates, which appear to be questioned by clients far less than the offshore rates. This also tempts the providers to leave more people onsite for longer periods than actually required. In the past, travel time from India to the USA or Europe was not usually charged and consultants were asked to travel over the weekend. Recently, I have seen Indian providers invoicing for travel time as well.
- *Inflation clauses*. Indian IT providers try to project stable rates for at least three to five years; however, they tend to build more and more clauses about inflation and cost-of-living adjustments (COLAs) into the contract, with calculation methods that are not always transparent. In the past few years, these adjustments should have been in the range of two to five per cent annually and from 2009 onwards they can be expected to be close to zero. My advice is to shun this type of clause; it should always be the provider's risk, and one of the reasons for outsourcing is to actually get cost predictability.

For the negotiation to be successful in the long term, you need to watch out that the offshore provider doesn't promise you the moon and the stars just to secure the deal. Even if everything is documented and signed by the provider's salesperson, the delivery people obviously won't be able to present you with the moon and the stars. So one: you need to make sure that you do not become unreasonable in your requirements; and two: you need to make sure that the right people are at the table. From the service provider side, these are the relationship manager(s) and responsible heads of the delivery teams. Not only should you watch the mood, the facial expressions and the reactions of the delivery team carefully, but you should also involve them in the discussion, asking for their opinions. Again, you will need to be familiar with conducting meetings with Indians and getting feedback from people who are lower down the hierarchy in front of their superiors. Also make sure that someone high enough in the (Indian) hierarchy to actually make decisions on the spot is participating. Otherwise, they will frequently need to go back to their bosses for decisions and the process will not be completed.

On your side, a number of people should participate to ensure the whole company is buying into all decisions being made. This includes an executive from the business area, a representative from the sourcing office, your relationship manager who will be the 'go to' person for the service provider, and someone very familiar with the business case. The negotiations should be led by an intercultural negotiation expert who is very familiar with India's offshore IT industry, supported in decision making by senior representatives from your organization.

Before you get to the negotiating table, make a list of issues and document your minimum acceptable position for each item. Also think about 'nice-to-haves' which you can trade with the provider. Every issue should have a clearly defined responsibility and decision-making authority attached to it so that your negotiation team presents a united front to the offshore provider.

When negotiating with Indians, forget about aligning the issues with a formal agenda. As we shall see in Chapter 7, Indians are by nature polychronic negotiators, who will first want to get an overview of all the issues on the table before they commit to decisions or concessions. This can initially be very confusing for agenda- and priority-oriented monochronic Westerners, which is precisely the reason why you should have an intercultural negotiator in the driving seat.

Once you have reached an agreement and selected a provider, the next step is to design a good contract that both sides can live with. It should balance security against scope for proactive actions to be taken on the spot. Chapter 5 covers offshore outsourcing contracts and the Indian perspective in more detail.

The last step towards living happily with the contract is measuring success to ensure that you and the provider are jointly heading in the right direction. For sourcing management please refer to the methods described in Chapter 6.

Designing the offshore outsourcing contract[26]

Some customers neglect prudent governing documents and contracts, shying away from the work involved and claiming to want a partnership and a good relationship with their offshore IT provider. Even if trust has been earned over the years, this is a high-risk approach! My sincere advice is to invest time in designing a good set of documents which help govern the relationship.

Cultural impact

When designing the offshore outsourcing contract and especially when entering into a contract with a firm incorporated in India, remember that India is a very different country. Its legal system may resemble the British one due to its colonial history, but that is many years ago and the historic legacy should not be overstated. India's laws and legal process are quite different.[27] You also need to understand the reality and difficulty of realizing contractual damages and repatriating them back home. The contract itself will not be the issue, assuming you have access to legal departments framing the text, but you need to understand the different cultural context in which the contract is agreed on.

India is a relationship-oriented society (see Chapter 7) where contracts are seen as a starting point for a business relationship, as a memorandum of understanding – and this understanding can change later depending on how things develop. It is interesting to know that Indian companies sometimes tell their lawyers to build ambiguity into contracts so that litigation proceedings can be started more easily.

Contract structure

The main idea of the S-LEAN RFP™ process is to create RFP documents which can go almost directly into the contract.

A typical outsourcing or offshoring contract is made up of three different views. The *legal view* consists of the contract documents, which are formally agreed upon prior to commencement of the contract. The legal conditions of the contract come at the top; they are written for interpretation by the legal community in case of disputes. The *commercial view* is part of the legal view and contains the project and pricing schedule. The pricing schedule is the provider's answer to the pricing framework which you included in the RFP. The *operational view* contains the governance schedule, human resources schedule, and the entry transition, innovation and exit plans as a kind of instruction handbook for the client and the provider to successfully operate the relationship.

The *preamble* or *introduction* is probably the most under-valued part of the contract; you should not scan and skim it, but craft or read it carefully. It can contain important elements which shift liabilities, declare the client an expert, or are central to the interpretation of the remainder of the contract.[28]

The contract itself needs to be well structured, indexed, and summarized in order to allow quick access to relevant parts. It is imperative that all parts of the contract are written in commercial English so that managers and executives on both sides can easily understand and interpret their meaning. The sole exceptions are the legal conditions, which should be written in legal English as they are to be interpreted by lawyers, arbitrators, and judges.

Indian judicial system

In accordance with the Indian Constitution, the judiciary on the subcontinent is independent. Legislative power is conferred on the parliament and state legislatures. Most of their enactments delegate the power to make rules and regulations to the executive, which has to lay them periodically before the union or state legislature.[29]

Important secondary sources of law are the judgments of the Supreme Court, the twenty-one High Courts and some specialized tribunals. Through these judgments they not only decide disputes, but in the process interpret and determine the law according to binding precedents.

Unwritten local customs and traditions are used to enact certain laws. For instance, family law is based either on Hindu or Muslim tradition. These differences have implications for the interpretation of law.

Indian law is based on the English *common law* system and is thus similar to the legal systems of Australia, the UK and USA.[30] It is governed by statutes, rules and case law.

When you enter an offshoring contract directly with an Indian company (and not with the front-office organization of an Indian pure player or a multi-national provider), then this contract transcends national boundaries. As a result, the legal regime of either your country or India becomes inadequate; two legal systems impinge on the contract and the rules of private international law come into play.

Indian contract law

Indian contract law is governed by the provisions of the *Code of Civil Procedure (CPC)*, under which parties are free to design the terms of their contract. They can also decide the jurisdiction and the law which is supposed to govern the contract; private international law rules are customarily followed. In the absence of any explicit mention, the law of the country with which the contract is most closely connected will be applied. This close connection is determined by a number of factors, such as the place of contracting, negotiating and execution, the currency of payment or the place of incorporation of the contracting companies. And if a dispute between two parties has already been resolved in a foreign court, then this ruling is binding in India as well.[31]

While the Indian Contract Act covers the issue of damages[32], the concept of extra-contractual damages (including punitive and exemplary damages) is not well established in Indian jurisprudence. The principle of restitution applies and the party suffering the loss is compensated so as to put it in the same position as if the contract had been completed; the compensation is directly related to the loss actually suffered and no compensation is awarded for any remote or indirect losses. Also, predetermined penalties (so-called liquidated damages) may not be awarded by courts if they are higher than the actual losses suffered. The customer as the innocent party is also required by the principle of mitigation of loss and damages to do everything possible to mitigate its losses in the face of the breach of contract.[33]

While laws are in place, the Indian legal system as such remains a concern. Delays are common, and it can take more than ten years for a case to be resolved. More than four million cases are pending in India's Supreme Court and the High Courts; in district and other subordinate courts across the country an astounding 26.7 million cases remain open, and the trend is rising.[34]

At first sight, these legal hurdles seem rather frightening. However, there is a rather elegant and easy way to avoid any direct interaction with the Indian legal system. First, if you are planning to contract with a multinational provider, your contract is going to be with the front office of this provider in your home country, and the contract will therefore be governed by, say, American, British, French, or German law. Your own legal department can agree on the offshoring contract with the MNC provider just as it would in a normal outsourcing contract within your country. Second, if you are planning to contract with a sizeable firm of Indian origin which also has multinational subsidiaries, you can insist on signing the contract with their international subsidiary in your home country. There is only one, albeit crucial, difference between this and the MNC scenario described above. The FIO may not have substantial assets in your home country, so any contract litigation and attempts to realize contractual damages may turn out to be fruitless.

6
Successfully Running the Offshore Project

After the contract is signed, successfully running the offshore project entails managing the relationship between your company and the Indian offshore provider continuously, proactively, and effectively. In order to do so, you need to first dispense with the cliché about the standard client–provider dichotomy, which fails to capture the complexity of the global relationship, and understand the various stakeholder groups involved, their relationship types, and how they develop after the contract has been signed. Second, you need to establish a measurement framework to continuously manage the relationship with the provider. These measures build on the project statement of work which has been developed as part of the RFP.

Managing stakeholder relationships

The dyadic client–provider relationship sheds only limited understanding on an outsourcing relationship;[1] and in my experience, the situation with a global offshore relationship is even more complex. Here I propose a model of stakeholder segments which has grown out of my specific analysis of many IT offshoring arrangements.

By stakeholder segment, I mean a group of people tending to have the same expectations, perceptions and goals. While the personality, charisma or abrasiveness of individuals can of course supersede these segmented stereotypes, they are still useful in identifying trends and tendencies.

In general, one can identify stakeholders at the client company, at the offshore service provider in India and at the offshore service provider onsite in a Western country. Distinguishing between the last two groups is important, as delivering offshore service is not only about working out of India. Multinational companies will engage their front-office relationship managers and consultants, Indian pure players are in the process of expanding their onsite presence and thereby directly competing with multinational companies or sending some of their staff as an onsite delegation. Moreover, the interests of Indian pure players and multi-national providers, as stakeholder segments, will differ slightly; Table 6.1 provides an overview of these segments.

Client company

- *Senior business managers* are responsible for achieving business results and getting value from IT expenditure. However, in many cases they have neither the knowledge nor the means to assess whether and how much value is added through information systems. This often causes them to focus mainly on IT costs.
- *Senior IT managers* have to strike a balance between providing excellence to the business users and the cost containment strategy of the IT department. In offshoring deals, their jobs are rarely lost but rather redefined, and they become valuable contributors not only to the evaluation and negotiation process, but especially to the ongoing relationship management with the Indian provider.
- *IT staff* at the client company are responsible for delivering the IT service. They tend to be enthusiastic about technology and try to please the business users while sometimes neglecting to watch out for cost containment. They fear that their jobs are potentially

Table 6.1 Stakeholder segments

	Indian pure player	*Multinational provider*
Client company	**Offshore provider (in India)**	**Front-office unit**
• Senior business managers • Senior IT managers • IT staff • IT users	• Business unit managers • Relationship managers • Sales managers • Engagement manager • Offshore team members	• Business unit managers • Relationship managers • Sales managers • Engagement manager • Front-office team members
	Offshore provider (onsite)	**Offshore subsidiary (in India)**
	• Sales managers • Project coordinators • Indian onsite members	• Project manager • Offshore team members

affected by offshoring deals and, when unionized, they can become quite vocal against 'cheap labour' from India.

- *IT users* need to execute their business responsibilities with the help of information systems; hence they focus on IT excellence and best-in-class business functionality. In many cases, they are enthusiastic about offshoring as they hope to get better service and more functionality at less cost. However, this initial enthusiasm often turns into a wall of disapproval if the offshore project execution processes are not managed correctly and they have to talk to Indian software developers directly.

Indian pure player

- *Business unit managers* and *relationship managers* are responsible for delivery execution, client satisfaction and profitability for a number of IT deals, for example, in a specific industry or technology sector. They are supposed to balance these three objectives, but as their key performance indicators (KPIs) are mostly about profitability they tend to attach the most importance to it.
- *Sales managers* can be located onsite in the home country of the customer base or offshore in India. Their KPIs are to close as many deals as possible at the best projected profitability. Hence they tend to overpromise and not think about the possible conflicts that their delivery colleagues will encounter.
- *Engagement managers*, together with the *offshore team members*, deliver the agreed scope of services. The engagement managers again face the conflicting priorities of satisfying their clients and keeping the project costs under control; they want to personally grow along with the engagement and hence additions to the project team size are more important to them than cutting costs, at least in an Indian career context. The junior team members are technical enthusiasts, who will both try to please their customers with good functionality and try to enlarge their technical domain expertise. The more senior team members look for an opportunity to grow into sub-project leaders and manage as many people as possible.
- *Project coordinators* coordinate the specification work and delivery acceptance with the client; they are typically based onsite in the client company's premises.
- *Indian onsite members* are sent to the client company's premises to support the project by interacting directly with client IT staff and business users. Their intrinsic motivation is mainly to gain international

experience, which they can later highlight on their CVs, and to earn some additional salary, mostly through generous daily allowances.

Multinational provider

A multinational provider's stakeholders are mostly the same as the Indian pure player's. However, the physical location of these roles is just the opposite. *Business unit managers, relationship, sales,* and *engagement managers* mostly belong to the front-office unit; only the *project manager* and the *offshore team members* work out of India. As a multinational player with traditional roots in the Western home countries, these providers need to engage their *front-office team members* as well; their job is to bridge the distance gap and ensure a smooth delivery from India. Naturally, just like the client's IT staff, they sometimes tend to fear for their jobs. However, in most cases, their job profile is upgraded from technical development to functional specification or coordination.

Relationship lifecycle

The client–provider relationship tends to be very dynamic; it is a myth that everything will be sweetness and light all the time. The only way to overcome the snags is to actively manage the relationship. Four prevalent relationship types occur along the lifecycle:[2]

- *Exploration.* When both parties have no shared offshoring history, they are initially unsure whether they have shared, complementary, or conflicting goals. The relationship manifests itself as a cautious one, sometimes showing a predisposition towards enthusiasm. Discussions are held to explore the possibilities of a partnership; however, there is no commitment yet and hence neither you nor the Indian IT provider is inclined to behave aggressively.
- *Collaboration.* A collaborative relationship occurs when both parties have shared goals. Even though the marketing talk will tell you a different story, this will by definition never be the case between you and your Indian IT provider. This kind of relationship can actually only occur if you are offshoring to your own captive centre (see p. 92) and if the captive centre is sufficiently well integrated into your company's global fabric.
- *Cooperation.* Offshoring relationships are typically based on the notion of an exchange – a fee for a service. It is probably clear that these are not shared goals leading to a collaboration, but both parties have

a vested interest in the other succeeding; in other words, they need something from each other in order to succeed in the relationship.
- *Conflict*. The relationship can turn adversarial when the goals of the two sides are in conflict. During the relationship lifecycle, there will be a conflict of interest on at least three occasions: (1) during negotiation of the contract, (2) when establishing precedents for contract interpretation in the early phases of the offshoring relationship, and (3) if the contract needs to be realigned or renegotiated midway through the initially agreed duration.

The key to reaching a cooperative relationship and avoiding conflict is to achieve the right balance of power between you and the provider. As soon as the provider gets more power, you will be dominated. And if you get too much power over the provider, there is a real danger that the provider will eventually lose money on your account, which will ultimately mean that your relationship is going to suffer.

Governing the offshore contract relationship

Although the day-to-day activities of managing the offshore project really only commence after the Indian IT service providers are chosen, the framework needs to be set up as early as possible, but certainly before contracts are signed with the providers.

So, what does a governance framework do? Offshore governance is really about assigning responsibilities and rights to manage the resources and all other services provided externally (or internally through captive offshoring). The objective is to follow your firm's sourcing principles (see Chapter 3), ensuring a seamless service and creating value by delivering results.

Offshore delivery coordination

Simply signing an offshore contract and assigning a manager is not governance. In fact, this is where chaos begins; the new managers realize that they have no clear rules to follow, no authority to make decisions, and no power to implement them.

Let me therefore introduce you to a generic offshore governance structure, which is depicted in Figure 6.1. It is driven by four principles:[3]

- *Symmetry*. Roles and responsibilities are set up in a symmetrical structure between customer and provider in terms of geographical location and hierarchy.

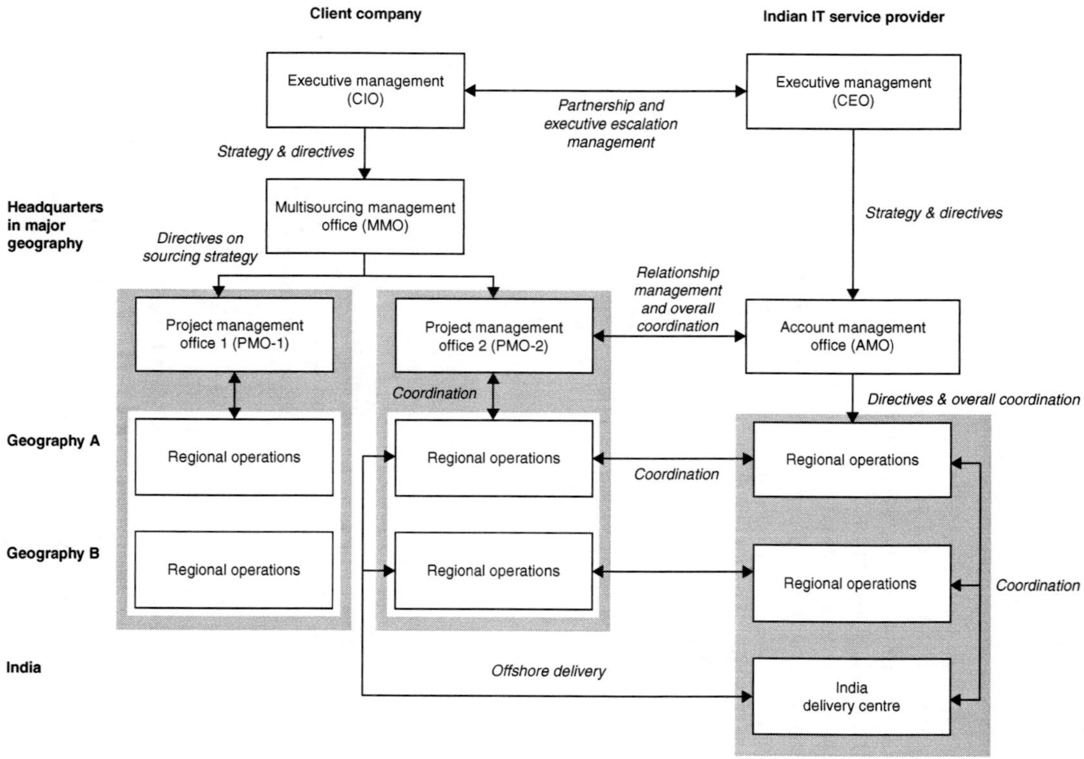

Figure 6.1 Offshore governance structure

- *Communication alignment.* Processes for communication are defined and the many possible channels are aligned.
- *Cascading hierarchy.* All levels from relationship strategy and coordination to the daily delivery are defined on both sides.
- *Proximity.* Communication is made easier through the Indian IT provider having local interfaces.

Your project management office (PMO) interacts with the provider's account management office (AMO); they are the highest level units on both sides. All strategic decision making, disagreements and conflicts are escalated to them; very occasionally they are escalated further to the executive levels, which would be the CIO in your company and the CEO (or one of the CEO's representatives) of the IT service provider. At the tactical level, your regional operations interact with the provider's regional customer interface as well as coordinating service delivery with the provider's India offshore operations.

In multisourcing environments your PMOs are governed by a multisourcing management office (MMO), from which they receive their instructions on sourcing strategy. The MMOs are a management layer in between the PMOs and your CIO. They evaluate and compare the relationship with different service providers and make decisions as to whether to increase the workload given to one specific service provider or move away to a different one.

Ideally, you should outline this diagram in the RFP package as part of the governance schedule (see p. 109). If a PMO unit has not been established in your company and you have an ongoing offshore contract, you should work together with the provider to set one up; it should be in the provider's own interest to have a strong unit at the customer's place as this will nurture the relationship and improve cooperation.

The next step is to create role profiles for sourcing management so that your company can put in the right people with the right mix of competencies. Then you should establish internal career paths so that you will be able to develop and retain your managerial staff. If you cannot find these skills within your own company, you have to consider recruiting them, even in turbulent economic times; these jobs are too important for the success of your offshoring endeavour for you to compromise on the competencies. A good place to fish for new employees is with multinational service providers with India operations; they have invested time and money in developing the necessary competencies with their (Western) managers.

Measurement framework

As much as governance is about authority to make decisions and be responsible for them, it also involves input to make the right decisions, and this input can only be generated through proper evaluation and measurement of the service delivery.

In many companies, offshoring measurements of this kind are either completely non-existent, not sufficiently precise or not relevant to what they are supposed to measure – the business outcomes of the offshore endeavour. The goal should be to create an integrated *Relationship Performance Dashboard* (RPD), which collects, tracks, aggregates, analyses, and communicates the results of engaging the Indian IT provider.

I have seen many companies and offshore projects that collect completely irrelevant metrics, sometimes mandated by the offshore provider's quality assurance team. Some examples are:

- It's all about pricing, keeping to effort estimates, and delivering on time. But the quality of what is delivered is not measured at all!
- The measures for service levels or software development productivity are too complicated, cannot be understood by management and are based on far too much confusing data – sometimes with the aim that everything will be levelled out and that the result does not look alarming. Frequently the only indicators measured are those which are easy to track, but irrelevant.
- The measurements are not dynamic, that is, they neither build in nor anticipate some improvement over time through learning, innovation and industrialization experience.
- The measurements are driven and made available by the IT service provider; hence they completely omit any metrics which are relevant to you as a customer.
- Last but not least, they ignore relationship factors, satisfaction and trust between you and the service provider.

The next thing which goes wrong are occasions when external companies are brought in to conduct one-off assessments. This can only be useful if your offshore project is completely derailed and has to be fixed immediately; even then the next step has to be the establishment of an RPD.[4] Filling the RPD with data has to be an ongoing process, not a snapshot. If you are evaluating an existing offshore relationship and do not have all these baseline metrics available, you need to first start collecting data. Begin measurement immediately, look at trends, compare with industry benchmarks and set new targets for improvement.

Let us now look in detail at how to design effective metrics for governing offshore IT relationships. You need to derive the necessary metrics from the business task. Unfortunately, there is no way of doing this deductively; you really need to look up lists, libraries, and publications[5] – or build them up from scratch. In their entirety they become a dashboard, which then needs to be verified or falsified; all this requires an engineering approach. Metrics should be:

- *Useful.* Your information need should match the content provided by the metric.
- *Exact.* Information provided should be reliable and correct.
- *Current.* Very little time should pass between collection and analysis of the data; the metric should be up-to-date.
- *Beneficial.* The costs of collecting the data and preparing the metric should not be higher than the benefits gained.
- *Simple.* You should not only be able to read the metric, but also understand its calculation and be able to act on it.

Of course, a list of one hundred or so different metrics does not help any manager to understand the situation; hence the metrics need to be grouped into categories and then displayed in the dashboard. Depending on the kind of business you are in, these categories will vary a bit. The following is a good starting point for your discussion:

- *Service levels (category 1).* Focuses on creating quality and business value by looking at how – and at what costs – relevant service levels are achieved.
- *Financials (category 2).* Considers the business owner's view of the offshore endeavour.
- *Alignment with provider (category 3).* Assesses the quality of your relationship with the provider.
- *Risk (category 4).* Monitors your firm's exposure to risk through offshoring.
- *Offshore team (category 5).* Appraises everything around the provider's offshore team assigned to your project.

The above are categories which you will need to collect by project, then aggregate by provider, and in a third step aggregate again on a multisourcing level. At the last level of aggregation, you can add the category of:

- *Offshore management (category 6).* Examines your firm's state of outsourcing resp. offshore utilization.

There are several RPD perspectives to these categories (see Figure 6.2). *Value* is what you really get for the money you spend. The *contextual* setting is a soft factor and is about how the work gets delivered, regardless of what is delivered and at what price. The *project and contract* perspective looks into achieving quality and service level achievements by strengthening the relationship with the provider. The *agenda* perspective depicts how the project or contract builds up the bigger picture which finally leads to category 6, the offshore management. The *people* perspective portrays the soft aspect of working with a culturally different team in a remote location. These five different perspectives finally build up to the *strategy* perspective, which really tells you how your organization as a whole is doing with its offshore management.

Let us now look at the categories in a little more detail.

Category 1: Service levels

Of course, the traditional indicators of service level and cost still find a place in the RPD. Review what has been put down in the contract as a result of the RFP evaluation and negotiation process (see Chapter 5) and select those measures which focus on creating business value. Bear in mind that you should monitor as few service level indicators as possible,

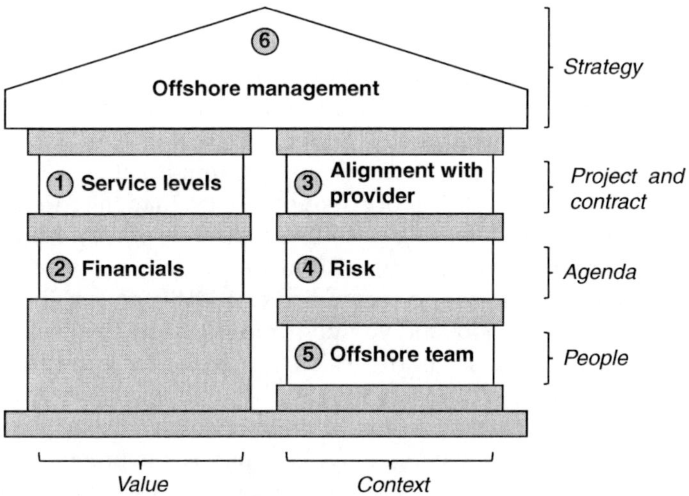

Figure 6.2 Categories and perspectives of the RPD
Source: The notion of perspectives for a RPD builds on the stakeholder perspectives of a contract scorecard in Cullen (2004), p. 20.

which really focus on relevant business outcomes. Especially when linking fee reductions to service level underachievement, having only a small set of service levels will help you to steer the service provider's performance in the right direction.

Looking only at how service levels achieve value is not sufficient; you need to consider the cost component as well. To evaluate the cost perspective, look at the baseline costs before offshoring, your business case projections and the trend over time. Are the costs coming down?

Category 2: Financials

Every section of the IT department is 'owned' by someone from the business; and this someone is putting in money in order to receive services. You need to evaluate how favourably the India offshore option performs as compared to other options the business owner may have to get the work done. You also need to judge the efficiency increase through offshore industrialization (see page 9) or the decrease in efficiency due to distributed delivery overhead as compared to the previous onsite and in-house option (see page 51). For captive centres, which operate as cost centres, another important measure is the percentage of (internally) billable costs as compared to the costs which stay with the captive unit.

Category 3: Alignment with provider

The quality of your company's relationship with the Indian provider is important to ensure that you stay on course with your offshore endeavour. Unlike the two categories above – service levels and financials – this is a qualitative measure, but nonetheless very important.

Turn back to your RFP process and the evaluation criteria you designed then for selecting your offshore partner (see p. 118). Remember that you are now in an ongoing relationship with the provider and it is only important to look into the outcomes of delivery; *how* it is being done is the provider's job, and you do not need to get involved. What remains of the criteria used in the selection process? From the after-deal perspective, we need to reword a little.

First, there is *customer satisfaction*. This is a key driver for the provider's performance. As we are talking about IT projects, the provider's direct customers are part of your organization. Hence you should not fall into the trap of including customer satisfaction as a measure in the first category (service levels). It is a more subjective measure which can be too easily manipulated by the IT provider, so it is more useful to include it in this category. I have seen some companies evaluating their satisfaction with every single developer of the provider's offshore team. There is definitely something fundamentally wrong with this approach; in an advanced industrialized offshore delivery model, IT colleagues in your company should not even be in a position to judge this; they should not have direct access to every single Indian programmer in the first place! Instead, consider the following list of questions to calculate a satisfaction index:

- How satisfied are you with the IT provider in general?
- Are you happy working together with your counterparts in India?
- How content are you with communication to and from India?
- Does the quality of deliverables meet your expectations?
- Is working with India getting on your nerves (reverse scored)?
- Would you rather interact with a local or in-house provider (reverse scored)?

Second, you can use the various components of *trust and confidence*[6] to analyse your relationship with the provider. Hand out a questionnaire to your key people working with the Indian provider asking them their opinions on the following:

- Does the provider have the capability to deliver? (*capability*)
- Is the provider's approach and culture compatible with our company? (*congruency*)
- Does the provider deliver on promises and to targets? (*predictability*)
- Is the provider dependable? Can you predict how the provider will react if a new situation comes up? (*dependability*)
- Does the provider show commitment to helping you achieve your goals? (*mutuality*)
- Does the provider communicate in a meaningful and timely way? (*communications*)
- Does the provider consistently follow processes, standards, and protocols? (*consistency*)
- If there is a hitherto unknown situation, is the provider able and willing to meet these new circumstances? Does the provider then make adequate new resources available or train the required skills? (*responsiveness*)
- Is the provider's approach and culture compatible with your company? (*compatibility*)
- How do you judge the provider's reputation in the market? (*reputation*)

Next, chart the average scores and add them up; this will give you a good measure of the current state of confidence in the relationship with your provider. But do not blindly add up the scores; look at the quality of trust at different levels of your organizational hierarchy. Sometimes you may find a high level of trust at the top of your firm, but a complete lack of confidence at the operational level. This is usually the case when the IT provider was chosen through an 'executive mandate', but did not arrive through a fair evaluation process in which all the important stakeholders participated and agreed on a vote. Of course, it can also be the other way round – your operations have a higher level of trust in the offshore provider's capabilities than the management. This shows a disconnect in your own organization between the employees who do the 'real' work and the management. Mostly, management does not receive, read or understand the RPD dashboard (which we are creating now) and bases its judgment entirely on a few escalation cases it has had to deal with. It may be a good idea to create a management view on the RPD so that the information is correctly passed up to the CIO.

If you find a low level of trust in the congruency and mutuality components, you may have entered into the wrong type of deal; your organization is probably looking at something completely different from what you have actually contracted.

But what do you do if trust is down on all components and across all levels in your organization right from operations up to the board? It is unfortunately virtually impossible to rebuild trust without committing a heavy investment of resources to this activity. In most cases, it is better to focus on an exit strategy and select a new provider following the S-LEAN RFP™ process outlined in Chapter 5 (p. 104).

Category 4: Risk

Risk is an adverse event which may occur in the future and cause damage. Unfortunately we do not know if or when it will happen or how great the actual damage will be. Hence we need to work with probabilities and damage estimates. You can then come up with actions to prevent such risks or reduce their effects. In Chapter 4 the risks of India offshore business were highlighted and business continuity management introduced as a way of normalizing the risk factors. At this juncture we need to consider all types of risks in outsourced offshore projects.[7] Coordinating and managing a team situated halfway across the globe, having another cultural mindset and working in a different time zone not only raises issues of quality and delivery, but also leads to a longer average lead time resolving issues and bridging gaps. Getting the right Indian employees with the right knowledge and attitude to work on your project is difficult in a fast market environment. And keeping them as part of your project team is even more difficult; current job contracts and project assignments hardly ever translate into lifetime (or even long-term) relationships. It is up to the business sponsors to decide how much money they want to spend on reducing risk – and whether this is financially viable at all.

In practical terms, this category is really about visualizing your risk exposure through:

- *Risk index*. Try to determine your risk portfolio explicitly by counting and monetarily evaluating the number of identified risks and the measures implemented, and judge their rentability.
- *Risk statistics*. Count the number of risk incidents that have affected your operations and evaluate them with respect to the damage they have caused and what it took to overcome the damage.
- *Indirect risk evaluation*. Collect information about (external) indicators to judge changes in the risk situation.
- *Implicit risk evaluation*. Consider the stakes of the risks (as per the risk index) on the minimum service levels and you will get an idea of how good your planning is.

Category 5: Offshore team

Even though we always use impersonal words like offshoring, industrialization or service providers, the India resources are actually not resources, but human beings. And humans are the most expensive part of any IT organization, even if the organization is located in a low-cost location like India. Hence it makes a great deal of sense to see the India offshore team as an investment and get a feel for their skills, satisfaction, motivation and training. All this should be monitored and, if required, acted on long before one is hit by the famous Indian attrition rate (see p. 25); of course, the offshore IT provider is the partner primarily responsible for this task, but remember, a dissatisfied team and attrition will also affect your bottom line.

How do you get all this information in real life? Obviously you cannot trust the IT provider to present it to you impartially; it will always be 'improved on'. Hence you need to get a feel for the employees yourself. I find it surprising that not many clients even attempt this. It is so easy: design a questionnaire, sign up with a web-based survey tool and send a link to every team member via email. Of course, you need to get this agreed with the service provider, having if possible already mentioned it in the RFP and the contract. You should also ensure full confidentiality for the Indian employees and run the survey anonymously; you may also choose not to share these results directly and unfiltered with your IT offshore partner in order to protect the employees from being reprimanded for giving bad feedback. If you ensure all this, you will be surprised what kind of open and honest feedback you get from your Indian team.

Category 6: Offshore management

Offshore management does not look at the individual activities required to successfully deliver, but it controls the process which drives the solution. In the context of the RPD, project management is about how effectively offshoring is utilized to support IT projects in your organization.

Look at the percentage of work offshored across all projects and as per the IT value chain (see Chapter 2, Figure 2.4), in other words, the individual phases of the project. Then relate it to industry best practices and you will get a good idea of where you stand in your offshore utilization; you will then also see the gap and how much cost efficiency you potentially miss out on.

Metrics to examine the health of your multisourcing relationships are the number of escalations to the MMO or executive levels, contract amendments, increases in charge-out rates, and so forth. The leverage of offshore can be calculated in terms of cost savings, efficiency increase and offshore resources versus own employees. In the case of a dedicated offshore team, the utilization rate not only affects the cost savings, but is also an early indicator of team morale and upcoming attrition. Indian employees do not like sitting idle; they need project action in order to hone their skills and upgrade their attractiveness for the job market.

Further metrics can count and track irregularities, such as deviation from scheduled performance, not keeping to deadlines, quality problems and budget overruns. Your company's offshore exposure should further be measured according to work done by business area, technology and phase of the IT value chain.

Adopting the offshore model in your company

Offshoring requires a new understanding and organization of roles and responsibilities in your company to bridge the distance between onsite design activities and offshore build tasks.

Case Study 9: Offshore relationship crisis

Parcel Co. is a pseudonym for a global provider of logistics and communication services, which offers its customers both standardized products and tailored solutions.

Its business unit Mail Services operates a data warehouse, which is based on four distinct technologies with a good number of interfaces to other applications. In 2008, the development phase was completed and Parcel Co. decided to outsource the maintenance to Warty Ltd., a pseudonym for a multi-national IT service provider with offshore operations of around 3,000 employees in India. Warty Ltd. was awarded an initial three-year contract.

In mid-2008, Warty Ltd. began a three month long incident-based knowledge transfer phase from Parcel's development team. Selected members of Warty's Indian maintenance team were sent onsite and joined Parcel's developers in solving incidents reported through trouble tickets. As a result, they figured out certain parts of the application, but failed to understand the whole picture: how the application is built up, how it is interlinked, and what functionality it really offers. When Warty took over the operational maintenance responsibility, it was not long before serious knowledge gaps surfaced and many tickets could not be solved; the agreed SLAs were not kept and Warty tried to fake the reporting by classifying non-measurable incidents as 'green'. For Parcel it meant additional and unbudgeted effort to continue supporting the provider's maintenance team. For Warty it was one of the first offshore maintenance projects from this region and its service provisioning managers did not have any prior experience of working together with India. Warty neither introduced appropriate communication channels between the onsite and offshore team, nor between Parcel's business users, the developers and the maintenance team.

By mid-2009 and more than one year into the project, no maintenance processes were created, no knowledge database was established, and no appropriate quality audits on the project were conducted. Summer 2009 even saw a week-long shut-down of the entire database caused by sheer technical incompetence. Warty as a company was more or less helpless and tried to resolve the situation by sending more and more Indians to onsite assignments. This measure negatively affected the motivation and work of the remaining offshore team and commercially brought the project into the red area.

I was then called in by Parcel Co. to help analyse the situation and propose a way forward. Applying the RPD methodology as proposed in this chapter, I examined the relationship between customer and provider and found all areas to be at great risk. Using a single slide, I summarized the situation for Parcel Co.'s management: Warty wanted to buy themselves into a reference project back in 2008, and in the process took Parcel Co. for a big ride, providing inexperienced resources, and failing to introduce any offshore best practices into the project. The three-year maintenance contract made Warty believe they had the upper hand in this relationship. Parcel Co. was running the risk of becoming fully dependent on Warty without a chance to switch providers. Within a few weeks, we discussed our view of the situation with Warty, both in India and onsite and called for a meeting of the relationship management board. Warty understood the urgency of the situation, came up with an improvement plan, and tried to mobilize resources to immediately improve service delivery. Notwithstanding these improvements, Parcel Co. regained operational independence from Warty, opening the way for a provider change once the contract comes up for renegotiation in 2011. The RPD slide I had created subsequently became the basis for an ongoing relationship monitoring and management process.

Role of the front office in offshore endeavours

The front office (FO) is the part of an offshore project which organizes between you as a customer and the back office (BO) offshore team in India. If you are contracting with a multi-national provider, it is very likely that the FO team will be mainly staffed by consultants from your own country and maybe a few Indian colleagues who are sent on an onsite assignment. However, when you are dealing with an Indian pure player, the FO team tends to be smaller and mainly staffed by consultants from India. Of course there is also the possibility of your IT department taking on the FO role, supported by some consultants from the provider.

The FO team sets the standards, is responsible for knowledge transfer to the offshore team, trains the client project team on distributed delivery methodologies, picks which parts of the project are to be delivered from offshore and which from onsite, ships those parts across to India and coordinates any issues during the delivery. It is important to note that the FO team does not have a monopoly on client contact. The middle man concept only leads to delays and distortions; the offshore teams should communicate directly with the client team in a coordinated manner and it is the FO team's job to orchestrate this interaction. The FO team is also not a post-box shipping work packages to India. Some parts of a project require intense discussions with the client and this can best be done by specialists from the FO team. This should not be misinterpreted as 'do not send complex and difficult things to India'; there is a subtle difference here. Complex activities can be done from offshore; however, the requirements need to be clearly described before sending the work to India. The FO team has to make the final call and decide what can be done where. Therefore it is important that the FO team consists not of 'content-free' facilitators, but experts who can architect and engineer solutions.[8]

Two main models for offshore delivery are available: the one-team and the factory model (see Figure 6.3).[9] The brief explanation which follows should enable you to understand the two concepts and their advantages in your discussion with offshore providers. It is really best to leave the final decision to your offshore provider.

In the *one-team model*, the organization of the FO team is mirrored at the offshore delivery location. For each and every part of the FO team, there is a corresponding BO team. The FO team takes the lead for BO and FO combined. Of course, resources can be shared across different streams; but for every assigned work package, a member of the FO or BO team will always report to one designated front-office team lead. Streams are secondary to the team organization and are supervised by the distributed delivery coordinator (DDC). Only the development stream is typically managed by the technical FO teamlead.

In a *factory model*, the streams become factories and take priority over the FO teams. Following the idea of offshore industrialization (see page 9), such factory units can work for multiple FO teams in different projects. The offshore factory heads report to an offshore factory manager in India, and on a dotted line to the distributed delivery coordinator in the front office.

Such a factory organization achieves tight process control, while sacrificing some of the context knowledge that offshore resources can easily gain through the one-team model. Mixed models are also possible; for example, data migration, testing and support can be run through a factory model, whereas GUI customizing could be operated via the one-team model. It really depends on the project situation and how advanced the offshore provider is in applying the industrialized factory model.

One-team model

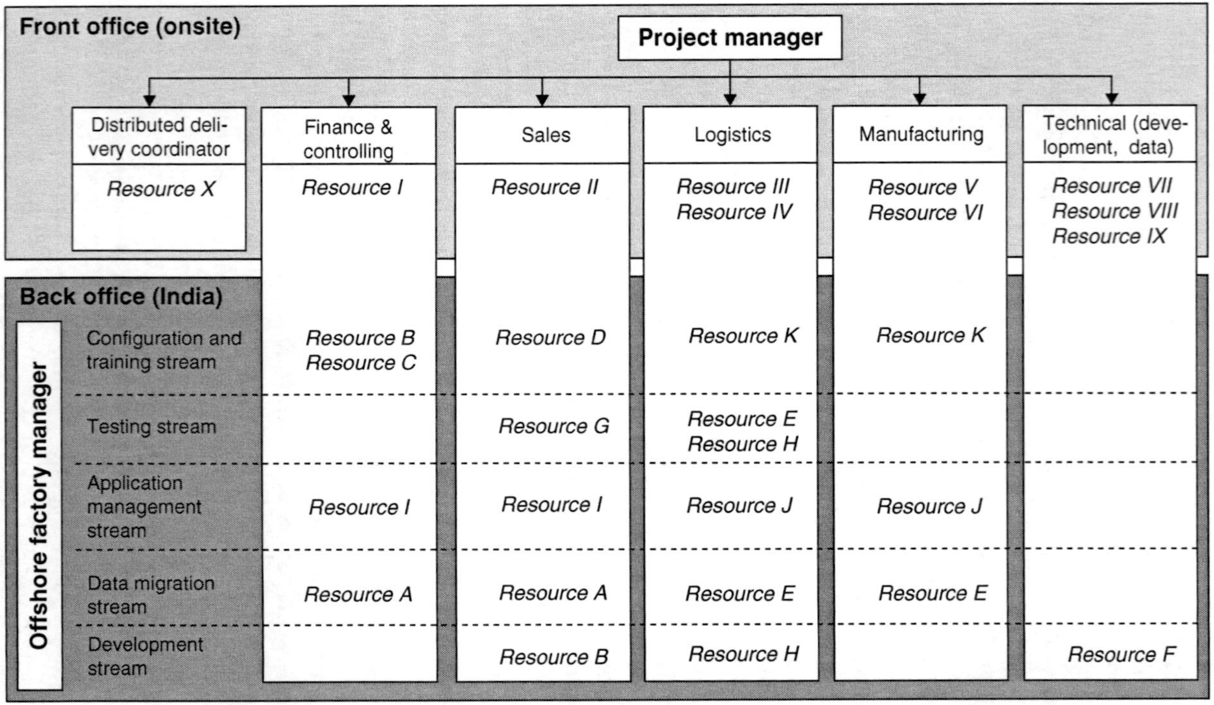

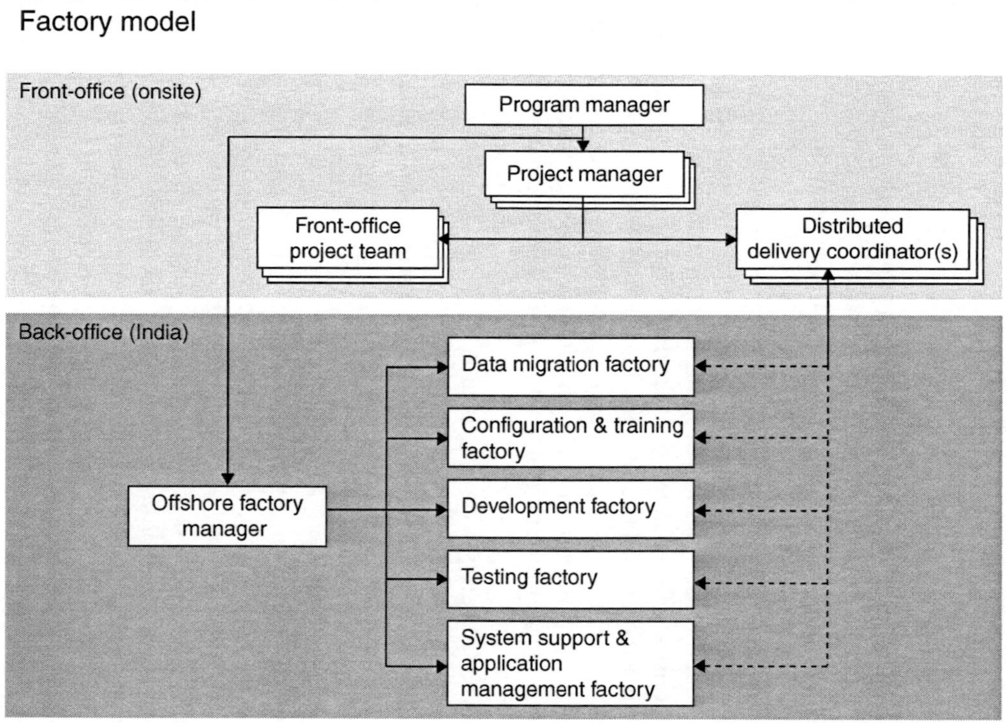

Figure 6.3 Offshore delivery models
Source: Adapted from Thun, 2008b, p. 80.

I have already mentioned the role of the *distributed delivery coordinators (DDCs)*; they are key people in setting standards, selecting templates and tools, and managing conflicts. In a factory model, they have direct resource and delivery responsibility for an offshore factory. In the one-team model however, they need to rely on their influencing skills and their cooperation with the project management to get things done.

New skills in the front office

New skills need to be deployed in the front office, in both your company and your external providers, be it with domestic outsourcing companies, multi-national IT providers with India operations, or simply with some of your freelancers. These new capabilities need to bridge distances halfway around the globe. One obvious aspect is technological support, but the real underlying challenge is how the organization adapts to build capabilities which shape different tasks, distribute them between 'onsite' and 'offshore', and facilitate ongoing communication. The different way of working, of course, also has an effect on job profiles and roles. Different soft skills are now required; face-to-face interaction is probably less important than carefully structuring communication, methodically preparing input and meticulously documenting it, thereby distinguishing between different target groups and levels of importance.[10] Needless to say, you cannot develop such new capabilities overnight or by management order; instead, you need to plot the way ahead on a transformation map similar to the one shown in Figure 6.4, and work your way to perfection step by step.

Organizational capabilities

The front office needs to be interwoven with the IT provider's standard delivery model so that the many handovers between streams or factories become smooth. Many individuals are involved in this and the model can only work if your colleagues change their behavioural patterns from attitudes like 'let me quickly fix this' to a careful and sometimes cumbersome documentation process. Even telephone conferences with the offshore partner will only deliver results if carefully prepared and documented. Communication across geographical and cultural distances simply leaves too much open to interpretation; Chapter 7 offers a glimpse of the challenges and some practical advice. Projects need to be controlled, based on measurable and meaningful KPIs, which are collected in a dashboard and allow drill-downs for fine-tuning of workloads and resource planning. The problem of accurate workload forecasting is a serious one in offshore projects. On one hand, keeping

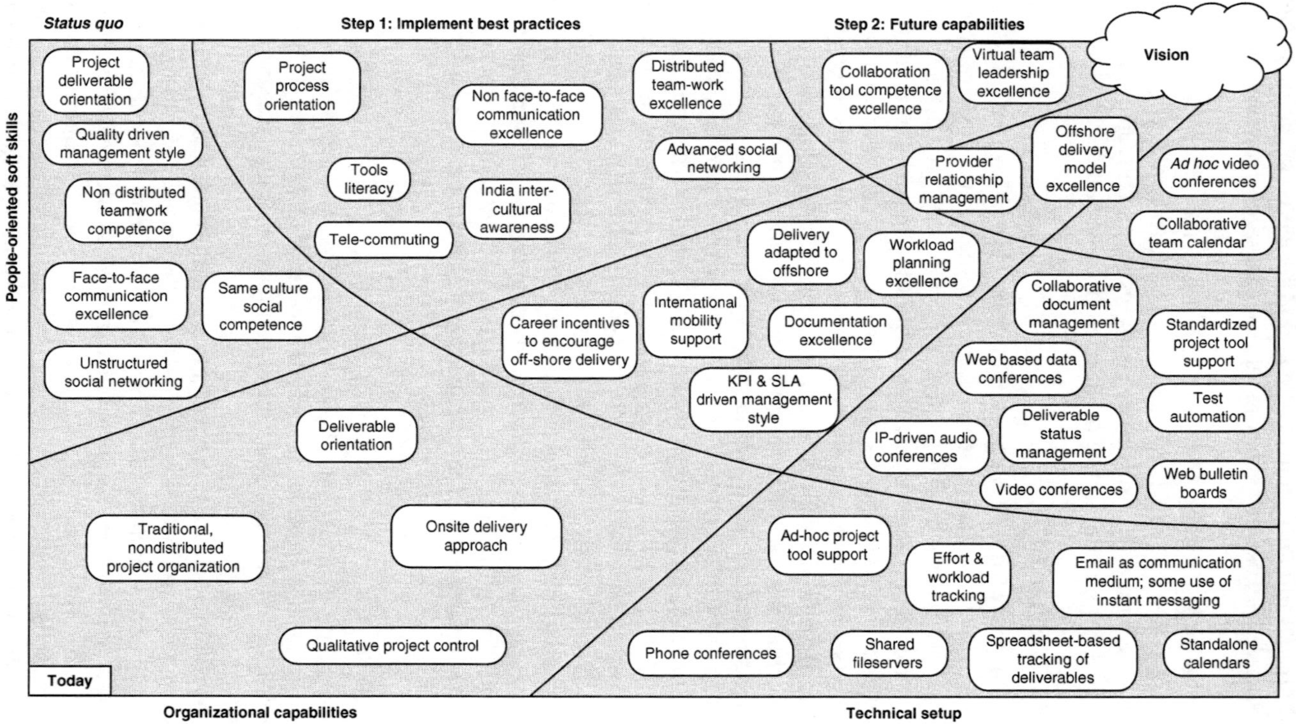

Figure 6.4 Example of a transformation map for the front office
Note: I acknowledge the contribution of my colleague Frank Thun at Capgemini who developed an earlier version of this transformation map.

a few additional Indian resources idle and available is not going to be very expensive because of very competitive cost rates. However, being idle and waiting for work to come in does not really fit in well with the career aspirations of young Indian IT engineers. Too many unutilized people on the offshore bench can quickly turn the mood in the project around to boredom, which will drive employees out of the project and out of the company resulting in the often-cited high Indian attrition rates.

People-oriented soft skills

As the main part of the IT delivery is shifted offshore to India, the IT employees in your company are forced to become designers, architects, and coordinators. Few may lose their jobs, but the remainder move much closer to the business areas. The front office becomes increasingly responsible for quality – and the back office in India will treat your people as experts and 'first aid' in case of problems or misunderstandings.

This move from delivery towards solution finding, together with the added challenges of offshore delivery, brings with it new requirements for soft skills. The lack of face-to-face communication needs to be compensated for by more effective and structured communication, an understanding of the polychronic Indian work style and Indian high-context communication (see Chapter 7). Your employees in the front office need to address the dichotomy between this more personal understanding of communication and at the same time no longer relying on personal impressions at all. Instead, KPIs, numbers and milestones have to replace experience-based judgments. Of course, these skills cannot be commanded, they need to be trained and slowly built; intercultural awareness and communication skills courses are a good start.

Technical setup

If everything is in place, but the technology remains inadequate to enable efficient and effective virtual management, distributed delivery will still fail. In many ways, technology can help to bridge gaps created by distance.

The good old telephone is hardly in use when it comes to coordinating offshore teams in India. For one, India's telecommunication market is still very much regulated, resulting in high international call rates.[11] And second, today's world offers much more sophisticated electronic communication tools, starting with voice-over IP (VOIP) telephone systems and various computer-based communication gadgets. They enable you to see who is at work and instantly accessible, set up conferences in an instant, and allow computer screens to be shared at any point in time.

Excel® spreadsheets and email attachments are not suitable tools for distributed development, nor are they actually good support tools for any professional project work. Surprisingly and disappointingly for the maturity of the industry, they can still be found in many offshore projects. Better collaborative applications provide a platform to store documents, access them from anywhere, integrate workflows to review and approve these, track and store deliverables, sound alerts on status changes, capture knowledge in wikis, discuss issues in forums. In addition, team members can record their time against various tasks and assignments. Various levels of testing can these days be automated or at least supported with predefined scripts in test automation tools; test defects are again made accessible across geographical boundaries to the entire test team, both in the front office and the Indian back office. Such collaborative platforms make sure that everyone is on the same page (single point of truth); they also serve as the base for a handover from application development to maintenance after go-live.

Knowledge transfer

When you start your offshoring project, you may find yourself pondering the question of how a selected provider can develop knowledge about your technical setup, industry domain and business processes in order to not only maintain the quality of services, but also provide efficiency increases, innovation and transformation? Looking at the high attrition rates in India's past IT history, how do you make sure that the know-how stays with the provider rather than walking out of the door? And where do you draw the line between freely passing on knowledge and keeping your market differentiating expertise to yourself?

Believe me, at the same time, the IT offshore providers are asking themselves very similar questions. How can one quickly develop expertise in hitherto unknown areas or technologies? How to overcome the hurdle of the source sitting halfway around the globe from the recipients of knowledge transfer? How can an organization retain knowledge when it resides in the brains of employees who tend to move quickly from one employer to the next?

Both parties realize that outsourcing and offshoring require the provider to have an in-depth understanding of the client's technical business domain. And here the disconnect usually begins. To the provider, domain expertise only means becoming familiar with your industry; however, to you domain expertise stands for a lot more, for understanding your particular business, your technology, your systems architecture, products, markets and processes. The key to outsourcing and offshoring is understanding this knowledge gap and closing it.[12]

In the early years of outsourcing and offshoring, senior Indian consultants were sent onsite to study the client systems, processes, and business (usually in that order, but not vice versa!), tasked with putting everything down in standardized templates, and, once back in India, given the responsibility of training their offshore colleagues. Not surprisingly, a huge glossary was always part of the knowledge transfer documents. In cases where the client provided the documentation, it was carefully examined with pre-fabricated review checklists and issues logs were used for seeking clarification. In those days, providers performed the knowledge transfer process with the main and often sole purpose of understanding the client's systems. This documentation would serve for future reference should a problem with the delivery arise or a new team member in India be inducted into the project team. Typically, new joiners were given a pile of documents and asked to go through them before they actually started doing anything on the project.

While documentation had its place in offshoring, and in many ways still retains its importance today, this approach missed a great opportunity for both sides as it was fully focused on the one client's existing systems. However, customers can well profit from leveraging expertise that offshore consultants have gained from working on similar projects for other customers, in other industry sectors, or in the same domain but in another country. The offshore provider can also make good use of such knowledge when starting projects with other clients, maybe also somewhere else in the world. Maybe some of these other clients are even your competitors? So what? Unless the Indian consultants are working on a real market-differentiating piece of software, the learning will go both ways and be beneficial for both you and your competitors. This is about treating the bottom layers of your IT systems as a commodity, making them cheaper, more robust and more agile at the same time.

These questions point to a major lesson for you as a customer of offshoring – you need to work together with your chosen provider(s) in order to successfully identify information, plan for transfer, conduct the knowledge transfer, absorb new information coming back from offshore and combine it with new information simultaneously generated in your company. This will be a closed loop knowledge management process in which you need to work together with the provider in order to drive his knowledge retention programme. It is all to ensure that knowledge stays alive, does not age or get lost. Let's be honest, in every outsourcing deal knowledge is lost, which is probably inevitable, so it is really important that you plan for the implications of such losses and try to avoid any damage they can cause to your agility and quality.

Let us look at what leading IT offshore service providers do with the knowledge they transfer from your company into their own organization. Figure 6.5 shows the two levels of knowledge management: at the project level and the organizational level.[13] The processes at the project level are vital for successfully delivering an engagement for a single client; they represent the provider's ability to quickly adapt to a new environment, absorb the knowledge, and deliver a tangible outcome. At the organizational level, knowledge management processes support the coordination of expertise and bring staffing suggestions to project teams promptly and at the appropriate time. All three processes interact and support each other.

At the project level, the IT service provider's first step is to *organize for knowledge transfer* by putting the organizational structure in place and selecting individual team members who have previous know-how in comparable environments. This not only significantly enhances the capability of quickly absorbing client knowledge; it also puts the

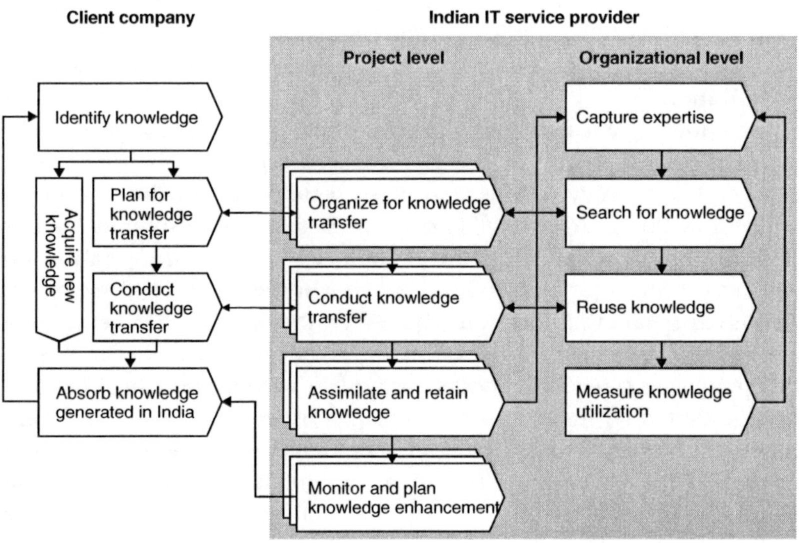

Figure 6.5 Offshore knowledge management process

service provider in the driving seat for a successful knowledge transfer. During the stage *conduct knowledge transfer*, communication channels are established and protocols ensure a successful transfer of your company's knowledge to the IT vendor. At this point it is important that a common language between the two sides is established; glossaries and standardized templates help in this matter. The *assimilate and retain knowledge* phase ensures that knowledge is not only documented, but really absorbed in the offshore team on a long-term basis. An explicit succession and back-up plan facilitates the process by assigning the project manager, every subject matter expert, and really every team member a back-up person, who can seamlessly take over should the first person decide to leave the project. This helps to avoid panic should an employee fall sick or resign. Devising this kind of succession plan not only requires involvement from all levels at the provider's site, it also commands your understanding and cooperation; sometimes you will simply have to accept that you need to deal with more than one person for back-up purposes. The purpose of the last step, *monitor and plan knowledge enhancement,* is really to continuously examine how knowledge is dispersed in the client–provider relationship and how it is absorbed in the project team as an organizational process. During the delivery cycle, the offshore team develops knowledge which needs to be passed back to your company and absorbed there as well in order to avoid any knowledge gaps between client and provider. If you have started with an application development project, this phase also ensures a smooth transition to the application maintenance support organization.[14]

The knowledge management processes at project levels are supported by an expertise process at the IT provider's organizational level. This process is about developing a strong capability to coordinate competences and knowledge. First, knowledge needs to be captured (*capture expertise*) by creating entries in directories providing information on who has done what for whom and who has what level of expertise. This is easier said than done; it requires a rather sophisticated employee knowledge database with relevant categories, good processes to ensure that employees regularly update their knowledge, and last but not least, good management processes to supervise the entry and normalize experience levels. During the *search for knowledge* stage, this database connects with a staffing management system showing the current and planned utilization of consultants; as a result, suitable consultants are proposed for a new client assignment. The *reuse knowledge* phase provides tangible benefits: it speeds up the delivery and adds to consistent quality by having the right people on board the team, drawing on earlier experiences and installing prefabricated solutions. This is a real driver for industrialization of offshore delivery (see page 9). At the end, the provider needs to *measure knowledge utilization* in order to judge the effectiveness of the knowledge management process by measuring to what extent expertise has helped to win new client projects, deliver with better quality and more favourable margins, and how the organization develops in terms of knowledge accumulation. Out of this analysis, new service offerings can be designed which allow the provider to proactively approach clients with new sales propositions.

This process sounds straightforward and simple. However, in real life, you will probably be surprised how many Indian IT providers struggle with their knowledge management processes, how long it takes them to fulfil a staffing requirement, and how basic the underlying directories and databases are. In fact, academic research[15] shows that IT providers need to come up with an even broader vision to manage expertise and knowledge, which also maps the communication between individuals into a network structure. A big challenge in all these systems is of course attrition and how to manage changes in the employee base. This, however, is a topic for another book, as it is something which does not affect you as a customer directly; it is something the Indian offshore industry needs to solve. You only need to understand how knowledge transfer to the other side of the globe works, and why it is important that you fully support your provider in this process.

7 Navigating Cultural Differences

In every cross-cultural collaboration there is scope and potential for misunderstanding. Some surveys go as far as to show that cultural differences are the biggest challenge in offshoring. While I would not fully agree with this point of view – since many other aspects highlighted earlier in this book have an important effect on the functioning of an offshore relationship as well – culture is certainly the most underestimated, neglected and often wrongly interpreted hurdle. The superficially similar aspects of culture (like English as a common business language, Western office dress or world-class business parks in India) may lull you into complacency, making you believe that you can easily navigate other differences. However, attitudes, work ethos and values of Indians are at first glance invisible to you, just as your attitudes, work ethos and values are initially hidden from your Indian colleagues. My simple advice is to not underestimate the differentness; it not only impacts the working and collaboration style, but brings with it serious business implications. When dealing with India, you need to expect similarities and differences, but you need to accept and respect the country's diversity.

International encounters

The difference between you (as a customer of an offshore service provider) and your Indian counterparts (who deliver the job from an offshore location) can be described via intercultural dimensions (see the relevant sections of the readiness assessment in Chapter 3, pp. 66–9). This very difference leads to a very complex construct of levels of intercultural understanding – and many misinterpretations of well-meaning behaviour. Let us start by sitting back for a moment and judging our own proficiency in the Indian business culture and society, as compared to the knowledge your Indian counterparts have about the Western business culture and society. The matrix in Figure 7.1 visualizes this mapping and helps to identify appropriate actions.

If you and your Indian peers both have low familiarity with each other's culture, a third person can be introduced to help bridge the gap; this can be an offshore deployment coordinator, someone more familiar with the foreign culture or even an external coach. By the term 'familiarity with a culture', I refer to someone's current knowledge of another culture and the ability to use that knowledge competently in collaborating with members of the other culture. Provided both parties share a similar moderate familiarity with each other's culture, you both need to sit down and talk about how the collaboration is to proceed. This coordinated adjustment can best be done explicitly at the start, but most often it happens implicitly as the cooperation moves along through a gradual blending of elements from both cultures. For those of you who are highly familiar with the Indian cultural baggage and happen to meet Indians who are well in tune with the Western culture, you

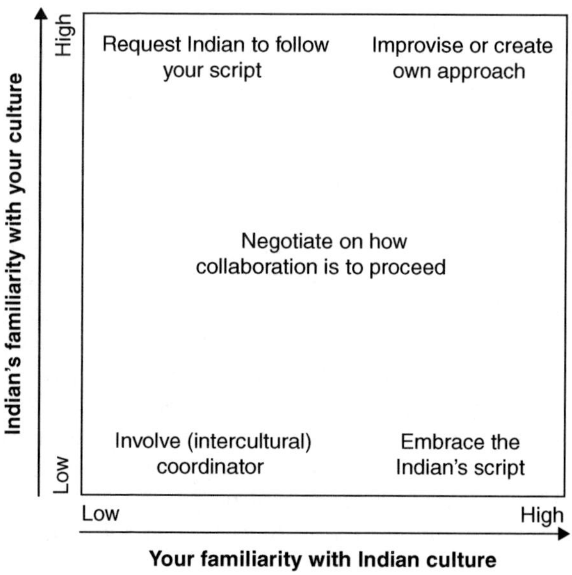

Figure 7.1 Intercultural responsiveness strategies

Source: Adapted from the strategic framework for intercultural negotiation in Weiss (1994a), p. 54 and Weiss (1994b).

may need to improvise during the collaboration process in a sensitive dialogue, taking each other's strengths, attributes and the circumstances into account; you will notice that you will both begin to create your own unique approach. However, if familiarity with each other's culture is very unequal, then the party who is more familiar with the other culture should adapt to it to a greater extent.

So, what constellation of intercultural familiarity do we mostly encounter in India offshoring collaborations? While the Americans and the British are fairly familiar working with Indians in their home countries, one should not forget that these types of emigré Indians no longer represent the culture of real Indians. Some Indians have been living abroad for long enough to be out of touch with cultural development and current business practices in India.[1] And on the subcontinent itself, Indians at an upper management level tend to believe that they know a lot about Western culture as they frequently travel on business. However, Indians at delivery level and sometimes even at project management level are yet to get this first-hand experience. Typically neither set receives the necessary training from their companies. Many managers do not want to attend soft skill training; in Indian business culture it is seen as a weakness to admit the need for soft skill training. Delivery employees are not sent on these training courses as their companies often do not want to invest in high quality intercultural training for their junior employees; such costs typically cannot be recovered from clients and thus reduce project or business unit margins.

In summary, a collaborative and synergistic style of working together is called for, involving considerable reflection on your own cultural preprogramming as well as a careful investigation of Indian culture. So, what happens when your company engages an Indian IT provider for the first time and when your team needs to communicate and work together with colleagues halfway round the globe?

Such intercultural encounters are typically accompanied by a shift of feelings over time. Initially, you will notice a short period of euphoria, followed instantly by the phenomenon of culture shock, then by acculturation, and finally by a stable state in which collaboration with India is found to be either something very normal, positive, or negative. (Note that this shift of feelings over time, as described here, does not of course apply to employees who have been made redundant due to offshoring to India.)

The first phase of *euphoria* can entail the excitement of job enrichment and maybe even getting an opportunity of travelling to India for the project kick-off. The *culture shock* (second phase) sets in when the project actually gains speed in the new distributed and international environment, or when one arrives in India. Many things have been hoped for but few actually turn out as expected. This difference between hope and reality can lead to frustration and even a sudden decline in the acceptance of offshoring as a strategic instrument. Expatriates in India often take to alcohol or even drugs in this phase to cope with the anger and frustration. This makes it really essential, from both an enterprise perspective and an individual point of view, to overcome the culture shock as quickly as possible. Companies need to set aside resources to counsel and coach individuals and the project team. The *acculturation* (third phase) begins when everybody has slowly learned how to collaborate with the other culture and the project is up to speed under the new conditions. The stable state (fourth phase) is reached when the project members have completely come to terms with the peculiarities of intercultural collaboration or have simply accepted their fate. These feelings can (a) remain negative, if smooth intercultural communication has not been established and there are problems with project deliverables. If it is (b) neutral, then the offshore collaboration model is seen to be just about as good as getting the job done at home. A positive feeling (c) about working together with Indians can only be achieved by acquiring intercultural abilities on the personal front and at the same time following a mature process model for international cooperation with established processes. Figure 7.2 shows this acculturation curve; feelings about working together with India are plotted on the vertical axis and the time is on the horizontal one.

Intercultural awareness can be learned through experience and also taught to some extent on intercultural training courses.[2] However, people with inflated egos, low uncertainty tolerance, with political sympathies for extreme parties or racism, and those who cannot distance themselves from their own cherished environment typically find it very difficult to keep prejudices aside and learn from what they see and experience. Before starting a project with an India offshore contribution, it is a good idea to offer intercultural awareness training[3] to the entire project team. As a C-level executive or project manager you should also invest these one or two days and join the training, because you need to understand the kind of challenges your team is going to face in the course of the offshore project. The remaining part of this chapter can only offer you a short glimpse and try to convince you that training and careful preparation will be your key to success.

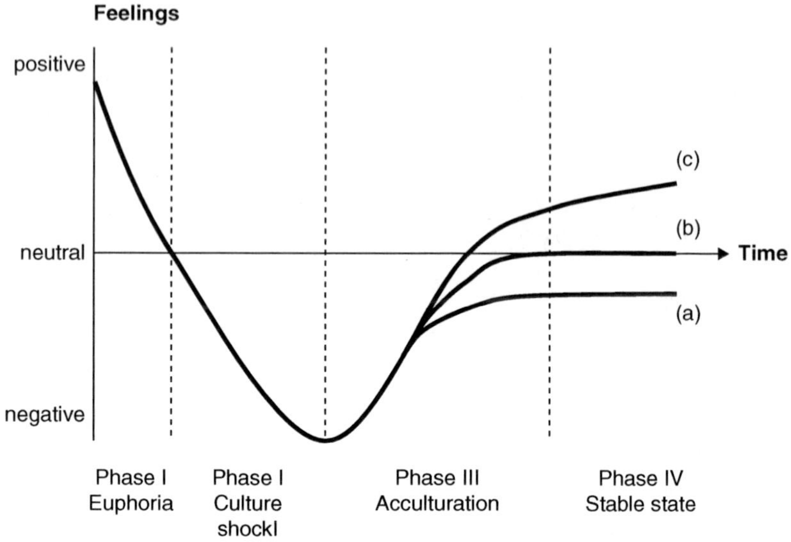

Figure 7.2 Acculturation curve for international encounters
Source: Hofstede and Hofstede (2005), p. 324.

Indian cultural specifics

Collectivistic value system

The key values of Indian traditional society are collectivistic and people-oriented, and they very much shine through in business interactions as well. The four most prominent ones are:

- *Dependability*. How do you get a job done in India? Not by discussing the approach and the desired outcome, but first and foremost by building up a dependable relationship with a person. This leads to a mutual feeling of trust and allows both parties to maintain a good business relationship. Through this feeling of trust, the job gets done – nor is the result going to be disappointing.
- *Spirituality*. In Hinduism, the ultimate purpose of life is to transcend the mortal physical existence of this world, renounce all its material aspirations, and be elevated to a state of spiritual consciousness. Indians believe in doing their best to reach this stage and manage a deliverance from the cycle of reincarnation – and leave the rest to fate. Translate this to real life and the IT industry, and one notices

that Indians do not get very worked up about something which does not go according to plan, as it is seen as part of fate.

- *Family*. Indians behave very collectivistically when interacting with their extended family or with members of their own community – family comes first. This can be seen in people not showing up for a scheduled business meeting because 'there was a problem at home' or a religious function had to be attended. However, when it comes to career advancement and personal benefit, Indians display considerable individualistic traits as well.
- *Hospitality*. Being welcoming, offering warmth and adjusting themselves to the convenience of others, has been engrained into Indian culture for centuries. You will notice the special attention given to you when you visit an Indian delivery centre as a customer; of course, some of it is attributable to the fact that the Indian provider is wooing you as a customer, but the welcoming atmosphere certainly also relates to an old adage about treating a guest like God.

These values are in stark contrast to the value system of Western countries which are typically more individualistic than collectivistic, and more task- than people-oriented, that is, the focus is generally on quality, orderliness, or punctuality. Again, we should all refrain from any kind of judgment as neither value system is better or worse, they are simply different and bring with them a different way of dealing with things.

High-context communication style

The modest and people-oriented culture of India results in a special kind of high-context communication style, found in face-to-face business discussions and telephone calls, as well as in emails. The language is quite indirect, very subtle, and may sometimes sound ambiguous to you. The real messages, for example, about deadlines not being met, about problems with the project delivery, or about staffing issues, are rarely explicitly stated; instead, they are implied 'between the lines' and hidden in the context. Coming from a Western and more low-context culture, your challenge is first to correctly decipher these implicit messages, and second not to upset your Indian counterpart with your explicit, direct, and commanding style of communication. You need to be especially careful about giving negative feedback; people do not want to hear it anywhere in the world, but in India it is perceived as closer to torture than to anything else and definitely not as an appropriate attempt to progress a project.

Polychronic understanding of time

There is ambivalence about time and punctuality in India. While many activities do occur within a predefined though somewhat more flexible timeframe, social activities often get delayed or postponed. In addition, the importance of family and social activities sometimes influences the happening of business activities.

While in the businesses and private sphere of the Western world the clock continuously ticks, everybody has an agenda, and everything constantly gets prioritized and re-prioritized, in India time seems to be moving in circles, agendas are flexible, and people tend to discuss everything at the same time, having seemingly never heard of priorities at all. This is the polychronic understanding of time where appointments or deadlines are not missed, but come around again should something else have got in the way. From an Indian point of view, an eleven o'clock appointment is due only at a quarter past eleven and only then should the previous meeting be over. When you enter into discussions with Indians you will need to learn how to interpret and adjust, at least to a certain extent, to these different behaviours.

Indian society and the caste system

In the many intercultural training sessions I have conducted, Western participants always want to know about the functioning and importance of the caste system in India. They are extremely disappointed when I tell them that, even though the caste system has officially been abolished since 1950 (shortly after India gained its independence) and while it nonetheless continues to have an effect on how society at large functions, it is completely invisible to anyone from outside India working together with India's IT industry. When interviewing employees, one is usually unaware of their caste; the best person for the job is recruited.[4] Software engineers tend to gloss over it at work, and most of them don't even know which caste their colleagues belong to.[5]

Much less well-known in the Western world, but very important for social life in India, are the 300 local communities (*jatis*), which are subsections of the castes. People of one *jati* share common religious rituals and food habits, and do not usually marry outside this defined group.

What is much more important for your understanding of working together with Indians is the importance of the family, which is at the heart of their life and one of the basic units of Indian society. In the Western world, family usually connotes a nuclear family of two adults and their children. In India, family always means extended family, including sometimes very distantly related aunts, uncles, and cousins. Family events are at the top of the priority list of every Indian software engineer. As a manager, one needs to take account of these private requirements in order not to lose the employee's trust – or worse, lose the employee altogether.

Women have equal rights and career prospects in the Indian IT industry. However, many still follow the traditional role model and after marriage become responsible for bringing up children, looking after the well-being of the extended family and socializing. For this reason, the number of women in project management or executive positions is less than at entry levels.

Surviving Indian meetings and negotiations

A lot has been written about how best to conduct meetings and negotiations in India; some of it is sheer nonsense and overemphasizes the implications of history, religion and culture for international business. Nonetheless, the following factors, drawn from my own experience, really influence Indians when conducting meetings:

- *Polychronic time concept.* A meeting appointment is at best tentative in India and getting a firm commitment is almost impossible. Having said this, if you are a customer of an Indian IT provider and you are to bring in good business, then the business sense will overshadow the polychronic habit and you can be pretty sure that your meeting will take place. Although there may be a little delay, it will happen.
- *Collectivism and people-orientation.* Meetings usually start with private discussions around cricket, tea or coffee and family. This is to get to know each other and establish a common ground of understanding. During discussion of business matters, the language used will mostly be soft and not very direct to avoid any controversy and allow everybody to 'save face'. This can make it very difficult for you to understand the real message as it might be hidden somewhere in the context. You will mostly be in the situation where, as a customer, you are handled extra carefully. The situation changes when the Indian believes himself to be in a superior hierarchical position; then the language used can be very derogatory and condescending, in line with the strong hierarchy index of Indian society.
- *Hierarchy consciousness.* Indians look up to their elders and bosses at work; in a meeting it is the boss who has the right to speak and make decisions. Subordinates are only present to support the boss, not to voice their own opinions. It is very difficult for you to find out what

subordinates, such as the project manager, the quality manager and some team members, really think about the progress of the project. Your best course is to engage an India intercultural expert to come up with the right wording of questions at the right moment to the right people.

- *Polychronic discussion*. There will be no agenda; Indians like to come to meetings with a blank sheet of paper. This does not imply disinterest or arrogance, but simply a different understanding of the purpose of a meeting. From an Indian context, a meeting is about establishing a common ground of understanding from which the activities can be started.
- *Coming to a conclusion*. When does an Indian meeting end? Definitely not when you leave the room and not even when you wave goodbye and get into the taxi to the airport. In fact, some new aspects will be added via email afterwards or as part of the meeting minutes. This is where the discussion really continues – and meeting minutes are also not seen as something which has been agreed upon, but as something which needs to be reviewed later when the context has changed.

8
Conclusion

Offshoring of IT can deliver benefits to your organization and help to achieve business priorities. However, these benefits are inherent neither in the act of offshoring nor in India as a destination for outsourced IT delivery.

If you want to realize the full value that offshoring can provide and at the same time balance the risks associated with doing business halfway around the globe, you need to make an informed decision, plan and execute the process carefully. My experience from many years of working with India and in India shows that good preparation and strong management is paramount to success and makes a difference to the results that you get out of the offshore endeavour. I have designed this book so that your organization does just that and thereby gets the maximum contribution from IT for achieving business priorities.

Offshoring is not a single transaction led by a contract. Instead, it is a series of governance decisions which are part of a lifecycle model; the contract is only one of them.

Offshoring is both science and art. The science part involves frameworks, methods and approaches which can guide you in developing your own offshore strategy. In this book, I have tried to introduce you to some of them which I find practical and effective. In addition, offshoring requires thoughtful management of relationships, both with the Indian IT provider and stakeholders in your own company. This is really an art and the human face of strategy. You will integrate the services of providers into your own company and by managing them successfully, provide your company with the possibility and agility to support the achievement of business priorities through IT.

For most companies, offshoring requires and deserves the attention of executive management. It is a change from the traditional way of IT delivery, be it application development, maintenance or infrastructure management. This transformation not only takes place in terms of the delivery locality, which already involves many challenges with respect to switching from face-to-face communication to stringent documentation, using collaborative tools, adapting to different cultures, values and aspirations, and normalizing risk for business continuity management. This change also affects and improves the way software is delivered in an industrialized fashion through standardization and segmentation. Offshore industrialization will soon be the new norm for efficient and effective IT delivery.

Given the discipline and effort required to successfully evaluate, plan, transfer and operate an India offshore cooperation model, you may be tempted to wait and in the meanwhile improve your current operations for efficiency and cost effectiveness. Alas, waiting is not an option in the currently changing business landscape. The forces of recession, cost and margin pressures, competition, globalization, and the need for supporting business priorities through a powerful yet agile IT will not allow you to omit to reap the benefits that offshoring to India can bring to you. The risks of remaining passive and of continuing to operate at comparative disadvantages are too high. Therefore the need to master offshoring is becoming increasingly important.

Throughout the book I have focused on a few key themes: understand both what India can offer and what its limitations are, connect with Indians and their unique culture, build your strategy to support business priorities through IT and enable it through offshoring, introduce governance into your company, manage and measure your relationship with offshore providers effectively, and – last but not least – don't forget to drive necessary changes through in your own company. Nobody says the roadmap is easy, but it is a proven path. Get started today, don't waste any more time, and don't allow the competition to get a head start.

Notes

Chapter 1 Offshoring: India's Playground

1. Definitions of outsourcing can be found in Cohen and Young (2006), p. 2.
2. Cf. Kaiser and Hawk (2004), pp. 70–71. The IT provider EDS refers to cosourcing as outsourcing deals in which the provider takes over an activity and gets paid for improvements in the client's business; cf. Cullen and Willcocks (2003), ch. 2.1.3.
3. Cf. Koulopoulos and Roloff (2006).
4. Marketing departments will use this type of expression to suggest that companies are doing something extraordinary and clever. For instance, the CEO of Deutsche Bank, Josef Ackermann, introduced the term smartsourcing to describe shifting jobs to locations with lower costs in an attempt to boost the bank's return on equity and share prices; see FAZ 0302 (2005) and von den Bergen (2005).
5. Cf. Nasscom and McKinsey (2009), p. 22.
6. The term 'offshoring' is not specific to information technology; previously and sometimes still today, the world of financial economics refers to 'offshore' to describe locations that serve as tax shelters for international investors.
7. Cf. Manning *et al.* (2008), p. 39.
8. Cf. Nunes *et al.* (2009), p. 6.
9. I am providing a practitioner's view of the offshoring fields. Academic literature and studies are not very clear about these fields and sometimes refer to them simply as IT work or IS services as noted by Westner (2007), pp. 7–8.
10. For a reference to the outsourcing levels, cf. for example Brown and Wilson (2005), pp. 20–25.
11. Cf. Kennedy (2009), p. 95.
12. Cf. Figure 1.8 and p. 20.
13. Cf. Vautier and Phypers (2007).
14. Cf. Thun (2008a), p. 57.
15. This figure does not include export-oriented BPO business and domestic software; see p. 20 and Figure 1.8 for a more detailed breakdown.
16. Cf. Jalote (2001).
17. Cf. the critique by Ghemawat (2007), p. 232.
18. Cf. Ghemawat (2007), pp. 33–54.
19. The following are examples of very recent books about India: Gupta and Wang (2008); Luce (2008); Meredith (2008); Müller (2006); Nilekani (2009). The term 'globalization apocalypse' was coined by Ghemawat (2007), whose view on the semi-globalization state of our world I strongly support.
20. Cf. CIAWorldbookIndia.
21. According to Unicef (2009) and a BBC report (Pandey, 2006), around 45 per cent of India's children below the age of three are too small for their age, 47 per cent are underweight (which is an astronomically high total of

57 million children), and at least 16 per cent are undernourished. The state of Madhya Pradesh records the highest rate of malnutrition (55 per cent) and Kerala the lowest (27 per cent).

22. Cf. *Liverpool Daily Post* 2603 (2009); Merrick (2009).
23. Cf. Hale *et al.* (2008).
24. Cf. Nasscom and McKinsey (2009), p. 23.
25. Cf. Thun (2008a), p. 3.
26. Data based on Nasscom industry analysis; see Messner (2009a), pp. 67–68.
27. Revenue productivity is defined as revenues (billions USD)/employees (thousands) and can be accepted as a good measure of competitiveness; see Umamaheswari and Momaya (2008), p. 128.
28. Cf. Messner (2009a), p. 71.
29. For a full analysis see Umamaheswari and Momaya (2008).
30. Cf. Mahalingam (2009).
31. Many newspaper articles have been published around this topic: see for example *Economic Times* 1301 (2009).
32. Note that the name Maytas is the semi-palindrome of Satyam.
33. A good overview of the unfolding of the Satyam story can be found in Post *et al.* (2009).
34. Cf. *Economic Times* 0901 (2009), p. 1.
35. I first heard the term 'flywheel of success' from Peter Schumacher, CEO of the Value Leadership Group; see Schumacher and Olsson (2009), p. 13.
36. See my my detailed calculations in Messner (2009a), pp. 78–81.
37. According to data released by the Department of Industrial Policy and Promotion (DIPP) (IBEF, 2009).
38. According to an UNCTAD study; compares calendar year 2008 with 2007, cf. IBEF (2009).
39. FDI is allowed up to 100 per cent in all manufacturing industries, except defence production (capped at 26 per cent). FDI is not allowed in a few service industries, including retail trading (except single brand), lottery business, and gambling. In the permitted services, foreign equity is allowed up to 50 per cent. FDI is currently allowed only up to 49 per cent in scheduled air transport services or domestic passenger airlines. Broadcasting services also have similar rules; up-linking of non-news television channels is the only broadcasting service permitted to have 100 per cent FDI after clearance by the Foreign Investment Promotion Board (FIPB). Majority foreign equity is not allowed in cable television networks and direct-to-home (DTH) operations. In print media, FDI is allowed only up to 26 per cent. In the area of financial services, such as private banks, FDI is allowed up to 74 per cent. The insurance industry, however, can get FDI only up to 26 per cent. Minority foreign equity up to 49 per cent is permitted in asset reconstruction companies (ARCs), stock exchanges, depositories, clearing corporations and commodities. Except for ARCs, FDI is capped at 26 per cent for these sectors. In telecommunication services – both basic and cellular – FDI is allowed up to 74 per cent (49 per cent allowed under the automatic route and the rest requiring approval from FIPB). Cf. IBEF (2009).
40. Cf. Messner (2009a), p. 80.
41. Cf. Farrell *et al.* (2006), p. 30. It is even worse for students with only generalist knowledge; here the shrinking factor is estimated at 90 per cent.

Interestingly, the situation is worse in China where only 10 per cent of the engineering graduates are deemed suitable for MNC employment.
42. Cf. Messner (2008), p. 28; Messner (2009a), p. 82; PTI (2008), p. 7.
43. Nasscom and McKinsey (2009), p. 22. As per the study, long-term relates to the year 2020. I have renamed some of the scenarios and highlighted the industrialization of IT delivery as an important aspect of innovation in this field.

Chapter 2 Considering Offshoring

1. I acknowledge the contribution of my colleague Frank Thun; together with him I have developed an earlier version of this lifecycle model at Capgemini. For another model on outsourcing with eight building blocks, refer to Cullen and Willcocks (2003), or to Willcocks *et al.* (2009, pp. 2–3) and Cullen (2006) for an updated version with four phases and nine building blocks.
2. For an example of a stringent project method for outsourcing IT in retail banking refer to Krause (2008).
3. Future costs are a result of upcoming strategies and need to be estimated, attached to probabilities, and discounted via the net present value (NPV) method.
4. For more details refer to p. 24.
5. Cf. Capgemini (2009), p. 5; Nunes *et al.* (2009); Rhodes and Stelter (2009); Tolido (2009); Charan (2009).
6. Cf. Accenture (2009), p. 2.
7. Many newspaper articles and books have been published about the Enron case; see for example Fox (2002).
8. Cf. Ryan (2007).
9. The idea is based on Capgemini's TechnoVision 2012; cf. Capgemini (2008, 2009). I have reduced the future perspective and brought it back to the actual situation in the industry. As a consequence, clusters are renamed and consolidated. For another perspective on offshoring in a recession see Lewin and Perm-Ajchariyawong (2009) and Lewin *et al.* (2009).
10. According to Kaplan *et al.* (2009), p. 16, 50–70% of server, 50–80% of network, 30–50% of mainframes, 50–80% of end-user devices and 50–80% of helpdesk related IT infrastructure operations can be offshored. I provide a higher number (90%), as under infrastructure management I also include application operations, which I consider to be different from application maintenance.
11. According to Forrester Research (see Apte, 2009, p. 14), offshore blended rates are between USD 21–35 per hour
12. A pure comparison of salary levels is interesting, but not very useful, as it does not cover higher workplace costs of Western employees.
13. As per an estimate published by Accenture (2007, p. 3); I can confirm this based on my offshore experience.
14. Black–Scholes is a partial differential equation that creates a range of possible outcomes based on the uncertainty of the market, the cost to take advantage of the option, and whether the results of the option will be worth more than the costs. Forrester Research (see Gliedman, 2008, and Gliedman, 2004), has

proposed transferring the formula to examine the flexibility of a portfolio of IT projects and simplified the formula for this purpose. A quantifiable metric is produced by the formula to see if the value of flexibility is worthwhile in the current market environment.
15. For more background please refer to p. 30. The HR implications are discussed in Ready *et al.* (2008) and Messner (2009b), p. 93.
16. For a short but more detailed discussion, refer to Messner and Weinert (2008) pp. 39–41. Aspray *et al.* (2006), and Agrawal and Farrell (2006), offer a more detailed analysis.
17. This case study is based on a number of business cases I have calculated for various clients. The company Comp AG and the circumstances are realistic, but fictitious.
18. Cf. Aspray *et al.* (2006), p. 79.
19. Cf. Agrawal and Farrell (2006).

Chapter 3 Readiness for India

1. Cf. Kennedy (2009), p. 4.
2. Alternatives to CMM are ISO or Six Sigma process/quality methods.
3. Between 1994 and 2004, a team of 170 scholars teamed up to study societal culture, organizational culture and attributes of effective leadership in 62 cultures. As part of this Global Leadership and Organizational Behavior Effectiveness (GLOBE) study, they surveyed more than 17,000 middle managers from 950 organizations. The results are published in two books, House *et al.* (2004), and Chhokar *et al.* (2007).
4. Cf. Messner (2009a), p. 25.
5. These are affective intercultural competences, namely open-mindedness, empathy, and non-ethnocentricm; cf. Gelbrich (2004), pp. 263, 266.
6. Cf. Martorelli and McCarthy (2004), pp. 4–5.
7. A good overview of evaluation criteria for application selection can be found in Westner and Strahringer (2008), who have not only evaluated the existing academic literature and practitioner publications, but have also conducted expert interviews. I present here criteria which are specific to an individual application and have not been covered in the section on organizational readiness.
8. In academic literature, documentation is sometimes referred to as codification.
9. Business domain knowledge is sometimes referred to as business specificity.
10. For example Lo Giudice and Moore (2008); Martorelli and McCarthy (2004); Vashishta (2006), pp. 129–30.
11. For definitions of multisourcing and sourcing strategy, see, for example, Cohen and Young (2006), pp. 19–20, 38; Davis *et al.* (2009); Robinson and Kalikota (2004), p. 45.
12. Cf. Davis *et al.* (2009).
13. Information about this case study has been compiled from publicly available sources: Gallagher (2004); Guardian Life (2009); Overby (2003); Robinson and Kalikota (2004).

14. For a short summary of the standoff between Pakistan and India see Messner (2009a), p. 45.

Chapter 4 Normalizing India's Country Risk

1. Cf. Moreau and Mazumdar (2008).
2. Cf. *Times of India* 1402 (2008); *Times of India* 2402 (2008).
3. Cf. BBC 1912 (2007); Bowring (2006); Singh (2009); Thapaliya (2007).
4. Cf. Howard (2002) and Messner (2009a), pp. 40–5, 85.
5. Cf. Pandit (2008).
6. Cf. Arya (2000).
7. Cf. for example, *Economic Times* 2904, (2009) and IANS (2009).
8. Cf. Kennedy (2009), p. 121.

Chapter 5 Selecting the Service Provider

1. Cf. Apte (2007), p. 6.
2. Cf. Iyengar (2006), pp. 2–3.
3. Cf. Messner (2009b).
4. Cf. Apte (2007), pp. 10–11.
5. Cf. Mitchell (2006).
6. Cf. Texas Instruments (2009).
7. Cf. Alkon (2008); Harvey (2009); Hayward and Raviart (2006); Hermelin and Spencer (2006); Kripalani and Brady (2006); Thomsen-Moore (2003).
8. I was working with Deutsche Software Ltd. on an expatriate assignment in 1998 and kept in touch with events around the acquisition by HCL. Most of the information is also available through publicly available sources, for example Grant (2007); Sachitanand (2001); Siliconindia (2004).
9. Information about this case study is based on an interview with John Knowles, CIO of Allianz Insurance, in 2009, and discussions with Rakesh Gupta, COO of ACIS, in 2008. Further information is collected from publicly available sources, for example, ACIS (2009); FE (2003); Jost (2009).
10. In 2005, 84 per cent of offshore IT delivery was performed by FIOs; see HSBC (2007), p. 8. However, MNCs' share is growing at the cost of FIOs'.
11. Cf. Umamaheswari and Momaya (2008), p. 123.
12. Cf. McCarthy (2006), p. 2.
13. Cf. McCarthy (2006), p. 2.
14. Cf. Umamaheswari and Momaya (2008), p. 117.
15. Cf. Messner (2009a), p. 77.
16. Cf. Cohen and Young (2006), p. 146.
17. Cohen and Young (2006), report (p. 148) Gartner Group benchmarks which show 50 per cent higher than market average costs for sole source negotiations across the entire outsourcing domain.
18. A fast track RFP process with four phases for outsourcing deals has been proposed by Cohen and Young (2006), pp. 143–69, of Gartner Group. In this chapter, I am following the principles of this process, but have adapted it to

the specialities of offshoring deals. S-LEAN RFP™ is my original trademark and is used for the first time in this book.
19. Cf. Cohen Young (2006), p. 162.
20. On earn-back provisions cf. Martorelli, B. (2009), p. 3.
21. This list is an extended version of that found in Cohen and Young (2006), p. 158.
22. The following concept, including Figure 5.3 with its three competencies and twelve capabilities for selecting outsourcing suppliers is, at its core, based on Cullen *et al.* (2009), pp. 281–4 and Feeny *et al.* (2005); I have adapted the concept to India IT offshoring.
23. An inadequate scale is also often used in customer satisfaction surveys leading executives to believe that '80 per cent of the customers rate us as four or five, let's move on!', without realizing that 80 per cent are at least somewhat satisfied, but have no means of expressing a concern on a limited scale. See Bortner (2008), p. 3.
24. Cf. Cullen *et al.* (2009), p. 294.
25. Cf. Moore *et al.* (2008).
26. This section is for reference purposes only. It is not a comprehensive treatment of all laws and regulations pertaining to offshoring and should not replace consultation with a legal adviser. The reader should seek specific legal advice before taking any action discussed here.
27. Cf. Kobayashi-Hillary (2005), p. 193.
28. Cf. Bäumer (2009), p. 4.
29. Cf. Vagadia (2007), pp. 33–6.
30. The other law form is *civil law*, which is codified. It is possible to distinguish between French civil law (found, for example, in France, Benelux, Italy, Spain), German civil law (Germany, Austria, Switzerland, Portugal, China), and Scandinavian civil law (Denmark, Norway, Sweden, Finland).
31. This principle is known as *res judicata*, that is, something over which judgment has already been reached.
32. Refer to §§ 73 and 74 of the Indian Contract Act, 1872.
33. Cf. Bäumer *et al.* (2007), pp. 42–4.
34. Cases pending as at 31st March 2009: Supreme Court, 50,163; High Courts, 3,955,224; district and subordinate courts, 26,752,193. Source: Supreme Court of India; see also Rahman (2009), p. 18; Headlines India (2007).

Chapter 6 Successfully Running the Offshore Project

1. As noted by Lacity and Willcocks (2009), p. 304.
2. Adapted from Lacity and Willcocks (2009), pp. 315–8.
3. Cf. Carmel and Beulen (2005), pp. 142–4.
4. The research company Gartner Group offers a Relationship Performance Assessment (RPA) for this purpose; cf. McClure and LeVasseur (2009).
5. A good overview of metrics from different sources is available in Kütz (2009), pp. 131–225, 227–326.
6. For components of trust in sourcing relationships see Cohen and Young (2006), p. 203.
7. Cf. for example, Hendel (2008), pp. 75–6; Nassimbeni and Sartor (2008), pp. 15–6.

8. Cf. Thun (2008b), p. 80.
9. For a more in-depth discussion of the one-team and factory model, see Thun (2008b), pp. 81–5.
10. Cf. Thun (2008b), pp. 85–98.
11. This is slowly changing. In the USA, the first flat-rate packages for calls to India were offered on the market in mid-2009. Europe, however, trails behind and the state-run telecom operators continue to charge up to USD 3 per minute to India while private carriers offer considerably less expensive, but also more unreliable, connections.
12. Cf. Rottmann and Lacity (2009), pp. 249–50.
13. Cf. Oshri *et al.* (2009), pp. 381–3.
14. For knowledge transfer from build to run in delivery factories, see Hendel (2008), p. 75.
15. Oshri *et al.* (2009), pp. 383–5, propose a transactive memory system (TMS) which combines individual memory systems and communication between individuals. Transactions between employees link their memory systems and through a series of processes (encoding, storing and retrieving) knowledge is exchanged.

Chapter 7 Navigating Cultural Differences

1. Cf. Messner (2009a), p. 158.
2. For a classification of intercultural training courses see, for example, the overview in Holtbrügge and Schillo (2008), pp. 137–9.
3. Cultural awareness training is different from traditional country briefings. It focuses on the cultural and mental programming of individuals, different value systems, and helps to get things done effectively in another culture.
4. There is a legal requirement, established only in 1990, for companies to report the percentage of their employees belonging to certain lower and backward castes to prove that they do not favour upper casts.
5. More detailed information about the caste system can be found in Chhokar (2007), pp. 974–5; Messner (2009a), pp. 51–3. The Brahmin (priest, teacher) is at the top of the caste ladder, followed by the Kshatriya (warrior, ruler, landholder). Third comes the Vaishya (businessman) and the Shudra (labourer, artisan) is last. Below these four castes are the casteless Untouchables and Tribals. This societal hierarchy is believed to data back to the Vedic period around 1,500 to 1,000 BC. Today, the Brahmins, Kshatriyas, and Vaishyas together make up about 15 per cent of the population, the Shudras account for 50 per cent, and the casteless ones around 20 per cent. Approximately 15 per cent are outside this caste ladder and do not belong to the Hindu religion.

References

Accenture (2009) *Outsourcing. Industrialize Your Applications Delivery to Achieve High Performance.* Retrieved 1 June 2009, from Accenture (podcast transcript): http://www.accenture.com/NR/rdonlyres/650F3E35-9894-4831-9E89-3162C353A479/0/185Accenture_Industrialize_Your_Applications_Delivery_Podcast_Transcript.pdf

Accenture (2007) *You're Offshoring. Now what?* Retrieved 16 September 2009, from Accenture: http://www.accenture.com/Global/Outsourcing/Application_Outsourcing/R_and_I/YoureOffshoringNowWhat.htm

ACIS (2009) *Allianz Cornhill Information Services.* Retrieved 13 October 2009, from ACIS: http://www.acis.co.in

Agrawal, V. and Farrell, D. (2006) 'Who Wins in Offshoring?' in D. Farrell, *Offshoring. Understanding the Emerging Global Labor Market* (pp. 57–66), Boston (MA): Harvard Business School Press.

Alkon, R. (2008) *Capgemini Extends Strategic Relationship with HSBC.* Retrieved 9 July 2009, from Capgemini: http://www.capgemini.com/resources/news/capgemini-extends-strategic-relationship-with-hsbc/

Apte, S. (2007) *Shattering the Offshore Captive Center Myth,* Forrester Research.

Apte, S. (2009) *Offshore Negotiation Toolkit: Ammunition to Help Sourcing Teams Cut Rates And Mitigate Risks,* Forrester Research.

Arya, A. S. (2000) 'Recent Developments toward Earthquake Risk Reduction in India', *Current Science, Special Section Seismology, 79* (9).

Aspray, W., Mayadas, F. and Vardi, Y. M. (2006) *Globalization and Offshoring of Software. A Report of the ACM Job Migration Workforce.* Retrieved 26 May 2009, from ACM Association of Computing Machinery: www.acm.org/globalizationreport

Bäumer, U. (2009). *Rechtliches zum Rightshore – Rechtliche Aspekte einer Offshore (Outsourcing) Partnerschaft.* Retrieved 12 August 2009, from Osborne Clarke: http://www.osborneclarke.de/publikationen/Rechtliches_zum_Rightshore.pdf.pdf

Bäumer, U., Webber, M. and Basu, S. (2007) 'IT Outsourcing and Global Sourcing: A Comparative Approach from the Indian, U.K. and German Legal Perspectives', *Indian Journal of Law and Technology, 3,* 25–60.

BBC 1912 (2007, 19 December). *Senior Maoist 'arrested' in India.* Retrieved 1 July 2009, from BBC News: http://news.bbc.co.uk/2/hi/south_asia/7151552.stm

Bortner, B. (2008) *Best Practices: Why Customer Satisfaction Studies Fail. How to Drive Bottom-Line Success with Effective Satisfaction Research,* Forrester Research.

Bowring, P. (2006, 17 April). *Maoists who Menace India.* Retrieved 1 July 2009, from *The New York Times*: http://www.nytimes.com/2006/04/17/opinion/17iht-edbowring.html?_r=1

Brown, D. and Wilson, S. (2005) *The Black Book of Outsourcing. How to Manage the Changes, Challenges, and Opportunities,* New Delhi: Wiley India.

Capgemini (2006) *European CIO Survey – Views on Future IT Delivery,* Capgemini Consulting Services.

Capgemini (2008) *Technovision 2012: Bringing Business Technology to Life.* Retrieved 22 April 2009, from Capgemini Thought Leadership: http://www.capgemini.com/resources/thought_leadership/technovision-2012/

Capgemini (2009) *Capgemini's TechnoVision: Survival Tool for the Downturn. Addressing the New Challenges – and New Solutions – Raised by the Downturn.* Retrieved 31 May 2009, from Capgemini: http://www.capgemini.com/resources/thought_leadership/capgeminis_technovision_survival_tool_for_the_downturn/

Carmel, E. and Beulen, E. (2005) 'Managing the Offshore Transition', in E. Carmel and P. Tjia, *Offshoring Information Technology. Sourcing and Outsourcing to a Global Workforce,* Cambridge: Cambridge University Press (pp. 130–48).

Charan, R. (2009) *Leadership in the Era of Economic Uncertainty,* New Delhi: Tata McGraw-Hill.

Chhokar, J. S. (2007) 'India: Diversity and Complexity in Action', in J. S. Chhokar, F. C. Brodbeck and R. J. House, *Culture and Leadership across the World. The GLOBE Book of In-Depth Studies of 25 Societies,* Mahwah (NJ): Lawrence Erlbaum Associates (pp. 971–1020).

Chhokar, J. S., Brodbeck, F. C. and House, R. J. (2007) *Culture and Leadership Across the World. The GLOBE Book of In-Depth Studies of 25 Societies,* Mahwah (NJ): Lawrence Erlbaum Associates.

CIA Worldbook (2008) *The World Factbook India.* Retrieved 6 March 2010, from https://www.cia.gov/library/publications/the-world-factbook/geos/in.html

Cohen, L. and Young, A. (2006) *Multisourcing. Moving Beyond Outsourcing to Achieve Growth and Agility,* Boston (MA): Harvard Business School Press.

Cullen, S. (2004) 'Hanging in the Balance. Contract Scorecard', *Information Economics Journal,* June, pp. 19–20.

Cullen, S. (2006) 'The Outsourcing Lifecycle: Womb to Tomb (and Back Again)', *Cutter Consortium Sourcing & Vendor Relationships Advisory Service* (7).

Cullen, S. and Willcocks, L. P. (2003) *Intelligent IT Outsourcing: Eight Building Blocks to Success,* Butterworth-Heinemann.

Cullen, S., Willcocks, P. L. and Lacity, C. M. (2009) 'Selecting and Leveraging Outsourcing Suppliers', in C. M. Lacity and P. L. Willcocks, *Information Systems and Outsourcing. Studies in Theory and Practice,* Houndmills: Palgrave Macmillan (pp. 280–302).

Davis, E., Parker, A. and Shanahan, A. (2009) *Service Integration Delivers Multisourcing's Promise. Multisourcing Q&A,* Forrester Research.

Economic Times 0901 (2009) 'Satyam a big lie. A Rs 7,000-crore hole in the books', *The Economic Times,* p. 1.

Economic Times 1301 (2009) *Wipro not the only company to be banned by World Bank.* Retrieved 31 March 2009, from Economic Times: http://economictimes.indiatimes.com/Wipro_Satyam_Megasoft_banned_by_World_Bank/articleshow/3966439.cms

Economic Times 2904 (2009) *Will Swine Flu be a Boon for Indian Generics?* Retrieved 21 July 2009, from The Economic Times: http://economictimes.indiatimes.com/News/News-By-Industry/Healthcare—Biotech/Pharmaceuticals/Will-swine-flu-be-a-boon-for-Indian-generics/articleshow/4464469.cms

Farrell, D., Kaka, N. and Stürze, S. (2006) 'Ensuring India's Offshoring Future', in D. Farrell, *Offshoring. Understanding the Emerging Global Labor Market,* Boston (MA): Harvard Business School Press (pp. 27–41).

FAZ 0302 (2005) *"Smartsourcing" bei der Deutschen Bank.* Retrieved 18 July 2009, from FAZ Frankfurter Allgemeine Zeitung: http://www.faz.net/s/RubE3BF7B6B26F443E5990C9BA42301A0C9/Doc~E54E033956C45413EB39FC722B609A993~ATpl~Ecommon~Scontent.html

FE (2003) *Allianz Cornhill to Set up Software Development Centre in Kerala.* Retrieved 13 October 2009, from Financial Express: http://www.financialexpress.com/news/allianz-cornhill-to-set-up-software-development-centre-in-kerala/70891/

Feeny, D., Lacity, C. M. and Willcocks, P. L. (2005) 'Taking a Measure of Outsourcing Providers', *Sloan Management Review, 46* (3), 41–8.

Fox, L. (2002) *Enron: The Rise and Fall.* Hoboken (NJ): Wiley & Sons.

Friedman, T. (2005) *The World is Flat. A Brief History of the Globalized World in the 21st Century,* London (UK): Allen Lane (Penguin Group).

Gallagher, J. (2004) *Uncovering Offshore Secrets.* Retrieved 29 June 2009, from Insurance & Technology: http://www.insurancetech.com/resources/competition/showArticle.jhtml?articleID=17701493&pgno=2

Gelbrich, K. (2004) 'The Relationship between Intercultural Competence and Expatriate Success: A Structural Equation Model', *Die Unternehmung, 3/4* (58).

Ghemawat, P. (2007) *Redefining Global Strategy. Crossing Borders in a World Where Differences Still Matter,* Boston (MA): Harvard Business School Press.

Gliedman, C. (2004) *Valuing IT Flexibility,* Forrester Research.

Gliedman, C. (2008) *The Total Economic Impact(TM) Methodology: A Foundation for Sound Technology Investments,* Forrester Research.

Grant, I. (2007) *Deutsche Bank Outsources to HCL Technologies.* Retrieved 29 June 2009, from ComputerWeekly.com: http://www.computerweekly.com/Articles/2007/11/08/227955/deutsche-bank-outsources-to-hcl-technologies.htm

Guardian Life (2009) *Who We Are.* Retrieved 26 June 2009, from Guardian Life: http://www.guardianlife.com/company_info/who_we_are.html

Gupta, A. K. and Wang, H. (2008) *Getting China and India Right. Strategies for Leveraging the World's Fastest Growing Economies for Global Advantage,* San Francisco (CA): Jossey-Bass (John Wiley).

Hale, K., de Souza, R., Brown, R., Potter, K. and Morikawa, C. (2008) *Forecast: Outsourcing Worldwide 2000–2012,* Gartner Dataquest Market Statistics.

Harvey, K. (2009) *Capgemini.* Retrieved 28 October 2009, from HSBC and Capgemini: Innovative Collaboration: http://www.capgemini.com/resources/videos/hsbc-and-capgemini-innovative-collaboration/

Hayward, D. and Raviart, D. (2006) *Capgemini Acquires Kanbay and Aims for 35,000 Staff in India by 2010.* Retrieved 2 July 2009, from Ovum Comments: http://www.ovum.com/go/content/c,67578

Headlines India (2007) *Over 3 Million Cases Pending in Courts.* Retrieved 10 August 2007, from Headlines India, VII/151: http://www.headlinesindia.com/main.jsp?news_code=41562

Hendel, A. (2008) 'Offshore ERP Services', in A. Hendel, W. Messner and F. Thun (eds), *Rightshore! Successfully Industrialize SAP Projects Offshore,* Heidelberg: Springer (pp. 63–77).

Hermelin, P. and Spencer, R. (2006) *Capgemini Acquires Kanbay.* Retrieved 2 July 2009, from Capgemini: http://investor.capgemini.com/assets/capgemini_acquires_Kanbay.pdf

Hofstede, G. and Hofstede, G. (2005) *Cultures and Organizations. Software of the Mind,* New York: McGraw Hill.

Holtbrügge, D. and Schillo, K. (2008) 'Managing from a Distance: Virtual Delegation to India', in A. Hendel, W. Messner and F. Thun (eds), *Rightshore! Successfully Industrialize SAP Projects Offshore,* Heidelberg: Springer.

House, R. J., Hanges, P. J., Javidan, M., Dorfman, P. W. and Gupta, V. (2004) *Culture, Leadership, and Organizations. The GLOBE Study of 62 Societies,* Thousand Oaks (CA): Sage Publications.

Howard, S. (2002) India and Pakistan Camped on Brink of War over Kashmir, *Disarmament Policy* (65).

HSBC (2007) *Rethinking the European Competitive Landscape,* HSBC Global Research.

IANS (2009) *16th Swine Flu Case; India Says no Need to Worry.* Retrieved 21 July 2009, from New Kerala: http://www.newkerala.com/nkfullnews-1-55004.html

IBEF (2009) *Foreign Direct Investment.* Retrieved 12 August 2009, from Indian Brand Equity Foundation: http://www.ibef.org/economy/fdi.aspx

Iyengar, P. (2006) *Critical Mass is Necessary for Captive Centers to Succeed,* Gartner Group.

Jalote, P. (2001) *The Success of the SPI Efforts in India.* Retrieved 16 June 2008, from Indian Institute of Technology Kanpur: http://www.cse.iitk.ac.in/users/jalote/papers/IndiaSPI.pdf

Jost, S. (2009) *Allianz. Einmal um die Welt versichert.* Retrieved 13 October 2009, from Welt Online: http://www.welt.de/finanzen/globalisierung-kinder/article3087284/Einmal-um-die-Welt-versichert.html

Kaiser, K. M. and Hawk, S. (2004) 'Evolution of Offshore Software Development: From Outsourcing to Cosourcing', *MIS Quarterly Executive, 3* (2), 69–81.

Kamarkhar, U. (2004) 'Will You Survive the Services Revolution?', *Harvard Business Review* (June).

Kaplan, J., Libarikian, A. and Morstead, S. (2009) Getting Infrastructure Offshoring Right, *McKinsey Quarterly* (16).

Kennedy, R. E. (2009) *The Services Shift. Seizing the Ultimate Offshore Opportunity,* Financial Times Press.

Kobayashi-Hillary, M. (2005) *Outsourcing to India. The Offshore Advantage* (2nd ed.), Berlin: Springer.

Koulopoulos, T. M. and Roloff, T. (2006) *Smartsourcing. Driving Innovation and Growth Through Outsourcing,* Avon (MA): Platinum Press.

Krause, E. (2008) *Methode für das Outsourcing in der Informationstechnologie von Retail Banken,* Berlin: Logos Verlag.

Kripalani, M. and Brady, R. (2006) *HSBC's Lessons in Outsourcing.* Retrieved 2 July 2009, from Business Week: http://www.businessweek.com/magazine/content/06_05/b3969426.htm

Kütz, M. (2009) *Kennzahlen in der IT. Werkzeuge für Controlling und Management* (3rd ed.) Heidelberg: Dpunkt.

Lacity, M. C. and Willcocks, L. P. (2009) 'Managing Relationships across the Life Cycle of an Outsourcing Agreement', in M. C. Lacity and L. P. Willcocks, *Information Systems and Outsourcing. Studies in Theory and Practice,* Houndmills, Basingstoke: Palgrave Macmillan (pp. 303–40).

Lewin, A. Y. and Couto, V. (2006) *Next Generation Offshoring. The Globalization of Innovation. 2006 Survey Report.* Offshoring Research Network (ORN), Duke

Center for International Business Education and Research (CIBER), Booz Allen Hamilton Inc.

Lewin, A. Y. and Perm-Ajchariyawong, N. (2009) *Getting Serious About Offshoring in a Struggling Economy.* Retrieved 29 April 2009, from Offshoring Research Network, Duke – the Fuqua School of Business: https://offshoring.fuqua.duke.edu/pdfs/Shared%20Services%20News_ORN.pdf

Lewin, A. Y., Massini, S., Perm-Ajchariyawong, N., Sappenfield, D. and Walker, J. (2009) *Wipro Technologies Industry Research, Experts Speak.* Retrieved 29 April 2009, from Getting Serious about Offshoring in a Struggling Economy: http://www.wipro.com/industryresearch/pdf/whitepaper/getting_serious_about_offshoring_in_a_struggling_economy.pdf

Liverpool Daily Post 2603 (2009) *Jaguar Land Rover Owner Tata Says Company 'Needs Guarantees not Bailout'.* Retrieved 3 April 2009, from Liverpool Daily Post: http://www.liverpooldailypost.co.uk/liverpool-news/motor-industry-campaign/latest-jaguar-land-rover-news/2009/03/26/jaguar-land-rover-owner-tata-says-company-needs-guarantees-not-bailout-92534-23235346/

Lo Giudice, D. and Moore, S. (2008) Assessing which Applications to Offshore. A Selection Framework, *Forrester.*

Luce, E. (2008) *In Spite of the Gods: The Rise of Modern India,* New York: Anchor.

Mahalingam, T. (2009) 'Where Dreams End... And Nightmares Begin. Chronicles of the Rise and Fall of the Indian Software Engineer', *Outlook Business,* pp. 46–57.

Manning, S., Massini, S. and Lewin, A. Y. (2008) A Dynamic Perspective on Next-Generation Offshoring: The Global Sourcing of Science and Engineering Talent, *Academy of Management Perspectives* (Aug), 35–54.

McCarthy, J. C. (2006) *India's Looming Offshore Midlife Crisis. Rising Complexity to Unhinge Offshore Players,* Forrester Research.

McClure, T. and LeVasseur, C. (2009). *Measuring Outsourcing Relationships.* Retrieved 15 July 2009, from Gartner Group: http://www.gartner.com/4_decision_tools/measurement/measure_it_articles/july01/mit_outsoucrcing_relationships1.html

Martorelli, B. (2009) *Observe the Limitations of SLA Penalty Clauses,* Forrester Research.

Martorelli, W. and McCarthy, J. C. (2004) 'Assessing Your Offshore Outsourcing Readiness. Not all Organizations have the Processes or Culture to Move at the same Pace', *Forrester Trends.*

Meredith, R. (2008) *The Elephant and the Dragon. The Rise of India and China and what it Means for All of Us,* New York: W. W. Norton & Co.

Merrick, R. (2009) *Jaguar Land Rover will get Vital Credit from Bail Out Fund.* Retrieved 3 April 2009, from Liverpool Daily Post: http://www.liverpooldailypost.co.uk/liverpool-news/motor-industry-campaign/latest-jaguar-land-rover-news/2009/01/20/jaguar-land-rover-will-get-vital-credit-from-bail-out-fund-92534-22732281/

Messner, W. (2008) 'Offshoring in India: Opportunities and Risks', in A. Hendel, W. Messner and F. Thun (eds), *Rightshore! Successfully Industrialize SAP Projects Offshore* Heidelberg: Springer (pp. 15–30).

Messner, W. (2009a) *Working with India. The Softer Aspects of a Successful Collaboration with the Indian IT & BPO Industry,* Heidelberg: Springer.

Messner, W. (2009b) 'Winning the Race for Talent in Emerging Markets' (Letters to the Editor), *Harvard Business Review, March*, 93.

Messner, W. and Weinert, S. (2008) 'Economic and Business Effects of IT Offshoring', in A. Hendel, W. Messner and F. Thun (eds), *Rightshore! Successfully Industrialize SAP Projects Offshore*, Springer (pp. 31–44).

Mitchell, A. (2006) *Apple Downscales in India – Raising Doubts about Offshoring*. Retrieved 3 July 2009, from CRMBuyer: http://www.crmbuyer.com/story/50931.html

Moore, S., Ross, C. F. and Thresher, A. (2008) *Understanding Indian Providers' Margin Defense Tactics*, Forrester Research.

Moreau, R. and Mazumdar, S. (2008) *The Pakistan Connection*. Retrieved 1 July 2009, from Newsweek: http://www.newsweek.com/id/171056

Müller, O. (2006) *Wirtschaftsmacht Indien. Chance und Herausforderung für uns*, Munich: Carl Hanser.

Nasscom (2009) *Indian IT-BPO Industry: NASSCOM Analysis*, Nasscom

Nasscom and McKinsey (2009) *Perspective 2020: Transform Business, Transform India*. Retrieved 31 May 2009, from McKinsey on India: http://www.mckinsey.com/locations/india/mckinseyonindia/pdf/NASSCOM_report_exec_summ.pdf

Nassimbeni, G. and Sartor, M. (2008) *Sourcing in India*, Houndmills: Palgrave Macmillan.

Nilekani, N. (2009) *Imagining India: The Idea of a Renewed Nation*, London: Penguin Press.

Nunes, P. F., Firstbrook, C. and Ellis, J. M. (2009) *New Choices for New Challenges. Managing in Extraordinary Times*. Retrieved 16 September 2009, from Accenture Outlook: http://www.accenture.com/NR/rdonlyres/1D9ADC85-69BE-4E8A-B0DD-EC4D52D35F11/0/Accenture_Outlook_Managing_in_Extraordinary_Times.pdf

Oshri, I., Kotlarsky, J. and Willcocks, L. P. (2009) 'IT Offshore Outsourcing: Supplier Lessons on the Management of Expertise', in M. C. Lacity and L. P. Willcocks, *Information Systems and Outsourcing. Studies in Theory and Practice*, Houndmills: Palgrave Macmillan (pp. 366–89).

Overby, S. (2003) *Offshore Outsourcing: The Guardian View*. Retrieved 26 June 2009, from CIO: http://www.cio.com/article/print/29749

Pandey, G. (2006) *Spotlight on India's Malnourished Children*. Retrieved 3 April 2009, from BBC News: http://news.bbc.co.uk/2/hi/south_asia/4962880.stm

Pandit, R. (2008) China's Deep-Sea Plans Alarm India, *Times of India*, p. 14.

Post, J. E., Varma, J. R., Menon, K., Desai, A., Raghavan, A., Srinivasan, V. *et al.* (2009). The Satyam Story: Many Questions and a few Answers, *Vikalpa, Indian Institute of Management Ahmedabad, 34* (1), March, 69–88.

PTI (2008) Hefty Pay May Eat into margins of Indian IT Cos. *The Economic Times*, p. 7.

Rahman, S. (2009) Lords on Trial, *India Today*, pp. 18–26.

Ready, D. A., Hill, L. A. and Conger, J. A. (2008) Winning the Race for Talent in Emerging Markets, *Harvard Business Review*, 36–44.

Rhodes, D. and Stelter, D. (2009) 'Seize Advantages in a Downturn', *Harvard Business Review, Feb*, 40–8.

Robinson, M. and Kalikota, R. (2004) *Offshore Outsourcing. Business Models, ROI, and Best Practices* (2nd ed.), Mivar Press.

Rottmann, J. W. and Lacity, M. C. (2009) 'Knowledge Transfer in Offshore Outsourcing', in M. C. Lacity and L. P. Willcocks, *Information Systems and Outsourcing. Studies in Theory and Practice,* Houndmills: Palgrave Macmillan (pp. 249–56).

Ryan, J. (2007) *Chiquita Pleads Guilty to Paying Terrorists*. Retrieved 22 April 2009, from ABC News: http://abcnews.go.com/TheLaw/story?id=2962981

Sachitanand, N. N. (2001) *HCL Tech, Deutsche Bank form JV*. Retrieved 29 June 2009, from The Hindu: http://www.hindu.com/2001/09/27/stories/06270009.htm

Schumacher, P. and Olsson, E. (2009). *European IT Companies in India. How European IT SMEs are Leveraging Offshore Capabilities to Reignite Growth, Improve Financial Performance, and Capture New Markets*. Retrieved 16 July 2009, from Value Leadership Group: http://www.value-leadership.com/download/vlg_european_study.pdf

Siliconindia (2004) *HCL to acquire Deutsche Software*. Retrieved 29 June 2009, from SiliconIndia: http://www.siliconindia.com/shownews/HCL_to_acquire_Deutsche_Software-nid-25005.html

Singh, J. (2009) *Why is India Scared to Take on Maoist Rebels?* Retrieved 1 July 2009, from Deccan Chronicle: http://www.deccanchronicle.com/op-ed/why-india-scared-take-maoist-rebels-822

Texas Instruments (2009). *Texas Instruments India Pvt. Ltd.* Retrieved 3 July 2009, from Media Kit: http://www.ti.com/in/media_kit.htm

Thapaliya, B. (2007) *Rising Maoists Insurgency in India*. Retrieved 1 July 2009, from The Global Politician: http://globalpolitician.com/22790-india

Thomsen-Moore, L. (2003) *HSBC buys 20% of Kanbay*. Retrieved 2 July 2009, from Computerworld. IDG Communications: http://www.computerworld.com.au/article/64431/hsbc_buys_20_kanbay?fp=512&fpid=1177881746

Thun, F. (2008a) 'Industrialization of Application Implementations', in A. Hendel, W. Messner and F. Thun (eds), *Rightshore! Successfully Industrialize SAP Projects Offshore,* Heidelberg: Springer (pp. 45–62).

Thun, F. (2008b) 'Transforming the Front-Office', in A. Hendel, W. Messner and F. Thun (eds), *Rightshore! Successfully Industrialize SAP Projects Offshore,* Heidelberg: Springer (pp. 79–100).

Times of India 1402 (2008) Maha Exodus: 10,000 North Indians Flee in Fear. *Times of India*.

Times of India 2402 (2008) North Indians Leave Pune. Realty Projects Hit. *Times of India*.

Toffler, A. (2000) *Interview with Alvin Toffler by James Daly*. Retrieved 25 June 2009, from Iranscope Ghandchi: http://iranscope.ghandchi.com/Anthology/Alvin_Toffler00.htm

Tolido, R. (2009) *Stop the Drooling: The Crisis Needs Technology*. Retrieved 22 April 2009, from Capgemini CTO Blog: http://www.capgemini.com/cgi-bin/blog/mt-tb.cgi/819

Umamaheswari, R. and Momaya, K. (2008) 'Role of Creative Marketing in 10X Journey. Case of IT Firms from India', *IMR Indian Management Review, 20* (1), 113–130.

Unicef (2009). *Children's Issues*, Retrieved 3 April 2009, from Unicef India: http://www.unicef.org/india/children_2356.htm

Vagadia, B. (2007) *Outsourcing to India - A Legal Handbook,* Berlin: Springer.

Vashishta, A. (2006) *The Offshore Nation. Strategies for Success in Global Outsourcing and Offshoring,* New York: McGraw-Hill.

Vautier, A. and Phypers, A. (2007) *Winning with Next Generation IT Industrialization. How Structured Measurement Transforms IT Services to Enable High Performance.* Retrieved 1 June 2009, from Accenture: http://www.accenture.com/NR/rdonlyres/C3031009-83BF-4848-B659-10F6DC89FA5F/0/124610_Industrialization_6.pdf

von den Bergen, H. P. (2005) *Smartsourcing – Personalabbau zur Erhöhung der Eigenkapitalrendite.* Retrieved 18 July 2009, from Cornelsen Aktualitätendienst Wirtschaft: http://www.cornelsen.de/sixcms/media.php/8/wirt_smartsourcing_didak.pdf

Weiss, S. (1994a) 'Negotiating with "Romans", part 1', *Sloan Management Review,* vol. 35, no. 2.

Weiss, S. (1994b) 'Negotiating with "Romans", part 2', *Sloan Management Review,* vol. 35, no. 3.

Westner, M. (2007) *Information Systems Offshoring. A Review of the Literature.* Retrieved 19 June 2009, from Dresdner Beiträge zur Wirtschaftsinformatik: http://www.tu-dresden.de/wwwiisih/Westner%202007%20Gelbe%20Reihe%20Nr%2051.pdf

Westner, M. K. and Strahringer, S. (2008) 'Evaluation Criteria for Selecting Offshoring Candidates: An Analysis of Practices in German Businesses', *Journal of Information Technology Management, XIX* (4), 16–34.

Willcocks, L. P., Cullen, S. and Lacity, M. C. (2009). *The Outsourcing Enterprise. The CEO Guide to Selecting Effective Suppliers.* Retrieved 24 July 2009, from LogicaCMG, The Cullen Group, & London School of Economics: http://www.cullengroup.com.au/images/stories/CG/Publications/Downloads/outsourcingenterprisereport-Selecting-Suppliers.pdf

Index